Macmillan Computer Science Series

Consulting Editor: Professor F.H. Sumner, University

A. Abdellatif, J. Le Bihan and M. Limame, *Oracle – A user's guide*
S.T. Allworth and R.N. Zobel, *Introduction to Real-time Software*
Ian O. Angell, *High-resolution Computer Graphics Using C*
Ian O. Angell and Gareth Griffith, *High-resolution Computer Graphics*
Ian O. Angell and Gareth Griffith, *High-resolution Computer Graphics Using*
M. Azmoodeh, *Abstract Data Types and Algorithms*, second edition
C. Bamford and P. Curran, *Data Structures, Files and Databases*
Philip Barker, *Author Languages for CAL*
A.N. Barrett and A.L. Mackay, *Spatial Structure and the Microcomputer*
R.E. Berry, B.A.E. Meekings and M.D. Soren, *A Book on C*, second edition
P. Beynon-Davies, *Information Systems Development*
G.M. Birtwistle, *Discrete Event Modelling on Simula*
B.G. Blundell, C.N. Daskalakis, N.A.E. Heyes and T.P. Hopkins, *An Introductory Guide to Silvar Lisco and HILO Simulators*
B.G. Blundell and C.N. Daskalakis, *Using and Administering an Apollo Network*
T.B. Boffey, *Graph Theory in Operations Research*
Richard Bornat, *Understanding and Writing Compilers*
Linda E.M. Brackenbury, *Design of VLSI Systems – A Practical Introduction*
Alan Bradley, *Peripherals for Computer Systems*
G.R. Brookes and A.J. Stewart, *Introduction to occam 2 on the Transputer*
J.K. Buckle, *Software Configuration Management*
W.D. Burnham and A.R. Hall, *Prolog Programming and Applications*
P.C. Capon and P.J. Jinks, *Compiler Engineering Using Pascal*
J.C. Cluley, *Interfacing to Microprocessors*
J.C. Cluley, *Introduction to Low Level Programming for Microprocessors*
Robert Cole, *Computer Communications*, second edition
Derek Coleman, *A Structured Programming Approach to Data*
E. Davalo and P. Naïm, *Neural Networks*
S.M. Deen, *Fundamentals of Data Base Systems*
S.M. Deen, *Principles and Practice of Database Systems*
C. Delannoy, *Turbo Pascal Programming*
Tim Denvir, *Introduction to Discrete Mathematics for Software Engineering*
D. England et al., *A Sun User's Guide*
A.B. Fontaine and F. Barrand, *80286 and 80386 Microprocessors*
J.B. Gosling, *Design of Arithmetic Units for Digital Computers*
M.G. Hartley, M. Healey and P.G. Depledge, *Mini and Microcomputer Systems*
J.A. Hewitt and R.J. Frank, *Software Engineering in Modula-2 – An Object-oriented Approach*
Roger Hutty, *Z80 Assembly Language Programming for Students*
Roger Hutty, *COBOL 85 Programming*
Roland N. Ibbett and Nigel P. Topham, *Architecture of High Performance Computers, Volume I*
Roland N. Ibbett and Nigel P. Topham, *Architecture of High Performance Computers, Volume II*
Patrick Jaulent, *The 68000 – Hardware and Software*
P. Jaulent, L. Baticle and P. Pillot, *68020–30 Microprocessors and their Coprocessors*
M.J. King and J.P. Pardoe, *Program Design Using JSP – A Practical Introduction*
E.V. Krishnamurthy, *Introductory Theory of Computer Science*
V.P. Lane, *Security of Computer Based Information Systems*

continued overleaf

A.M. Lister and R.D. Eager, *Fundamentals of Operating Systems, fourth edition*
Elizabeth Lynch, *Understanding SQL*
Tom Manns and Michael Coleman, *Software Quality Assurance*
A. Mével and T. Guéguen, *Smalltalk-80*
R.J. Mitchell, *Microcomputer Systems Using the STE Bus*
R.J. Mitchell, *Modula-2 Applied*
Y. Nishinuma and R. Espesser, *UNIX – First contact*
Pim Oets, *MS-DOS and PC-DOS – A Practical Guide, second edition*
A.J. Pilavakis, *UNIX Workshop*
Christian Queinnec, *LISP*
E.J. Redfern, *Introduction to Pascal for Computational Mathematics*
Gordon Reece, *Microcomputer Modelling by Finite Differences*
W.P. Salman, O. Tisserand and B. Toulout, *FORTH*
L.E. Scales, *Introduction to Non-Linear Optimization*
Peter S. Sell, *Expert Systems – A Practical Introduction*
A.G. Sutcliffe, *Human–Computer Interface Design*
Colin J. Theaker and Graham R. Brookes, *A Practical Course on Operating Systems*
M.R. Tolhurst *et al.*, *Open Systems Interconnection*
J-M. Trio, *8086-8088 Architecture and Programming*
A.J. Tyrrell, *COBOL from Pascal*
M.J. Usher, *Information Theory for Information Technologists*
B.S. Walker, *Understanding Microprocessors*
Colin Walls, *Programming Dedicated Microprocessors*
I.R. Wilson and A.M. Addyman, *A Practical Introduction to Pascal – with BS6192, second edition*

Non-series

Roy Anderson, *Management, Information Systems and Computers*
I.O. Angell, *Advanced Graphics with the IBM Personal Computer*
J.E. Bingham and G.W.P. Davies, *Planning for Data Communications*
B.V. Cordingley and D. Chamund, *Advanced BASIC Scientific Subroutines*
N. Frude, *A Guide to SPSS/PC+*
Percy Mett, *Introduction to Computing*
Barry Thomas, *A PostScript Cookbook*

Modula-2 Applied

R. J. Mitchell

Department of Cybernetics
University of Reading

© R. J. Mitchell 1991

All rights reserved. No reproduction, copy or transmission of
this publication may be made without written permission.

No paragraph of this publication may be reproduced, copied or
transmitted save with written permission or in accordance with
the provisions of the Copyright, Designs and Patents Act 1988,
or under the terms of any licence permitting limited copying
issued by the Copyright Licensing Agency, 33–4 Alfred Place,
London WC1E 7DP.

Any person who does any unauthorised act in relation to this
publication may be liable to criminal prosecution and civil
claims for damages.

First edition 1991

Published by
MACMILLAN EDUCATION LTD
Houndmills, Basingstoke, Hampshire RG21 2XS
and London
Companies and representatives
throughout the world

Printed in Hong Kong

British Library Cataloguing in Publication Data
Mitchell, R.J.
 Modula–2 applied. – (Macmillan computer science series).
 1. Computer systems. Programming languages: Modula–2 language
 I. Title
 005.13
 ISBN 0–333–55453–1

Contents

	Preface	ix
1	**Introduction**	**1**
	1.1 The programs	2
	1.2 Modules	3
	1.3 Libraries	5
	1.4 Style	6
	1.5 Algorithms	7
	1.6 Multiple exits from loops and procedures	10
2	**Introductory Program**	**12**
	2.1 The HEX problem	12
	2.2 The backtracking technique	13
	2.3 The program structure and development	14
	2.4 The HEX module	15
	2.5 The HEXSOLVE module	15
	2.6 The HEXGRAPH module	23
	2.7 The HEXPRIM module	27
	2.8 Drawing lines	32
	2.9 Filling triangles	35
	2.10 All solutions	38
3	**Diagram Package - Introduction**	**42**
	3.1 Package overview	42
	3.2 The main commands	44
	3.3 File structure	48
	3.4 Syntax of the programming language	50
	3.5 Modules that form the diagram package	55
4	**Low Level Primitives**	**59**
	4.1 Screen control on a PC	59
	4.2 Sets	61
	4.3 Accessing screen memory	62
	4.4 Text routines	65
	4.5 Higher level graphics	68

	4.6	Look-up tables	74
	4.7	Windows	75
5	**Array Used for a Keyboard Buffer**		**79**
	5.1	Keyboard buffer	79
	5.2	Interrupts and polling	81
	5.3	Aborting and returning to a safe state	82
6	**Arrays for Selecting Commands**		**85**
	6.1	Commands	85
	6.2	Keyboard handling	87
	6.3	Command selection algorithm	88
7	**Transformations and Clipping**		**92**
	7.1	Transformations	92
	7.2	Clipping	99
	7.3	Bezier curves	103
8	**String Handling**		**107**
	8.1	Strings	107
	8.2	Simple processing	108
	8.3	Numerical conversion routines	113
	8.4	String edit routine	114
	8.5	Procedure variables	116
9	**Variant Records**		**119**
	9.1	Records	119
	9.2	Variant records	120
	9.3	Variant record in the diagram package	122
	9.4	Location of an item	127
10	**Use of Files**		**130**
	10.1	Files	130
	10.2	Saving a diagram into a file	132
	10.3	Loading a diagram	134
	10.4	File names, paths and directories	135
	10.5	Binary files	137
	10.6	Random access	138
	10.7	Simple database	139

11 Plotting the Diagram — 143
- 11.1 Plotting requirements — 143
- 11.2 Accessing the printer through the ports — 144
- 11.3 Local modules used as drivers — 147
- 11.4 Reverse Polish notation — 148
- 11.5 PostScript — 150
- 11.6 The PostScript module — 153
- 11.7 The HP-GL plotter module — 155

12 The Heap and One-way Linked Lists — 158
- 12.1 The heap — 158
- 12.2 Allocating and deallocating GCommands — 160
- 12.3 Linked lists — 162

13 Help Utility: Stacks and Linked Lists — 171
- 13.1 Stacks — 171
- 13.2 Sorted linked lists — 172
- 13.3 The help facility — 174

14 Two-way Linked Lists — 179
- 14.1 Two-way linked lists — 179
- 14.2 The selection application — 181
- 14.3 Selection routines provided — 186

15 Editor — 189
- 15.1 Basic methods — 189
- 15.2 Editor data structure — 190
- 15.3 Edit procedure — 192

16 Lexical Analysis — 198
- 16.1 Separation of items — 198
- 16.2 Identification of names — 203
- 16.3 Hashing — 204

17 Trees — 206
- 17.1 Linked lists and trees — 206
- 17.2 Tree structures — 207
- 17.3 Balanced trees — 213
- 17.4 Trees in the diagram package — 216
- 17.5 Multiway trees — 217

18 Expression Trees — 219
- 18.1 Expression trees — 219
- 18.2 Forming an expression tree — 222
- 18.3 Expression trees in the diagram package — 228

19 The Analyser — 232
- 19.1 Data structures — 232
- 19.2 Results of the expression analyser — 234
- 19.3 Checking compatible types — 235
- 19.4 Checking next tree is appropriate — 239
- 19.5 Obeying the program — 246

20 Miscellaneous Examples — 251
- 20.1 Sierpinski curves — 251
- 20.2 Fractals — 257
- 20.3 Three-dimensional shapes — 260

Index — 269

Preface

Programming is a skill which requires knowledge of both the basic constructs of the computer language used and techniques employing these constructs. How these are used in any given application is determined intuitively, and this intuition is based on experience of programs already written. One aim of this book is to describe the techniques and give practical examples of the techniques in action: to provide some experience. Another aim of the book is to show how a program should be developed, in particular how a relatively large program should be tackled in a structured manner.

These aims are accomplished essentially by describing the writing of one large program, a diagram generator package, in which a number of useful programming techniques are employed. This novel approach has a number of advantages. First, it shows the various techniques in real applications, rather than being abstract. Second, by the use of exercises, different applications where the techniques may be useful are described, so greater experience is provided. Also, the book provides a useful program, with an in-built manual describing not only how the program works, but also how it does it, with full source code listings. This means that the user can, if required, modify the package to meet particular requirements.

A floppy disk will be available from the publishers containing the program, including listings of the source code.

All the programs are written in Modula-2, using JPI's *Top Speed Modula-2* system running on IBM-PCs and compatibles. This language was chosen as it is an ideal language for implementing large programs and it is the main language taught in the Cybernetics Department at the University of Reading. There are some aspects of the TopSpeed implementation which are not standard, so suitable comments are given when these occur.

Although implemented in Modula-2, many of the techniques described here are appropriate to other languages, like Pascal or C, for example.

The book and programs are based on a second year undergraduate course taught at Reading to Cybernetics students, entitled *Algorithms and Data Structures*. Useful techniques are described for the reader to use, applications where they are appropriate are recommended, but detailed analyses of the techniques are not given. The book is aimed, therefore, at people who wish to use computers to help solve problems, not specifically at Computer Scientists, though they should find the techniques useful.

A knowledge of simple software engineering techniques, in particular top-down structured programming, and the language Modula-2, are assumed. Thus the reader should be aware of the basic constructs, IF, FOR, etc., PROCEDUREs, VARs, TYPEs, CONSTs, MODULEs, ARRAYs, RECORDs, etc. This book describes ways in which these constructs can be used in practical applications. References to suitable texts are given where appropriate.

x Preface

The specification for the diagram package is as follows. The user should be able to create a diagram interactively in a user-friendly manner. It should appear on the screen, but hardcopy should be obtainable. It must be possible to modify the diagram, to store it in a file and subsequently retrieve it. A diagram may consist of a series of built-in items, such as lines, circles, strings, etc., whose position is determined interactively. In addition, the user should be able to define his own items (made up of lines, circles, etc., and his own items) which can be included at any position, size or rotation. An advanced feature of the package allows the user to define an item by a program, rather than by a series of items. The package contains facilities for entering and analysing such a program.

In the book, the techniques are presented either in Modula-2 or in a pseudo code, which is similar in style to Modula-2, but often contains English statements. So that these can be distinguished, and stand out from the main body of the text, different fonts are used:

```
This font used for pseudocode
```
This font used for Modula-2

Description of the book

The book begins with an introductory chapter, reviewing top-down programming, modules and algorithms. It describes various rules recommended for programming and these are illustrated by a few practical algorithms.

The second chapter describes a shorter program which shows the development of a non-trivial program, illustrates the approach of the author to programming, gives a few useful techniques and provides a nice eye-catching demonstration. The techniques include the backtracking method, graphical algorithms and sorting. In this chapter only are program listings given in detail, the interested reader can find other listings on the associated disk. It is intended that this chapter will show enough of the style of the author to allow the reader to follow the later techniques, and ease the reader gently into the main task of writing a large program.

The rest of the book describes various techniques and how they are used in the diagram package. The aim is to describe the technique, and then show it in a specific application. The chapter outlines are as follows.

The Diagram Package

This chapter describes the package from a user's viewpoint, giving the commands provided and defining its programming language.

Low level primitives

This describes the handling of the screen, including the use of text and graphics, and windows, in which the screen is divided into separate areas. Other useful techniques, including sets and opaque types, are described.

Arrays and the use of a keyboard buffer

This describes the use of a simple array as a keyboard buffer. This is required because the user must be allowed to 'type ahead' and also be allowed to interrupt the program, if the program loops for example. In this case a means of returning to a 'safe' state is required.

Arrays and selection of commands

This chapter describes a simple method of allowing the user to select one command from many by moving a cursor up and down a list of commands. This is implemented using an array. A later chapter describes a more general method, using a more advanced technique, which can handle any number of commands.

Transformations, windowing and clipping

This describes the use of arrays for various transformation matrices, which are needed for drawing shapes at different sizes and positions, and for zooming in and out of the diagram to look at parts in more detail. This leads on to considerations of clipping the picture. Bezier curves are also described.

String handling routines

A string is a special type of array. Useful routines for processing strings, including comparison and editing are given here. Also included is a section on procedure variables which are very useful in producing general library modules.

Variant records

An item in the diagram is defined to be a line, circle, string, user defined item, etc., and each requires different parameters. It is convenient to define one variable type to describe an item, and this is best achieved using a variant record. Suitable definitions are given for this problem and routines described for entering and modifying them interactively.

File handling

This shows how text files can be used to store and retrieve diagrams in files and the use of binary files for defining characters used for strings.

Plotting: including reverse Polish

This shows how the diagrams can be plotted on printers and plotters and includes methods of controlling printer ports. Drivers for HP-GL plotters and PostScript printers are provided. PostScript is a language which uses the reverse Polish or Postfix notation, so this is described with a few exercises using routines for handling reverse Polish expressions.

The heap and one-way linked lists

The diagram is a series of items and the number of items in the diagram can vary. This is best achieved with a linked list structure. This chapter describes such a structure and routines for using it, including methods of using the heap.

Help facility using stacks and sorted one-way lists

This chapter describes an advanced help utility provided with the package which is implemented using another data structure, a stack, and sorted linked lists. Random access to files is also described.

Two-way linked lists

An application of these is in routines which allow the user to select a command by moving a pointer up and down a list. This is how options are selected in the final version of the diagram package.

Editor

This is the first chapter describing techniques which allow the user to define a shape by a program. Here a simple text editor is described which is used to enter such a program.

Lexical analysis

The first stage in the analysis of the program is to divide the program into separate items which can be processed subsequently. Identifiers produced by the lexical analyser must be stored suitably so that they can be referenced later. Hashing, one method used for this purpose, is described here.

Tree structures

Sorted trees, an alternative to hashing, are described here. These are in fact used in preference to hashing in the diagram package.

Expression trees

The next stage of the analysis uses expression trees to hold the statements and arithmetic expressions in the program. Elegant routines for handling these are described. These trees are used to store the program in a form which the interpreter can use directly.

The analyser

The final data structure used in the analysis is a combination of tree structures and linked lists. This structure, and routines for handling it, are described here, showing the final stages of the analyser.

Fractals and other programmable pictures

These routines provide example programs which the analyser can process to produce some elegant effects.

In conclusion, this book describes a number of programming techniques which should prove useful to programmers in a wide variety of applications.

Acknowledgements

The author wishes to thank the many people who have helped in the production of this book (known affectionately as 'son of book', and briefly entitled 'Modula-2 Applied Within' !): to other colleagues in the Cybernetics department, including Professor Kevin Warwick, and especially Dr Mark Bishop, for his various ideas, suggestions and cups of tea; to Malcolm Stewart; to family and friends; and to all Cybernetics students who have endured(!) the associated lectures.

Reading 1990

1 Introduction

The computer language Modula 2 was designed by Niklaus Wirth as a successor to his earlier language Pascal. Pascal was first written as a teaching language with the aim of introducing the student to the concept of structured programming. Since then many people have also been using Pascal to write large programs. Such programs tend to become unmanageable unless they can be divided into smaller parts each acted upon separately. Pascal does not have the facilities to do this properly, though certain extensions to the standard language, notably Turbo Pascal, have attempted to deal with this problem. Modula-2, however, does have these facilities. One objective of this book, therefore, is to show how reasonably sized programs can be designed and developed.

Programming is a skill which can only partially be taught, more is learnt by experience. The student can be shown the basic constructs of the language (PROCEDUREs, IF statements, FOR loops, data types, etc). These are the tools of the trade. How these should be used in any given application, the appropriate algorithms and data structures, is decided by intuition often based on past experience: a particular program already written is similar to the required one, so a similar technique is used. A parallel can be drawn in the design of electronic circuits: knowing the existence and properties of resistors, transistors, etc., does not in itself allow the designer to produce a stereo audio amplifier. However, such a design is likely to be based, at least in part, on other existing amplifiers.

Therefore, it is a good idea to know of various programming techniques. Hence another object of this book is to describe such techniques. These include not only various algorithms, but also data structures; as Wirth put it: *Algorithms + Data Structures = Programs.*

The aim is to achieve these two objectives by describing a large program in which such techniques are employed. In this way the techniques do not appear to be abstract, but actually useful. This novel approach has the additional advantage that it provides a useful program as well. Hence readers may wish to obtain a floppy disk containing the program.

Thus the techniques are described in a particular application. However, it is important to realise that these techniques can be used in other applications. Therefore copious exercises are provided in which the reader can see some of these other applications.

In this book it is assumed that the reader is conversant with programming and the syntax of the language Modula-2. However, a few general points will be given in this introduction, and less common aspects of the language will be described in detail as and when they are needed. All the programs given in the book have been implemented in *Top Speed Modula-2*.

1.1 The programs

As an introduction to the approach of the author to programming, a small, though non-trivial, program is described first. It also describes the backtracking technique and some useful algorithms in computer graphics.

The main program is a package that allows the user to draw diagrams. This is clearly useful (and has been used to produce all the diagrams in the book!). It introduces various techniques, including linked list and tree data structures. It is also a powerful package, not only allowing the normal interactive circuit schematic design, but also allowing more complicated diagrams, like graphs, to be produced by writing a program using a small interpretive language.

Program development

A computer is a tool, a device to aid the solution of a problem. To solve a problem, therefore, the programmer must produce a series of instructions to process the appropriate data. This requires the correct algorithm and data structure. Selecting these is not always easy. The most reliable approach is called top-down design (see for example Sommerville[1]).

As it is difficult to think about the whole problem all the time, it is a good idea to divide the problem into smaller parts and act on each separately. For example, to program a robot to make coffee, the problem should be divided into three parts. So the program is:

```
PROGRAM Make Coffee
BEGIN
  Boil water
  Put coffee in cup
  Add water to coffee
END
```

The first stage can be considered independently of the others, so part of the program, a procedure to boil the water, is:

```
PROCEDURE Boil Water
BEGIN
  Put water into kettle
  Switch kettle on
  Wait until boiling
END
```

The first of these actions is another procedure:

```
PROCEDURE Put Water In Kettle
BEGIN
   Put kettle under tap
   Turn tap on
   Wait until kettle sufficiently full
   Turn tap off
END
```

etc. This philosophy can be implemented directly in Modula-2.

The idea therefore is to successively divide the problem into parts until a part is sufficiently simple to be implemented. Each part can be acted upon separately. In practice, particularly for large problems, the design is not strictly top-down. This is because programmers base the design on previous knowledge: they use their experience. Therefore there tends to be an element of bottom-up and middle-out design. However, as an approach to programming new problems, the top-down method is recommended.

When working on one part, the rest can be ignored, except when they interact. The interaction should be minimised because, for example, if many different parts can change a particular variable, and that variable is given an unacceptable value, work is required to discover which part of the program corrupted the variable. Interaction is best minimised by using local items (variables, types, constants, procedures). In this way all the relevant items are associated only with the appropriate part. This approach is exemplified in object orientated programming (see Hewitt and Frank[2]). This leads to the philosophy that when working on one part, the user needs to know what another part does, but not how it does it. Modula-2 allows this by providing, in addition to procedures, the concept of modules.

1.2 Modules

A procedure is a series of statements which accomplish a particular action, possibly acting on parameters passed to the procedure, possibly returning a result either as a return value, or by changing variable parameters or global variables. As stated above, it is good practice to use local variables wherever possible. However, if a variable is to keep its value between successive calls to the procedure, that is if it is to exist always, it cannot be made local: it must be global and so potentially corruptable by other procedures. Another problem is that it is sometimes required that a variable be accessible by a group of procedures, but only by those procedures. Modules help to solve these problems.

A module is a collection of associated elements (procedures, variables, types, constants and modules). The programmer can specify which of these elements are accessible from outside the module. Any variable made local to the module can be changed only by the procedures within that module (just like a local variable in a procedure), but that variable exists always, so it keeps its value between successive calls to procedures in the module. Also, such a variable is accessible only to those procedures within the module. An example where this can be used is the generation of pseudo-random numbers.

Many programs wish to operate on random data and this can be achieved by generating a set of random numbers. Most methods used actually generate a sequence of values which appear to be random, but after a period the sequence is repeated: the numbers are said to be *pseudo random*. However, this is no problem provided that the sequence length is sufficiently long. The basic idea is that the next random number is obtained by processing the last one using a suitable algorithm. One method is the linear congruential method. To implement this, therefore, a variable is needed for storing the last random number (called the seed), and this must exist always. Also required is a procedure for initialising the seed and one for calculating the next number in the sequence. In the linear congruential method this is achieved by a calculation of the form:

seed := (seed * multiplier + constant) MOD modulus

The constants are crucial (see Knuth [3]). This produces numbers in the range 0..modulus-1. A module to achieve this which calculates cardinal values between 0 and 65535 (for which MOD 65536 is inherent) is:

```
MODULE Random;

EXPORT SetSeed, NextRandom; (* specify those elements accessible *)

VAR Seed : CARDINAL;(* this is local & can't be accessed outside *)

  PROCEDURE SetSeed (InitialValue : CARDINAL);
  BEGIN
    Seed := InitialValue;
  END SetSeed;

  PROCEDURE NextRandom() : CARDINAL;
  CONST Multiplier = 58653;
        Constant = 13849;
  BEGIN
    Seed := Seed * Multiplier + Constant;   (* Calculate new seed *)
    RETURN Seed
  END NextRandom;

BEGIN
  SetSeed (0); (* initialise the local variable at program start *)
END Random.
```

The above is an example of a self contained module which can be included in a program module. There are two parts to the module, the action(s) of the module and how the module interacts with other modules. This interaction is the EXPORT statement which specifies the parts of the module accessible from outside. Also allowable is an IMPORT statement, which defines elements from other modules which are accessed by the given module. Note that constants and types, as well as procedures and variables, can be IMPORTed or EXPORTed.

An important point to note in the above is that the local variable, Seed, can only be directly altered by the procedures in the module. In general, wherever possible, this practice should be followed.

Note, the numbers generated by the above will always be the same, as the Seed is always initialised to zero. For some applications this is desirable, but for others a useful technique is to initialise the Seed with a value based on the time of day.

1.3 Libraries

Although local modules can be used, in general a better method is to have library modules. By dividing a program into a series of parts, it is often the case that the programmer produces code for the given program, but which could also be useful in a different program: the above random number module, for example, could equally be used in a Monte-Carlo simulation as well as a program to assess the performance of a control system in reducing noise disturbance.

In fact, the libraries provided with the compiler for input/output, processing strings, mathematical functions, etc., are, in Modula-2, library modules which the user can use in his own program, and are no different from library modules written by the programmer himself. A program consists of a main program module and a series of library modules. Each of these could contain their own local modules.

Library modules are stored in separate files and must be compiled before use. Once compiled, however, the module can be used in other programs and need not be recompiled for each program. As each library module is compiled separately, if one library module only is changed, only that module needs recompiling.

Library modules have two parts: a DEFINITION module and an IMPLEMENTATION module. In the former is a list of those parts which can be accessed from outside, in the latter is the code which does the action. The DEFINITION module for Random would be:

```
DEFINITION MODULE Random;

  PROCEDURE SetSeed (InitialValue : CARDINAL);
  (* This procedure is used to initialise the sequence *)
  PROCEDURE NextRandom() : CARDINAL;
  (* This returns the next random number in the sequence *)

END Random.
```

The implementation module is the same as that given above except that the word IMPLEMENTATION precedes MODULE and there is no export statement.

1.4 Style

Programs should be written so that they can be understood: they should be readable and not include crafty programming tricks. Programming style contributes greatly to its readability. Points to be considered include the use of appropriate names, constants and types, layout of the program and the use of comments.

Programs are written to solve 'real' problems. One reason why high level languages are used, instead of writing in machine code, is that it enables the programmer to write a program in terms of the problem being solved, and not in terms of the machine.

Therefore, appropriate names should be assigned to objects; that is modules, procedures, variables, constants and types (identifiers) should be given names which illustrate their action. In the above example of random numbers, the module was called *Random*, the procedures were *SetSeed* and *NextRandom*, and the seed variable was called *Seed*. In general in this book, identifiers consist of one or many words concatenated together, with the first letter only of each word being a capital letter, as in SetSeed. This has the additional advantage that these identifiers stand out from the reserved words in Modula-2: IF, MODULE, BEGIN, etc.

The use of appropriate constants and types is also recommended. If a program had for its data the days of the week, these could be represented by the numbers 1 to 7, with 1 being sunday, 2 being monday, etc. This would not be helpful, as the reader would have to know that 1 was sunday and not monday. A better method would be to assign a series of constants, like:

```
CONST Sunday = 1; Monday = 2;
```

etc. However, this is couching the program in terms of numbers, not days of the week, which is what the program was about. Therefore the best method is to define a type for handling days of the week:

```
TYPE DayOfWeek = (Sunday, Monday, Tuesday, Wednesday,
                  Thursday, Friday, Saturday);
```

This has an extra advantage in that the program cannot cause a variable of type *DayOfWeek* to go out of range.

The layout of a program is also important in making the program readable. Liberal use of blank lines to distinguish between separate parts of the program is recommended. Indenting a section of code between a BEGIN and an END, or the THEN and ELSE parts of an IF statement etc., helps readability and understanding: it is immediately apparent which actions are undertaken if the boolean is true, and which are done otherwise. Also by putting the END in the same column position as the BEGIN, etc., reminds the programmer if he has forgotten the END. Modula-2 helps here as each control statement has a beginning and an end: for each IF, and each WHILE, etc., there is an END. Compare the following version of the Random module with the earlier well laid out version: which is easiest to read ?

```
MODULE Random; EXPORT SetSeed, NextRandom; VAR Seed : CARDINAL;
PROCEDURE SetSeed (InitialValue : CARDINAL);
BEGIN Seed := InitialValue; END SetSeed;
PROCEDURE NextRandom() : CARDINAL;
BEGIN Seed := Seed * 58653 + 13849; RETURN Seed END NextRandom;
BEGIN SetSeed (0); END Random.
```

There is always a certain amount of personal preference in layout, but the above comments should be used as guidance. The programs given in this book are deliberately laid out carefully.

Comments are also important. These should explain what the code is achieving, and perhaps indicate why a particular algorithm was used. Comments which state the obvious, like 1 assigned to x after x := 1, are pointless. Using appropriate names usually reduces the number of comments.

1.5 Algorithms

In the book the algorithms are often produced in a pseudocode, which is a cross between English and an informal version of Modula-2. The final implementation of the code is sometimes given in full in the book, but often only on the disk. The programs are fully commented (as is good practice).

In general algorithms are implemented as directly as possible, although some considerations of efficency are made. For example, an algorithm for drawing lines is given which uses integer calculations only, as these are usually faster than calculations using floating point numbers. Direct implementation often involves recursion: the process whereby a procedure to solve a problem does so by calling itself. Although for some problems recursion is inefficient and an iterative solution is better, for many other problems a non-recursive implementation is opaque (Wirth[4]). Recursion is a topic which is not liked by many new programmers. Thus, as many of the algorithms presented here are recursive, the following comments should prove reassuring.

Experience has shown that recursion is only a problem if you worry about it or a poor programming technique is used. For example, consider the Tower of Hanoi problem, probably the simplest sensible example of recursion.

Three disks are placed on one of three pegs in ascending order of size, the largest being on the bottom. The problem is to move these three disks from one peg to another peg, but only one disk can be moved at a time and a larger disk cannot be put on a smaller one. The third peg may be used in the course of the operation of the program. The solution of this problem illustrates well the top-down approach. Moving three disks is difficult: so the problem is broken down.

```
To move 3 disks from peg A to peg C, the other peg is B:
  move 2 disks from A to B, spare peg C
  move 3rd disk from A to C
  move 2 disks from B to C, spare peg A
```

So, the algorithm can be encoded:

```
PROCEDURE Move (3 disks, source, destination, spare)
BEGIN
  Move (2 disks, source, spare, destination)
  Move 3rd disk from source to destination
  Move (2 disks, spare, destination, source)
END Move;
```

Moving 2 disks is complicated, so that is broken down in the same manner:

```
PROCEDURE Move (2 disks, source, destination, spare)
BEGIN
  Move (1 disk, source, spare, destination)
  Move 2nd disk from source to destination
  Move (1 disk, spare, destination, source)
END Move;
```

Clearly, the procedure Move has the same form whether it is moving 3 or 2 disks, hence it can be generalised to move any number of disks:

```
PROCEDURE Move (nDisks, source, destination, spare);
BEGIN
  IF nDisks > 0 THEN
    Move (nDisks-1, source, spare, destination)
    Move nth Disk from source to destination
    Move (nDisks-1, spare, destination, source)
  END
END Move
```

(It should be noted that the problem is based on a legend where there are 64 golden disks on three pegs, and that one disk is moved each day. It is said that when the last disk has been moved the world will end. So as not to tempt fate, all versions of the program written by the author have limited the maximum number of disks to 15!)

To understand this recursive procedure it should be read thus:

```
To move n disks from source to destination with spare peg:
  IF n > 0 THEN
    move n-1 disks from source to spare
    move nth disk from source to destination
    move n-1 disks from spare to destination
  END
```

The action is obvious from these statements, and should be read directly with the reader accepting that n-1 disks are moved, but not worrying how this is achieved. This is no different from reading any structured program, the robot coffee maker, for example

```
To make coffee:
  boil water
  add coffee to cup
  add boiling water to cup
```

Therefore, recursion is no different from other programming constructs. Care is required, of course, with recursion to ensure that the routine terminates, but that is also required for loops. Here the recursion ends because at each stage the Move procedure is called acting on a smaller part of the problem: to move n disks it processes n-1 disks, and eventually the program ends because the procedure is called to act on 0 disks.

It is also important to use local variables in recursive procedures where appropriate, but this is encouraged also when writing non-recursive programs. Why it can be essential in recursion is illustrated by the *Quicksort* sorting algorithm. More details of the algorithm can be found in Wirth [4], but the essential details are given below.

The data to be processed are stored in an array in any order and the object of the algorithm is to rearrange them so that the array contains sorted data. This it does by partitioning the array into two parts, the first containing all values less than a particular value, the other part containing the rest. If each part were sorted somehow, then, clearly, the whole array would be sorted. Thus the next stage of the algorithm is to sort these two parts, and this is achieved by using the same procedure. Hence the algorithm can be implemented using a recursive procedure, *QSort*, which sorts the elements in the array between points *left* and *right*. Note that the recursive calls to *QSort* are always on a smaller version of the problem, on a smaller part of the array, thus the procedure terminates. The algorithm is shown below:

```
PROCEDURE QuickSort (VAR data : ARRAY)

  PROCEDURE QSort (left, right);
  (* sort data between data[left] and data[right] *)
  VAR leftlim, rightlim
  BEGIN
    Partition array;
    (* set leftlim and rightlim so that all items less than
    one value are between data [left] and data [rightlim],
    & the rest are between data[leftlim] and data[right] *)
      IF left<rightlim THEN QSort (left, rightlim) END;
      IF leftlim<right THEN QSort (leftlim, right) END
  END QSort;

BEGIN
  QSort (1, MAX size of array)
END QuickSort;
```

When *QSort* calls itself recursively, between limits *left* and *rightlim*, it is important that the values *leftlim* and *right* are not changed, so that a valid call to *QSort* between limits *leftlim* and *right* can be made subsequently. This is achieved in the above automatically because *rightlim* is a local variable, that is, every time *QSort* is called, it has its own version of both *leftlim* and *rightlim*. This would not be the case if *leftlim* and *rightlim* were global variables. This is of course no problem. Good programming practice requires that variables are made as local as possible, so *leftlim* and *rightlim* are made local, hence once again recursion is not a problem if the proper technique is adopted.

1.6 Multiple exits from loops and procedures

It is considered bad programming practice for a program to have many exits from a loop, or returns from a procedure. This is because it is more difficult to prove that such programs will operate correctly on all occasions, and to track the program operation. In this book, therefore, the author usually abides by this rule. However, on certain occasions, algorithms implemented in this manner are more opaque or unnecessarily clumsy than when multiple exits are used. Therefore, where appropriate, multiple exits are used, though the reader is advised that if he is writing programs where guaranteed operation is required, this practice should be avoided.

As a general rule, multiple exits should be avoided, but like all general rules, there are exceptions (except to this rule!).

Examples where multiple exits are used include the string comparison routine in chapter 8. In that case the author feels that the procedure should terminate as soon as the result is known, so the algorithm is implemented directly.

Conclusion

The aim of this book is to present various programming techniques in useful applications and show how large programs can be managed easily if they are broken down into separate parts each acted upon independently. This top-down philosophy will be illustrated by the writing of a large program. However, writing a large program is daunting, so a smaller program will be considered first, in which the above ideas are put into practice.

Exercise

Write a program to sort an array of random numbers using the Quicksort method: that is, complete the procedure shown on page 10. For this, an algorithm is required for partitioning an array, that is, to find the values of leftlim and rightlim. Consider the following:

```
midvalue := data [(left + right) DIV 2];
leftlim := left; rightlim := right;
REPEAT
  WHILE data[leftlim] < midvalue DO INC (leftlim) END;
  WHILE data[rightlim] > midvalue DO DEC (rightlim) END;
  IF leftlim <= rightlim THEN
    swap (data[leftlim], data[rightlim];
    INC (leftlim); DEC (rightlim)
  END
UNTIL leftlim >rightlim;
```

References

1 Ian Somerville *Software Engineering* Addison-Wesley 1989

2 J. A. Hewitt & R. J. Frank *Software Engineering in Modula-2* Macmillan Education 1989

3 D. E. Knuth *The Art of Computer Programming Vol 2* Addison-Wesley 1969

4 Niklaus Wirth *Algorithms and Data Structures* Prentice-Hall 1986

2 Introductory Program

The program described in this second chapter is designed to illustrate various points. First, it introduces the style of the programs presented here and the method of programming reasonably sized programs, showing how the problem is divided into separate, manageable parts, so that a solution is obtained easily. Second, it illustrates how the program should be divided into suitable parts: both the algorithms and data are placed in suitable modules, so that the appropriate data only are accessed by the relevant routines. Finally, the program illustrates a useful technique, backtracking.

2.1 The HEX problem

The program given here is to solve a puzzle in which there are 7 hexagons, each made up of 6 triangles of different colours, with the same colours on each hexagon, but in different orders. The problem is to arrange the 7 hexagons with one in the middle, and the others equally spaced around it, such that adjacent triangles on different hexagons have the same colour. The program should show its operation graphically. One solution to the problem is shown in figure 2.1. To solve the problem, the program must select which hexagon should go in each position and the orientation of each hexagon.

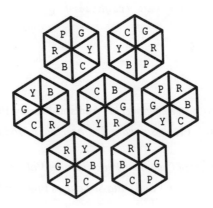

(R=Red, G=Green, B=Blue, Y=Yellow, C=Cyan, P=Purple)

Figure 2.1 One solution to the HEX problem

The program can be solved using the general purpose, problem solving, backtracking method, which is a useful technique not just restricted to solving silly puzzles. There are numerous examples where the technique is applicable, a few of which are listed below. This particular example was chosen as it provides a graphical display of the technique in action, it illustrates some other useful techniques, and it is a good demonstration.

Many books which introduce the technique illustrate the method with the Knights Tour or the Eight Queens problems. The former is to find a way of moving a knight on a chess board, using the knight's move of two along and one at right angles, such that it lands on each square of the board once only. The latter is to position eight queens on the chess board such that no queen is in check of any other.

Other more practical problems include finding a route through a maze, or along a map, and verification that a program is syntactically correct. The programming language PROLOG uses the technique to search its database in order to test the rules that make up the program. It can be used in solving various problems in 'artificial intelligence'. Other examples are described in the exercises at the end of the chapter. See also Wirth [1].

2.2 The backtracking technique

The technique is quite straightforward. The problem to be solved is divided into a number of small parts, and the parts are solved iteratively in a trial and error process. When one part is solved, the next one is attempted. If a solution to the next part cannot be found, then the particular solution to the original part must be erroneous, so the program goes back (*backtracks*) and tries to find an alternative solution to that part.

In the hexagon problem, the separate parts are to try to place a hexagon in each position. In the *Eight Queens* problem, there are eight separate parts, putting a queen on each row. In the *Knights Tour* there are sixty four parts: positioning a knight on each square.

Thus a routine is needed to try to put (in this case) a hexagon at a specified position. This it does by trying each hexagon in turn until it finds one that can be placed. Then that piece is positioned there. If this is the last position, then a solution to the whole problem has been found. Otherwise the program tries to put a hexagon in the next position. If a hexagon cannot be found to go in the next position, then the current selection is wrong, so the routine must continue its search for a hexagon that is acceptable. If no such hexagon can be found, then the routine fails. Thus the procedure terminates when either a solution has been found, or each hexagon has been tested (and found not to be acceptable). A pseudo-code procedure to do this is shown below:

```
PROCEDURE Try (Position);
VAR Hexagon;       (* must be local *)
BEGIN
  Initialise count of which Hexagon;
  REPEAT
    Select next Hexagon;
    IF Acceptable THEN
      Put It There;
      IF Position = Last THEN
        SolutionFound := TRUE
      ELSE
        Try (Next Position);
        IF NOT SolutionFound THEN Remove Hexagon END
      END
    END
  UNTIL SolutionFound OR Tried All Hexagons
END Try
```

This procedure is in a general form which can be adapted for other problems with ease. When the procedure tries to put a hexagon in the next position, it does so by calling the procedure *Try*, that is, it calls itself recursively. It is therefore important that the variable *Hexagon* should be local to the procedure for the algorithm to work correctly. Good practice would require it to be local, of course, as it is only associated directly with the attempt to put a hexagon at the particular position specified by the parameter passed to the procedure.

It is of course not the whole story. Routines are needed for deciding if a particular hexagon can be put there, for putting a hexagon there and for removing the hexagon. As the problem requires that its operation should be displayed graphically, the routines for putting and removing a hexagon should draw or erase the hexagon on the screen. Routines are also needed for initialising the problem, specifying how the hexagons are represented, etc. However, as is good practice, these more complicated routines are written separately.

2.3 The program structure and development

The program is made up of a number of modules. The main module, HEX, contains the main body which sets the program running and the Try routine. A separate module, HEXSOLVE, contains the routines for deciding if a piece can be positioned there and for putting and removing the hexagons. Associated with this module, therefore, is the way in which the hexagons are represented. This module uses another, HEXGRAPH, which is responsible for drawing the hexagons. How this is achieved, in the final analysis, depends on the graphics facilities, so a specific low level graphics driver, HEXPRIM, is provided for actual drawing of the shapes and for any initialisation. The program also calls other library modules, for example IO, the Top Speed Modula-2 Input/Output library.

The program was developed in a top-down manner, with suitable debugging statements (writing values to the screen, etc.) where appropriate. By forcing the routine *Acceptable* to return TRUE, the program would, if routines were available, draw the hexagons in the seven positions of the screen. Thus the HEX module was written first and dummy routines for *Acceptable*, *RecordIt* and *EraseIt* written in module HEXSOLVE. This was done without much worry as the *Try* routine is in the same form as other such routines written by the author, so the algorithm was known to be correct.

Then *RecordIt* was modified to call routines for drawing the hexagons. This required routines to calculate the coordinates of the triangles which form the hexagon and then draw the outline of the triangles. A routine in module HEXGRAPH, called *DrawTriangle*, was written which calculated the coordinates and then called routines for drawing lines provided in the TopSpeed library *Graph*. Then considerations for the representation of the hexagons were made, so that *RecordIt* drew hexagons of the correct colour.

The next stage was to write the routines *Acceptable* and *EraseIt*, and complete the action of *RecordIt*. The final stage was to draw the triangles properly, that is to fill them in the correct colour, rather than just draw their outlines: module HEXPRIM was written to replace the TopSpeed module Graph.

In this way the program was developed quickly and without much problem. Detailed development of each part is given in the following sections.

2.4 The HEX module

The main module, HEX, is as shown in program 2.1. This is in the same form as the algorithm presented earlier in pseudocode. Note in the module the use of appropriate names: the procedure *Try*, which tries to put a *Hexagon* at the specified *Position*, and sets the boolean *SolutionFound* if a solution to the problem has been found. These names, or identifiers, are meaningful, which makes the program much easier to read. Also, note the layout and comments which follow the guidance given in the introduction.

2.5 The HEXSOLVE module

This module contains the routines for deciding whether the specified hexagon can be put at the given position, *Acceptable*, for putting it there, *RecordIt*, and for removing it if it is found subsequently that it should not be there, *EraseIt*. These routines, and the constant *NumberOfHexagons*, are defined in the definition module HEXSOLVE.DEF. Note the use of the constant so that the main program could be used to solve any hexagon problem, not just this specific one. The definition file is listed in program 2.2. Note that the definition file contains a description of the facilities provided by the module so that the user knows how to use the module without needing to know how the constituent routines work.

16 Modula-2 Applied

```
MODULE Hex;
  (* to solve the hexagon problem, using the back-tracking method *)

FROM IO IMPORT WrStr, WrLn;
FROM HexSolve IMPORT NumberOfHexagons,Acceptable,RecordIt,EraseIt;

VAR SolutionFound : BOOLEAN;

  PROCEDURE Try (Position : CARDINAL);
     (* This procedure tries to put a hexagon in place 'Position' *)
  VAR Hexagon : CARDINAL;
          (* This variable is used to identify which hexagon tried *)
  BEGIN
    Hexagon := 0;            (* Initialise selection (of hexagon) *)
    REPEAT
      INC (Hexagon);                          (* Choose next one *)
      IF Acceptable (Hexagon, Position) THEN  (* Ok to put here ? *)
        RecordIt (Hexagon, Position);         (* Yes, so do so *)
        IF Position=NumberOfHexagons THEN     (* If placed last one *)
          SolutionFound := TRUE               (* Have a solution *)
        ELSE
          Try (Position + 1); (* Try to put hexagon in next pos'n *)
          IF NOT SolutionFound THEN     (* If could not put there *)
            EraseIt (Hexagon, Position)(* This one wrong so erase *)
          END                           (* and try another *)
        END
      END
    UNTIL SolutionFound OR (Hexagon=NumberOfHexagons);
                          (* Stop if got solution or tried all *)
  END Try;


BEGIN
  WrStr ('Hexagons'); WrLn;  (* Good to tell user program started *)
  SolutionFound := FALSE;                  (* Initialise variable *)
  Try (1);            (* Try to put hexagon in first position *)
  IF SolutionFound THEN
    WrStr ('Solution Found'); WrLn
  ELSE
    WrStr (' No Solution '); WrLn
  END;
END Hex.
```

Program 2.1 Main program module for HEX problem

```
DEFINITION MODULE HexSolve;

CONST NumberOfHexagons = 7;

PROCEDURE Acceptable (Hexagon, Position : CARDINAL) : BOOLEAN;
(* This tests if the given Hexagon can be placed in the Position *)

PROCEDURE RecordIt (Hexagon, Position : CARDINAL);
(* This puts the Hexagon at the given Position, and draws it *)

PROCEDURE EraseIt (Hexagon, Position : CARDINAL);
(* This removes the Hexagon and deletes it from the screen *)

END HexSolve.
```

Program 2.2 Definition file for HEXSOLVE module

For the implementation of the module, the first stage is to decide how the Hexagons are to be represented. For each Hexagon we need to know the colours of its 6 triangles, whether that triangle has been used and, if so, the orientation of the Hexagon. A RECORD can be used:

```
CArray = ARRAY [1..6] OF Colour;
Piece  = RECORD
           Colours  : CArray;
           Rotation : CARDINAL;
           BeenUsed : BOOLEAN;
         END;
```

Colours contains the colours of the 6 triangles in anti-clockwise order. *Rotation* has a value in the range 0..5: 0 means no rotation, with *Colours[1]* being to the right of the middle of the hexagon, 1 means a rotation anticlockwise by one triangle, so that *Colours[6]* is to the right of the middle, etc. The triangle numbers are shown in figure 2.2.

The 7 hexagons are an array of *Piece*:

```
Pieces : ARRAY [1..NumberOfHexagons] OF Piece;
```

We also need to know which *Piece* is placed in which of the 7 positions:

```
WhichPiece : ARRAY [1..NumberOfHexagons] OF CARDINAL;
```

18 Modula-2 Applied

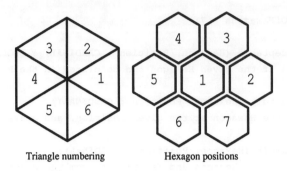

Figure 2.2 Numbering of hexagons

WhichPiece[1] will be the *Piece* put in the centre, number 2 will be the one to the right of this, and numbers 3..7 will be in anti-clockwise order around the centre piece: this is also shown in figure 2.2.

Note that these variables are only needed in this module. Therefore they are declared inside the module. The complete implementation module is listed in program 2.3, below.

```
IMPLEMENTATION MODULE HexSolve;

FROM HexGraph IMPORT
  Colour, Black, Red, Yellow, Purple, Green, Blue, Cyan,
  DrawTriangle;


TYPE CArray = ARRAY [1..6] OF Colour;
     Piece = RECORD                    (* This defines a hexagon *)
               Colours : CArray;   (* The 6 colours of the hexagon *)
               Rotation : CARDINAL;(* Its orientation when placed *)
               BeenUsed : BOOLEAN;   (* Has the hexagon been used *)
             END;


VAR Pieces : ARRAY [1..NumberOfHexagons] OF Piece;
       (* This defines all the hexagons *)
    WhichPiece : ARRAY [1..NumberOfHexagons] OF CARDINAL;
       (* This indicates which Hexagon is in which position *)
```

Introductory Program 19

```
PROCEDURE InitialiseHexagons;
BEGIN        (* This initialises the seven hexagons of the problem *)
  Pieces[1] := Piece (CArray (Blue,Yellow,Red,Green,Purple,Cyan),
                      0, FALSE);
  Pieces[2] := Piece (CArray (Blue,Red,Purple,Green,Yellow,Cyan),
                      0, FALSE);
  Pieces[3] := Piece (CArray (Red,Green,Cyan,Yellow,Blue,Purple),
                      0, FALSE);
  Pieces[4] := Piece (CArray (Yellow,Green,Purple,Red,Blue,Cyan),
                      0, FALSE);
  Pieces[5] := Piece (CArray (Purple,Blue,Yellow,Green,Cyan,Red),
                      0, FALSE);
  Pieces[6] := Piece (CArray (Green,Yellow,Red,Blue,Cyan,Purple),
                      0, FALSE);
  Pieces[7] := Piece (CArray (Green,Blue,Cyan,Purple,Yellow,Red),
                      0, FALSE)
END InitialiseHexagons;

PROCEDURE GetColour (Triangle, Position : CARDINAL) : Colour;
(* For the Hexagon at the given Position, returns actual value of
   colour of the Triangle, given the Hexagon's current Rotation *)
VAR num : CARDINAL;
BEGIN
  WITH Pieces[WhichPiece[Position]] DO
    num := 6 + Triangle - Rotation;    (* add 6 so num never < 0 *)
    WHILE num > 6 DO DEC (num, 6) END;
    RETURN Colours[num]
  END
END GetColour;

PROCEDURE Acceptable (Hexagon, Position : CARDINAL) : BOOLEAN;
(* Returns TRUE if can put the Hexagon in the specified Position *)

  PROCEDURE GetFacingColour;
  (* This rotates the hexagon until the appropriate side of the
     Hexagon faces the middle Hexagon *)
  BEGIN
    WITH Pieces[Hexagon] DO
    Rotation := 0;
    WHILE GetColour(Position+2,Position)#GetColour(Position-1,1) DO
      INC (Rotation)
    END
    END
  END GetFacingColour;
```

```
    PROCEDURE CheckAdjacent (Posn1, Posn2 : CARDINAL) : BOOLEAN;
    (* Do adjacent faces of adjacent Hexagons have the same colour? *)
    BEGIN
      RETURN GetColour (Posn1+3, Posn1) = GetColour (Posn1, Posn2)
    END CheckAdjacent;



BEGIN (* of Acceptable *)
  WhichPiece [Position] := Hexagon;    (* Mark hexagon in position *)
  WITH Pieces[Hexagon] DO
    IF Position=1 THEN
      Rotation := 0;
      RETURN TRUE      (* Can always put Hexagon in middle position *)
    ELSIF BeenUsed THEN
        RETURN FALSE   (* is already used, so cannot use it again *)
    ELSE
      GetFacingColour;                (* Rotate Hexagon suitably *)
      IF Position=2 THEN
        RETURN TRUE          (* Can always put in second position *)
      ELSIF Position=NumberOfHexagons THEN
        RETURN CheckAdjacent (Position, Position-1) AND
             CheckAdjacent (2, Position)
              (* Last Hexagon, check fits with 6th and 2nd Hexagon *)
      ELSE
        RETURN CheckAdjacent (Position, Position-1);
                  (* Check this Hexagon fits with previous one *)
      END
    END;
  END
END Acceptable;



PROCEDURE RecordIt (Hexagon, Position : CARDINAL);
(* This installs Hexagon at the current Position, and draws it *)
VAR ct : CARDINAL;
BEGIN
  FOR ct := 1 TO 6 DO
    DrawTriangle (Position, ct, GetColour (ct, Position) )
  END;
  Pieces[Hexagon].BeenUsed := TRUE
END RecordIt;
```

Introductory Program 21

```
PROCEDURE EraseIt (Hexagon, Position : CARDINAL);
(* This removes the Hexagon, and deletes it from the screen *)
VAR ct : CARDINAL;
BEGIN
  FOR ct := 1 TO 6 DO
    DrawTriangle (Position, ct, Black)
  END;
  Pieces[Hexagon].BeenUsed := FALSE
END EraseIt;

BEGIN
  InitialiseHexagons;              (* First define the Hexagons *)
END HexSolve.
```

Program 2.3 Implementation module for HEXSOLVE

Initialisation

The variable *Pieces* needs to be initialised, and this must be done in the module. As initialisation must occur at the start of the program, the obvious place to do it is in the main BEGIN..END clause of the module. Hence a call to the procedure *InitialiseHexagons* is placed there. Each *Piece* in the array *Pieces* is a record, and each can be initialised in one statement, thus:

```
Pieces[n] := Piece ( < contents of the record > )
```

This is a specific example of how a variable (a record, array, etc.) can be initialised:

```
variable := TYPE of Variable (  contents of variable )
```

In this case, the contents of the record are the array *Colours*, the cardinal *Rotation* and the boolean *BeenUsed*. The value of the array of colours is specified by:

```
CArray ( <6 colours> )
```

When doing such a statement, the type, in this case *CArray*, must be an explicit type. This is why the separate definition for CArray was made, rather than defining the Colours as being an ARRAY [1..6] OF Colour in the definition of a Piece. So, for example, the first piece is initialised by:

```
Pieces[1] := Piece (CArray (Blue,Yellow,Red,Green,Purple,Cyan),
                    0 ,FALSE)
```

Acceptable

The function *Acceptable* returns true if the particular hexagon can be placed at the specified position. The algorithm is as follows:

```
IF Position=1 THEN
   Can always put Hexagon here, do so with Rotation 0
ELSIF BeenUsed THEN
   Cannot put here as already been used
ELSE
   Rotate Hexagon so correct colour faces middle hexagon.
   IF Position=2 THEN
      Can always put Hexagon here
   ELSIF Position=LastHexagon THEN
      Test that both the adjacent triangles on this and the
         previous hexagon have the same colour
      AND the adjacent triangles on this and the second
         hexagon have the same colour
   ELSE
      Test that the adjacent triangles on this and the
      previous hexagon have the same colour
   END
END
```

The actual code for this, which is shown in program 2.3, follows this structure with calls to procedures to implement the more complex functions.

One such function is *GetFacingColour*, which seeks to find the orientation of the hexagon such that the triangle of the correct colour faces the middle hexagon. This is achieved using the routine, *GetColour*, which returns the actual colour of the triangle at the specified position given the rotation of the particular hexagon. For *GetFacingColour*, the appropriate triangle of the middle hexagon is the one at *Position-1*: for triangle 2 it is position 1, for triangle 3 it is position 2, etc. The pertinent triangle for the outer hexagon under test is at *Position+2*: for position 2 it is triangle 4, etc. Hence the procedure *GetFacingColour* is essentially:

```
Rotation := 0;
WHILE GetColour(Position+2,Position) # GetColour(Position-1,1) DO
   INC (Rotation)
END
```

GetColour is passed the notional triangle of interest, *Triangle*, and the position of the hexagon, *Position*, and calculates the actual colour given the rotation of the hexagon. The actual hexagon under consideration is:

```
Pieces [ WhichPiece [Position] ]
```

If the *Rotation* is 0, the colour required is *Colours[Triangle]*, if the *Rotation* is 1, the colour is *Colours[Triangle-1]*, etc., thus, in general, the colour required is *Colours[Triangle-Rotation]*, though care is needed to ensure that the index into the array is in the correct range. *Triangle* has a value in the range 1 to 6 and *Rotation* is in the range 0 to 5.

The final procedure, *CheckAdjacent*, checks that the two adjacent triangles of successive outer hexagons have the same colour. This operates on two hexagons at positions *Posn1* and *Posn2*. The two facing triangles are those at *Posn1+3* on the hexagon at *Posn1* and at *Posn1* on the hexagon at *Posn2*. Hence the routine returns:

```
GetColour (Posn1+3, Posn1) = GetColour (Posn1, Posn2)
```

RecordIt

This procedure installs the hexagon and draws it on the screen. The particular hexagon is marked as having been used and then each triangle is drawn, the colour of which is found using *GetColour* again. Hence the code is

```
Pieces[Hexagon].BeenUsed := TRUE;
FOR ct := 1 TO 6 DO
   DrawTriangle (Position, ct, GetColour (ct, Position) )
END
```

EraseIt

This procedure marks the hexagon as not being used and erases it from the screen (by drawing it in the background colour, black). Hence:

```
Pieces[Hexagon].BeenUsed := FALSE;
FOR ct := 1 TO 6 DO
   DrawTriangle (Position, ct, Black)
END
```

2.6 The HEXGRAPH module

This module contains the routine for drawing the triangle of a hexagon, and it defines the constants for each colour. The definition file is listed in program 2.4. The *DrawTriangle* routine draws the specified triangle of the hexagon at the given position, and then draws a white border around it. The routine assumes a graphics system of size *ScreenSize* square. The actual size of the screen depends on the graphics system being used, so this module calls a lower level primitive module,

HEXPRIM, which scales the coordinates to the actual screen size and contains the low level routines for drawing lines, etc.

```
DEFINITION MODULE HexGraph;

CONST Red = 12;            (* Define codes for the Hexagon's colours *)
      Yellow = 14;
      Purple = 13;
      Green = 10;
      Blue = 9;
      Cyan = 11;
      Black = 0;
      White = 15;

TYPE Colour = CARDINAL;

PROCEDURE DrawTriangle (Position,Triangle:CARDINAL; Col:Colour);
(* This draws a triangle of the hexagon at the specified Position.
   The orientation of the triangle is determined by Rotation.
   The colour of the triangle is specified by the Colour Col *)

END HexGraph.
```

Program 2.4 Definition module for HEXGRAPH

There are two parts to the module, the setting of the size of triangles and the drawing of the triangles. As a constant screen size is assumed, the size of the triangles can be determined by a series of CONST definitions at compile time, and these are stored in constant arrays. The complete listing of the module is given in program 2.5.

```
IMPLEMENTATION MODULE HexGraph;

FROM HexPrim IMPORT ScreenSize, FillTriangle, Line;

TYPE HexArray = ARRAY [1..7] OF INTEGER;

CONST
  MidScreen = ScreenSize DIV 2;    (* Now Calculate pertinent sizes *)
  TriSize = ScreenSize DIV 6;
  HalfTriSize = TriSize DIV 2;
  Root3TriSize = TriSize + (TriSize * 7) DIV 10; (* 1.7 * TriSize *)
  HalfRoot3TriSize = Root3TriSize DIV 2;
```

```
                         (* Arrays for position of hexagons *)
  XPos = HexArray (MidScreen, MidScreen + 2 * TriSize,
             MidScreen + TriSize, MidScreen - TriSize,
             MidScreen - 2 * TriSize,
             MidScreen - TriSize, MidScreen + TriSize);

  YPos = HexArray (MidScreen, MidScreen, MidScreen - Root3TriSize,
             MidScreen - Root3TriSize, MidScreen,
             MidScreen + Root3TriSize, MidScreen + Root3TriSize);

         (* Arrays for relative position of corners of hexagons *)
  XRot = HexArray (HalfRoot3TriSize, HalfRoot3TriSize, 0,
             -HalfRoot3TriSize, -HalfRoot3TriSize,
             0, HalfRoot3TriSize);

  YRot = HexArray (HalfTriSize, -HalfTriSize, -TriSize,
             -HalfTriSize, HalfTriSize, TriSize, HalfTriSize);

PROCEDURE DrawTriangle (Position,Triangle:CARDINAL; Col:Colour);
        (* Draw triangle of Hexagon at given position and colour *)
VAR XTriangle, YTriangle : ARRAY [0..2] OF INTEGER;
  (* These are used to store the X,Y coordinates of the triangle *)
BEGIN
  XTriangle[0] := XPos[Position];   (* Calc' vertices of triangle *)
  XTriangle[1] := XTriangle[0] + XRot[Triangle];
  XTriangle[2] := XTriangle[0] + XRot[Triangle+1];

  YTriangle[0] := YPos[Position];
  YTriangle[1] := YTriangle[0] + YRot[Triangle];
  YTriangle[2] := YTriangle[0] + YRot[Triangle+1];

  FillTriangle (XTriangle, YTriangle, Col);

                (* Now draw white border around it *)
  Line (XTriangle[0],YTriangle[0],XTriangle[1],YTriangle[1],White);
  Line (XTriangle[1],YTriangle[1],XTriangle[2],YTriangle[2],White);
  Line (XTriangle[2],YTriangle[2],XTriangle[0],YTriangle[0],White)
END DrawTriangle;

END HexGraph.
```

Program 2.5 Implementation module for HEXGRAPH

Constants

The hexagons are specified by two sets of arrays. The first gives the coordinates of the centre of each hexagon, the second gives the relative coordinates of the vertices of the hexagon from the centre.

The hexagons are made up of 6 equilateral triangles. The length of the sides of each triangle is defined by a constant, *TriSize*. So that the problem fills almost the whole screen, a suitable size for the triangle is a sixth of the screen, that is *ScreenSize DIV 6*.

The middle hexagon should be at the centre of the screen, so its origin should be at *ScreenSize DIV 2, ScreenSize DIV 2*. Hexagons at positions 2 and 5 should be displaced from the origin to the right and left, respectively, by *2 * TriSize*. This leaves a suitable gap between the hexagons (as shown in figure 2.1). The middle of the other hexagons should also be displaced from the centre by *2 * TriSize*, so simple trigonometry shows that the horizontal and vertical displacements should be *TriSize* and *TriSize * SquareRoot(3)*, respectively. *SquareRoot(3)* is approximately 1.7. Given the useful constants of

```
MidScreen = ScreenSize DIV 2;
TriSize = ScreenSize DIV 6;
Root3TriSize = ScreenSize + ScreenSize * 7 DIV 10;
```

the 2 constant arrays for the x and y coordinates of the centres of the seven hexagons are easily given: see program 2.5.

The coordinates of the vertices are *TriSize* away from the centre of the hexagon. Thus two are *TriSize* directly above or below the centre, and the others offset in the horizontal direction by *TriSize * SquareRoot(3) DIV 2* and by *TriSize DIV 2* in the vertical direction. These are also stored in arrays. For the triangle at a given Rotation, the vertices are elements *Rotation* and *Rotation+1*. Hence the arrays contain 7 coordinates, the first one being duplicated in the seventh position.

DrawTriangle

This routine calculates, in two sets of arrays, the x and y coordinates of the vertices of the given *Triangle* at the specified *Position*:

```
XTriangle[0] := XPos[Position];
XTriangle[1] := XTriangle[0] + XRot[Triangle];
XTriangle[2] := XTriangle[0] + XRot[Triangle+1];
```

and similarly for *YTriangle*. These coordinates are then passed to the *FillTriangle* primitive routine which draws the triangle in the specified colour. Then the outline of the triangle is drawn in white, by calling the *DrawLine* routine. The reason for doing this is that a skeleton of the hexagon is left when it is erased which shows that the program has indeed backtracked, and also how close the program has come to finding a solution.

2.7 The HEXPRIM module

The contents of this module depend on the graphics system used. Routines are needed to initialise the graphics system, to scale coordinates from the general *ScreenSize* square to the actual screen size, and for drawing lines and filling triangles. In the disk which accompanies this book, the complete module for using the program on an IBM PC or compatible is provided. In program 2.6 the definition module is given, and in program 2.7 is a listing of the more general routines only.

```
DEFINITION MODULE HexPrim;

CONST ScreenSize = 1024;              (* Notional size of screen *)

PROCEDURE FillTriangle (x, y : ARRAY OF INTEGER; colour : INTEGER);
  (* This routine fills the triangle specified by the 3 X,Y
     coordinates stored in the arrays *)
PROCEDURE Line (x1, y1, x2, y2, colour : INTEGER);
  (* This draws a line between the specifed coordinates *)

END HexPrim.
```

Program 2.6 Definition module of HEXPRIM

```
(* Start of Program 2.7: part of module HEXPRIM *)

PROCEDURE XScale (VAR x : INTEGER);   (* Scale x to fit on screen *)
BEGIN
  x := INTEGER( (LONGINT(x) * LONGINT(Graph.Width) ) DIV ScreenSize)
END XScale;

PROCEDURE YScale (VAR y : INTEGER);   (* Scale y to fit on screen *)
BEGIN
  y := INTEGER( (LONGINT(y) * LONGINT(Graph.Depth) ) DIV ScreenSize)
END YScale;

TYPE LineRec = RECORD          (* Line record to describe a line *)
              decision, incr1, incr2, alwaysIncr, S, A : INTEGER;
              UpS, UpA : BOOLEAN;
              END;
```

28 Modula-2 Applied

```
PROCEDURE SetLineRec (a1, s1, a2, s2 : INTEGER; VAR L : LineRec);
(* This procedure initialises the LineRec L. The a parameters are
the x/y coordinates which always change, the s's are the y/x
coordinates which change only sometimes *)
VAR da, ds : INTEGER;
BEGIN
  WITH L DO
    da := ABS (a2 - a1);           (* difference of always variable *)
    ds := ABS (s2 - s1);           (* difference of sometimes variable *)
    alwaysIncr := ds DIV da;
    incr1 := 2 * (ds MOD da);
    decision := incr1 - da;
    incr2 := decision - da;
    A := a1;                       (* A set to first of always variable *)
    S := s1;
    UpA := a1 <= a2; (* indicate if A should be changed each time *)
    UpS := s1 <= s2
  END
END SetLineRec;


PROCEDURE NextLine (VAR L : LineRec);
(* this calculates next 'X,Y' position of line defined by L *)
BEGIN
  WITH L DO
    IF decision < 0 THEN
      INC (decision, incr1);
      IF UpS THEN
        INC (S, alwaysIncr)
      ELSE
        DEC (S, alwaysIncr)
      END
    ELSE
      INC (decision, incr2);
      IF UpS THEN
        INC (S, 1+alwaysIncr)
      ELSE
        DEC (S, 1+alwaysIncr)
      END
    END;
    IF UpA THEN INC (A) ELSE DEC (A) END
  END
END NextLine;
```

```
PROCEDURE Line (x1, y1, x2, y2, colour : INTEGER);   (* draw line *)

  PROCEDURE ActualLine (a1, s1, a2, s2 : INTEGER; swap : BOOLEAN);
(* This actually draws the line, processing always and sometimes
     variables a1, a2 and s1, s2. swap is true if the a variables
     are y and s are x (that is x and y have been swapped) *)
  VAR L : LineRec;

    PROCEDURE dot;                 (* draw dot at specifed position *)
    BEGIN
      WITH L DO
        IF swap THEN
          Plot (S, A, colour)
        ELSE
          Plot (A, S, colour)
        END
      END;
    END dot;

  BEGIN
    SetLineRec (a1, s1, a2, s2, L);
    dot;                           (* draw dot at start of line *)
    WHILE L.A <> a2 DO             (* now go around and draw loop *)
      NextLine (L);
      dot;                         (* draw dot at current position *)
    END;
  END ActualLine;


BEGIN (* of Line *)
  XScale (x1);                     (* First scale coordinates *)
  YScale (y1);
  XScale (x2);
  YScale (y2);

  IF ABS (x1 - x2) >= ABS (y1 - y2) THEN
    ActualLine (x1, y1, x2, y2, FALSE)
       (* Draw line by changing x always, y sometimes *)
  ELSE
    ActualLine (y1, x1, y2, x2, TRUE)   (* change y always *)
  END
END Line;
```

```
PROCEDURE FillTriangle (X, Y : ARRAY OF INTEGER; colour : INTEGER);
(* This fills the triangle, whose coordinates are given in the two
   arrays, with the specified colour *)
VAR ct : CARDINAL;

  PROCEDURE Order (less, more : CARDINAL);
  (* This is used to check that the coordinates in the Y array are
     in the correct order: it ensures Y[less] < Y[more] *)
  VAR temp : CARDINAL;
  BEGIN
    IF Y[less] > Y[more] THEN
      (* The elements in Y array are in wrong order, so swap them *)
      temp := Y[less];
      Y[less] := Y[more];
      Y[more] := temp;

      temp := X[less];                (* and swap associated Xs *)
      X[less] := X[more];
      X[more] := temp
    END
  END Order;


  PROCEDURE Fill;
  (* This fills triangle with coordinates ABC (stored in X Y
     arrays), with A at top, C at bottom *)
  VAR y : INTEGER;
      L1, L2 : LineRec;


    PROCEDURE HLineMinMax;
    (* This calculates the coordinates of the next line and draws a
       horizontal line between them *)
    BEGIN
      NextLine (L1);          (* update variables for each line *)
      NextLine (L2);
      IF L1.S < L2.S THEN     (* join leftmost L1 and rightmost L2 *)
        HLine (L1.S - L1.alwaysIncr DIV 2, y,
               L2.S + L2.alwaysIncr DIV 2, colour)
      ELSE           (* between right most of L1, left most of L2 *)
        HLine (L2.S - L2.alwaysIncr DIV 2, y,
               L1.S + L1.alwaysIncr DIV 2, colour;
      END
    END HLineMinMax;
```

```
  BEGIN (* of Fill *)
    SetLineRec (Y[0], X[0], Y[2], X[2], L1);           (* Line AC *)
    IF Y[0]=Y[1] THEN
       HLine (X[0], Y[0], X[1], colour)                (* Ya=Yb so join AB *)
    ELSE
       SetLineRec (Y[0], X[0], Y[1], X[1], L2);        (* for line BC *)
       Plot (X[0], Y[0], colour);                      (* draw first dot *)
       FOR y := Y[0]+1 TO Y[1] DO HLineMinMax END      (* fill part tri *)
    END;
    IF Y[1] < Y[2] THEN
       SetLineRec (Y[1], X[1], Y[2], X[2], L2);        (* line BC *)
       FOR y := Y[1]+1 TO Y[2] DO HLineMinMax END      (* fill rest *)
    END
  END Fill;

BEGIN (* of FillTriangle *)
  FOR ct := 0 TO 2 DO                    (* First scale coordinates *)
    XScale (X[ct]);
    YScale (Y[ct])
  END;

  Order (1, 2);          (* Now sort so in increasing order of Y *)
  Order (0, 1);
  Order (1, 2);

  Fill;                                  (* and fill the triangle *)
END FillTriangle;
```

Program 2.7 Listing of part of HEXPRIM module

Scaling

It will be assumed that the actual size of the screen is defined by two constants, *Width* and *Depth*. Then any x coordinate will be scaled by:

```
x := INTEGER ( (LONGINT (x) * LONGINT (Width) ) DIV ScreenSize)
```

and any y coordinate will be scaled by:

```
y := INTEGER ( (LONGINT (y) * LONGINT (Depth) ) DIV ScreenSize)
```

x and *Width* are made LONGINT as their product may exceed MAX(INTEGER). After the division they are small enough to be returned as INTEGERs.

2.8 Drawing lines

There are various algorithms for drawing lines, some directly use the basic formula for a line, $y = mx + c$, but these require floating point arithmetic. Better algorithms use only integer calculations, the best of which was derived by Bresenham. This is an iterative algorithm. Given the coordinates of one point on the line, a simple efficient procedure is used to calculate the next point on that line, etc. For more information, see Foley and Van Dam[2].

On graphics systems, the dots on the screen are arranged in a regular matrix. Therefore the dots that make up the line must be drawn as such, so that a line is not straight but jagged. Bresenham's line drawing algorithm calculates the points on the matrix which are closest to the actual line. If the modulus of the gradient of the slope of the line is less than unity, the x coordinate of the line is changed at each iteration, and the y coordinate sometimes: as in line a of figure 2.3. Otherwise the y coordinate changes each time, and the x sometimes (line b of figure 2.3).

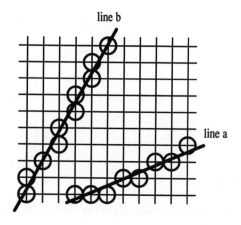

Figure 2.3 Detail of a Line

A derivation of the line drawing algorithm is given in Foley and Van Dam[2]. A procedure for the case of the line whose gradient is between 0 and 1 is shown below. Each time round the loop, the x coordinate is incremented and the variable *decision* is used to decide whether the y coordinate should be incremented. The decision variable is itself changed by one of two constants, *increment1* and *increment2*, which are calculated at the start of the procedure. The routine below draws the line in the specified colour, and uses the routine *Plot* to draw each dot.

```
PROCEDURE BresenhamLine (x1, y1, x2, y2, colour : INTEGER);
  (* For the case x1 < x2, y1 < y2, and that x2-x1 > y2-y1 *)
VAR decision, increment1, increment2, x, y : INTEGER;
BEGIN
  increment1 := 2 * (y2 - y1);          (* First initialise *)
  decision := increment1 - (x2 - x1);
  increment2 := decision - (x2 - x1);
  x := x1;
  y := y1;
  Plot (x, y, colour);    (* Draw dot at the start position *)
  WHILE x < x2 DO
    IF decision < 0 THEN              (* update position *)
      decision := decision + increment1
    ELSE
      decision := decision + increment2;
      y := y + 1
    END;
    x := x + 1;
    Plot (x, y, colour)   (* and draw dot at new position *)
  END
END BresenhamLine;
```

In the above, x is always incremented, y sometimes. A more general routine needs to handle the case where y is changed always and x sometimes, and where x and/or y is decremented. This can be handled elegantly by defining a record to handle the variable which always changes and that which changes sometimes. Such a record is as follows:

```
LineRec = RECORD
            decision, increment1, increment2,
            alwaysIncr, S, A : INTEGER;
            UpS, UpA : BOOLEAN;
          END;
```

decision, *increment1* and *increment2* are the same as above. *alwaysIncr* is needed for filling shapes (see below). *S* and *A* are the sometimes and always changed variables, and the booleans *UpS* and *UpA* indicate whether the changes are positive or negative. With routines to initialise (*SetLineRec*) and then use (*NextLine*) such a record, a general line drawing routine is as follows (the routine also uses the procedure *Plot*):

```
PROCEDURE Line (x1, y1, x2, y2, colour : INTEGER);

  PROCEDURE ActualLine (a1, s1, a2, s2 : INTEGER; swap : BOOLEAN);
    (* a1,a2 are the end coordinates of variable always changed.
       s1,s2 are for the variable sometimes changed.
       swap indicates whether a is X and s is Y, or not *)
  VAR L : LineRec;

    PROCEDURE dot;                       (* actually draw the dot *)
    BEGIN
      IF swap THEN
        Plot (L.S, L.A, colour)          (* use assumed routine *)
      ELSE
        Plot (L.A, L.S, colour)
      END
    END dot;

  BEGIN
    SetLineRec (a1, s1, a2, s2, L);      (* set LineRec *)
    dot;                                 (* draw first dot *)
    WHILE L.A <> a2 DO                   (* loop until reach end point *)
      NextLine (L)                       (* calculate next point *)
      dot                                (* draw next dot *)
    END
  END ActualLine;

BEGIN         (* first test to see whether x or y always changed *)
  IF ABS (x1-x2) >= ABS (y1-y2) THEN
    ActualLine (x1, y1, x2, y2, FALSE)
  ELSE
    ActualLine (y1, x1, y2, x2, TRUE)
  END
END Line;
```

The procedure *SetLineRec* is passed the end coordinates (a1 and a2) of the variable which always changes by 1, and (s1 and s2) for the variable which sometimes changes. In the above application, the sometimes variable will change by 0 or +/-1 at each iteration, as ABS (a1-a2) >= ABS (s1-s2). However, there are some applications (in filling triangles, below) where this is not true, which is where the *alwaysIncr* field of the record is needed. Also, the record must handle lines of negative slope, etc. Thus the initialisation of the *LineRec* is slightly more complicated than the code given above for simple lines with slope between 0 and 1. The *SetLineRec* procedure is given in program 2.7.

The procedure *NextLine* updates the *LineRec* using the decision variable to decide how much to change the sometimes change variable, *S*, and decision, and it changes the always variable, *A*, by 1. See also program 2.7.

Thus for this particular Hexagons problem, the line drawing routine first scales the end coordinates of the line, and then calls Bresenham's line drawing algorithm procedure to actually draw the line.

2.9 Filling triangles

As a general rule, procedures which fill areas should do so by drawing either horizontal or vertical lines. This is because of the discrete nature of dots on a graphics screen: when two parallel lines are drawn at an angle, there may be gaps between them. This is shown in figure 2.4. There are also advantages to using such lines: the positions of dots on them are calculated easily and, in some circumstances, because of the way in which graphics images are stored in memory, many dots can be written into memory in one go. For example, on some graphics modes in PCs, a line of graphics dots is stored in a series of bytes of memory. Therefore, to set one dot, the associated byte must be read, one bit of that byte set, and the byte written back. However, if a horizontal line is drawn for which all bits of that byte must be set, all that is necessary is to set and then write the appropriate byte to memory. Thus the following routine assumes the procedure *HLine* which draws a horizontal line of the specified colour between two x coordinates with the same given y coordinate.

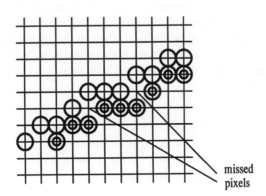

Figure 2.4 Missed pixels problem

The basic idea of the *FillTriangle* routine is as follows: for all y coordinates between the top and the bottom of the triangle, to calculate the x position of the two lines of the triangle which exist at that y coordinate, and to draw a horizontal line between them. Thus, referring to figure 2.5, the algorithm starts at position A, and then progresses down the lines AB and AC, calculating the x coordinates on these lines for each y value, and drawing horizontal lines between them, until point

36 Modula-2 Applied

B is reached. Then the procedure continues in the same manner, still on line AC, but now also on line BC, until point C is reached.

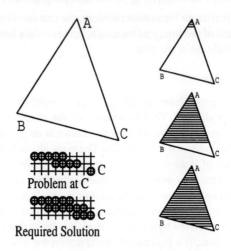

Problem at C

Required Solution

Figure 2.5 Illustration of triangle fill algorithm

To calculate the x coordinates on the lines, Bresenham's algorithm can be used again. So a *LineRec* is needed for each of the lines AB, BC and AC, and for each of these the y coordinate is changed always. This may mean (as in line BC of figure 2.5) that *alwaysIncr* will be non zero. Then, as the algorithm progresses along the lines, the appropriate LineRecs are updated accordingly and the horizontal lines drawn. Care is required for handling a triangle which has a horizontal side. The algorithm is:

```
SetLineRec (on line AC);
IF y coordinate of A equals that of B THEN
    (* a special case, just draw a line from A to B *)
    HLine (between A and B)
ELSE
    SetLineRec (on line AB);
    draw dot at A;
    FOR y := y coordinate of A + 1 TO that of B DO
        NextLine (LineRec AB);
        NextLine (LineRec AC);
        HLine (AB.X, AC.X, y)
    END
END
```

```
(* This has now filled the upper triangle:
   see middle triangle in figure 2.5 *)

IF y coordinate of B less than that of C THEN
   SetLineRec (on line BC);
   FOR y := y coordinate of B + 1 TO that of C DO
      NextLine (LineRec BC);
      NextLine (LineRec AC);
      HLine (BC.X, AC.X, y)
   END
END
```

There is a slight problem with this for triangles with shallow lines. The detailed section around point C, also shown in figure 2.5, illustrates what happens: a gap can occur between the last dot and the rest of the triangle. This is because the *alwaysIncr* field of the record is non zero, so that the x coordinates returned by *Nextline* are not those which would be calculated using the line drawing algorithm. For the line on the left we must estimate the 'leftmost' x coordinate for the given y value, and for the other line the 'rightmost' x coordinate must be estimated. Thus, for the line on the left (in this case BC) we need the x coordinate of the line when the y coordinate is first reached, and for the right line (AC), we need the x coordinate when the next y coordinate is reached. These can be guessed as being *Left.S - Left.alwaysIncr DIV 2* and *Right.S + Right.alwaysIncr DIV 2*. The effect of this change is also shown in figure 2.5.

FillTriangle is passed the X,Y coordinates of the triangle as arrays, and the colour with which the triangle is to be filled. The algorithm is:

```
scale the coordinates
sort them in increasing values in y
fill the triangle
```

The sorting is done using a simple version of Bubblesort (see also Wirth [1]): to sort n items in an array the algorithm is:

```
FOR i := 0 TO n - 2 DO
   FOR j := n - 1 TO i + 1 BY -1 DO
      IF element [j-1] > element [j] THEN swap them END
   END
END
```

38 Modula-2 Applied

As n is 3, elements 1 and 2 are tested, then elements 0 and 1, and finally elements 1 and 2. This action is encoded as three calls to the procedure *Order*: note that when two y coordinates are swapped, their x coordinates must also be swapped. The complete procedure is shown in program 2.7.

2.10 All solutions

The backtracking algorithm given above finds one solution to the problem, but with a few very simple changes, it can be made to find all solutions. The way this is done is to change the *Try* routine such that it does not stop when it finds a solution, it just carries on. Thus the algorithm is:

```
PROCEDURE Try (Position);
VAR Hexagon;
BEGIN
   FOR each Hexagon in turn DO
      IF Acceptable THEN
         Put It There;
         IF Position = Last THEN
            Say have a solution
         ELSE
            Try (Next Position)
         END;
         Remove Hexagon
      END
   END
END Try;
```

Exercises

1) Implement the Hexagon program on your system.

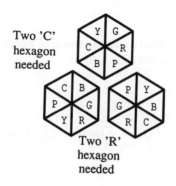

Two 'C' hexagon needed

Two 'R' hexagon needed

Figure 2.6 Problem with Hex program

Introductory Program 39

2) The Hexagon puzzle could be improved: an outer hexagon may be placed such that for the next hexagon to fit, it must have two triangles of the same colour, and none do so. This problem is illustrated in figure 2.6. This also shows where this problem can be most time wasting: placing a hexagon at position 2 and requiring that the hexagon at position 7 has two triangles of the same colour. Modify the procedure *Acceptable* to prevent this occurring.

3) Modify the procedure *Try* so that the program finds all solutions.

4) The Eight Queens problem is a good exercise in programming. Write a program to solve this problem and display the results graphically, as was done here for the Hexagon problem. The following procedure is recommended for program development:

Write a program with a procedure to draw a chess board.

Modify the program so that it can draw a queen on the board. If the queen is drawn on a black square, a white queen should be drawn, otherwise a black queen should be drawn.

Now solve the rest of the problem.

5) Modify the program so that it finds all 92 solutions to the puzzle.

6) Most of these solutions are rotations or mirror images of each other. Modify the program to find the 12 distinct solutions only.

7) Write a program to find one solution to the Knights Tour problem starting from one corner of the board. Develop the program on a 5*5 chess board, and then gradually increase the size of the board. Beware: the program gets very slow, very quickly, as the board size increases.

8) Another puzzle, a *Cryptarithm*, and its solution are shown below.

```
        A                           2
    M E R R Y                 9 7 4 4 5
    X M A S                     6 9 2 8
    ---------                 ---------
    T U R K E Y               1 0 4 3 7 5
```

Here each letter represents a different digit in the range 0..9, and the whole puzzle is a sum. The problem is to find which number is represented by each letter. Write a program to solve it.

40 Modula-2 Applied

9) Write a program to solve the following Cryptarithm:

```
    S E N D
    M O R E
    G O L D
    ―――――――
  M O N E Y
```

10) The problem, one solution to which is illustrated in figure 2.7, is to arrange the 12 numbers, 1 to 12 in the star shape such that the sum of the 4 numbers in each row of the star is 26. Write a program to solve this.

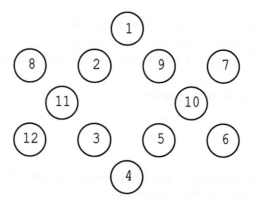

Figure 2.7 The star problem

11) Other puzzles which the author has programmed are the Pentaominoes problems (mentioned in Arthur C Clarke's *Imperial Earth*, and in great detail in Solomon W Golomb's *Polyominoes*), of positioning the twelve distinct shapes made up of five squares: these twelve pentaominoes and one of the distinct 65 solutions to the version of the puzzle in which the shapes are put in an 8*8 square excluding the middle four squares, is shown in figure 2.8. There are over a thousand solutions to the problem of putting the shapes in a 10*6 rectangle, but only two for the 3*20 rectangle.

These require a slight change to the Try routine: as all permutations must be tried, there need to be many nested loops, not just one. The author tried two methods of solving the 8*8 puzzle (one took an 8-bit computer 4 weeks of working days to find the 65 solutions, the following only 2 weeks). To find all solutions the routine should be of the form:

Introductory Program 41

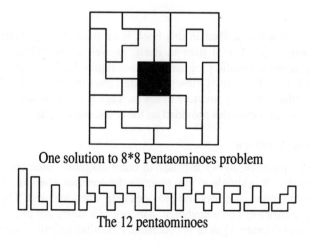

One solution to 8*8 Pentaominoes problem

The 12 pentaominoes

Figure 2.8 A pentaominoes problem

```
PROCEDURE Try (Pentaominoe);
VAR XPos, YPos, Orientation;
BEGIN
  FOR XPos := 1 TO 8 DO
    FOR YPos := 1 TO 8 DO
      FOR Orientation := 0 TO 7 DO
        IF Acceptable THEN
          etc
        END
      END
    END
  END
END Try;
```

The 8 orientations are the four 90 degree rotations for each side facing up. Write a program to find one solution (or all 65 if you have the time!).

References

1 Niklaus Wirth *Algorithms and Data Structures* Prentice-Hall 1986

2 J.D.Foley & A. Van Dam *Fundamentals of Interactive Computer Graphics* Addison-Wesley 1983

3 Diagram Package - Introduction

The main program described in this book is an interactive diagram generation package, which is a useful item in itself, as well as providing a vehicle for describing numerous useful programming techniques. In this chapter the package is described from the point of view of the user, showing the various facilities and the user interface, and the structure of the package is given, to allow the reader to follow the program modules provided on the accompanying disk.

3.1 Package overview

The diagram package allows the user to enter diagrams interactively in a user friendly manner. It is simple to use, prompts the operator when input is expected, allows the correction of errors and provides help when required. The data can be input using cursor keys on a keyboard, a mouse or a tablet. An important requirement of a user-friendly system is consistency: similar activities are signalled by similar actions.

A diagram consists of various standard items, such as lines, circles, arcs, strings of characters, etc., and the user is able to define and edit his own shapes (these can also be made up of lines, circles, etc., as well as other shapes) and be able to include these in the diagram at any position, size and orientation. For example, for logic circuits, a NAND gate can be defined as being an AND gate with a circle at the end, where an AND gate is a shape defined as an arc connected to three sides of a rectangle.

When editing the diagram, it is possible to examine parts of it in detail by zooming into a specific area. Another useful facility provides a regular grid on the screen which helps the user to position objects at regular intervals and to align objects.

Once an object (line, circle, shape, etc.) has been entered, the user is able to modify it: this is achieved by selecting the item to modify and then editing it in the same way that shapes are input initially. It is also possible to group together a number of objects to move them, copy them, erase them, etc.

An advanced feature of the package enables the user to describe a shape by a program rather than a series of lines, etc. This can be used to produce a graph, for example, and then suitable labels can be added interactively. Another use would be to draw a three-dimensional, wire-frame model. For this purpose a simple language has been defined, which is a cut down version of Modula-2. The package therefore contains an editor to enter the program and suitable code to analyse the program and so generate the appropriate lines, circles, etc. Note that once such a shape has been defined it can be included in other shapes, both those defined interactively and by a program, and can itself call other shapes.

The user can store the diagram in a file, so that it can be edited subsequently. It is also possible to define a library of shapes which the user can include in his program, and to concatenate a number of diagrams. The data are stored in text files so that they can be edited, or generated by another program. Hardcopy of the diagram is available on a plotter or a printer: drivers for other hardcopy devices can be produced easily.

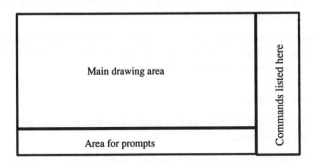

Figure 3.1 Windows on the screen

Appearance

As the user should be prompted suitably, the user interface is friendly and so the screen is partitioned into separate parts or windows, one for the actual diagram, one for prompts and one for commands: this is shown in figure 3.1. The main area contains the actual diagram being entered interactively, or the program describing a shape. Below this is a small area where suitable prompts are given. Finally, on the right of the screen, is an area where the commands are listed so that they can be selected.

All options for the program are listed in the 'command' window. The user is presented with the appropriate list of commands, one of which is highlighted. Then the user can move up and down the list using the mouse or cursor keys, until the correct item is highlighted, and this can then be accepted by pressing the Enter key or the left mouse button. This is used in various places in the package; for example, to choose the appropriate command (insert a line, a circle, etc., modify an item, plot the diagram, etc.), or select a file from a list of files already on the disk, etc.

When the program is first run, the command window has three options: to load an existing diagram from the disk, to specify where a diagram could be found and then load it, or to start a new diagram. If the first choice is selected, the user is given a list of files to choose from (as described above). For the second choice the user specifies the disk drive and/or directory and then the list of files there is given. Otherwise, the user is prompted for the name of the new diagram. Then the main loop is entered in which the appropriate commands are listed. If the current shape being edited is described by a program, the commands are to edit, draw or save the program, or change shape. Otherwise the commands are to allow the user to enter an item interactively, modify commands, change shape, etc.

44 Modula-2 Applied

The 'main' window is usually used for displaying the current shape being generated. Lines, circles, etc., are drawn as they are input. When the shape is one produced by program, then the window is used to display the program so that it can be edited, as well as to draw the shape when the program is analysed.

The 'prompt' window is used to give messages or report errors. The program analyser reports syntactical errors in the window, for example.

In addition, when the user asks for 'help', a suitable window appears in the middle of the screen in which an appropriate help message is shown. The user reads the message, then hits a key and the window disappears.

3.2 The main commands

When editing a shape interactively, rather than being in program mode, the commands are as follows:

enter an item: where an item is a Line, Circle, Arc, Rectangle, Diamond, String, Usershape or Bezier curve

modify an item

move, copy, generate a mirror image, delete or block a group of items

change the shape being edited

set options: change current colour and feature

exmine the picture: zoom in/out for more detail

add a grid

specify a new diagram

enter the file menu

plot a diagram

get some help

quit.

Entering / modifying an item

The user specifies that a line, circle, etc., is to be entered from the main command loop by selecting the command Line, Circle, etc. The user is then able to specify aspects of the item interactively: this is described below.

If the Modify command is selected, the user is allowed to select an item to be modified, by moving the crosshair until it is nearest the item to be changed; modify the last item entered; or select the item chosen previously. Having selected the item, the user is able to modify the current aspects of the item.

The aspects of an item are as follows. A line is defined by its end coordinates; a circle by its origin and radius; an arc by its origin, radius and the start and end angles of the arc; a rectangle by the coordinates of two corners; a diamond by the coordinates of two corners; a Bezier curve by two end points and two points which form tangents to the curve at the two end points; a string by a series of characters, its origin, size and rotation; and a usershape by the shape, its origin, size and rotation.

To define or change a shape, its aspects must be specified. This is done by first changing the first aspect by moving the mouse in the appropriate direction, or entering cursor movement keys on the keyboard. When one aspect is correct, pressing the right button on the mouse, or the space bar, moves on to the next aspect. This carries on in sequence, and will return to the first aspect. When the shape is correctly defined, the user presses the left button or Enter. As changes are made, so the shape appears on the screen as it will finally appear (the two exceptions to this are strings and usershapes: here a box around the shape is drawn only). For strings, the first aspect is the sequence of characters: the user types these at the keyboard, can delete characters with Del and move about in the string using the cursor keys.

For moving an aspect of an item or a crosshair, the keys are as follows:

The arrow keys move the aspect by a small amount up, down, left or right. This amount can be increased by pressing the + key and decreased by pressing the - key. When specifying angles of arcs or rotation, these amounts are degrees.

Home, PgUp, End and PgDn move by larger amounts in the corresponding directions. When specifying angles, these amounts are +/- 45 degrees.

Ctrl-Home, Ctrl-PgUp, etc. move by even larger amounts. (Ctrl-xxx means holding down the Ctrl key and pressing the xxx key).

At any time when editing, the user can look in more detail at part of the diagram by pressing the Ins key, and zoom out by pressing the Del key. In each case the current position becomes the centre of the window. To recentre around the current position, the user presses the * key.

Group commands

The group commands allow the user to select a group of items for processing. The processing options are to move the selected items, copy them, draw a mirror image, delete them, or install them as a usershape. The group can be selected in various ways:

The user can select an item by moving a cursor so that it is nearest the item to be chosen, select all items within a window, include the last item entered into the diagram, select the previous choice, or affect every item. Any combination of these choices is allowed. When an item is selected, it is redrawn on the screen highlighted. When all the items are chosen, the user can abort or accept the choices.

The move command allows the user to specify the amount by which the selected items should be moved: the 'move from' position is specified by moving a crosshair then the 'move to' position is given: the differences between the two are the amount by which the selected items are moved.

The copy command also uses two positions, specified in the same manner, and then duplicates all selected items, but puts them in the position offset from the original by the specified amount.

The mirror command allows the user to get a mirror image of the selected items. The user specifies the mirror point, whether a horizontal or vertical translation is required, and opts whether the original shape should be deleted or kept.

When items have been selected to be deleted, the user is asked whether he wants to quit without deleting, delete all the items specified, or be asked if each selected item is to be deleted. In the last case, each shape under consideration is redrawn in a different colour, and the user asked if it is to be deleted.

The block command allows the selected items to be transferred from the current shape and inserted in a new shape. The user is prompted for the name of the new shape.

Other commands

The EditShape command allows the user to select a different shape to be edited: a list of the current shapes is given, the last one of which is the main diagram, followed by two other choices: edit a new shape, or edit a new program. The user selects the appropriate command in the usual way. If the new command is an interactive shape, the above commands are listed: if it is a program, the appropriate commands are given (these are described in detail below).

The Options command allows the user to change features of items. An item can have one of 8 colours and 4 features. For strings, the four features are whether the characters are normal, bold, italic, or bold and italic. For other items, the features are 4 thicknesses of lines, circles, etc. When an item is first entered it is given the current colour and feature. The Options command allows the user to select the current colour or feature, or to change the current colour and/or feature of a group of items selected by the user.

A Grid consists of a regular series of dots on the screen. The Grid option allows the user to specify the distance between dots (0 means no Grid at all). The default size of the screen is 4096 by 4096, thus a Gridfactor of 256 gives 8 rows and columns of dots.

The Examine option allows the user to zoom in/out of the picture, by moving the cursor around and pressing Ins or Del. Enter is used to end the command.

The New command clears the current diagram and allows the user to start a new diagram, or load a new diagram from the disk. The user should save the current diagram first if he does not want to lose it!

The File commands allow the user to Load a new file, Insert an existing file into the current diagram, Save the current diagram in a file, specify the Path whereby the package searches for files, or load a file in to be Edited by the inbuilt editor. For saving a file, the user is asked to specify the name of the file (the default name is that of the diagram). For loading or inserting a file, a list is given of the current files on the disk, and the user selects the appropriate file. When a file is

Inserted, its contents are added to the existing diagram: if this results in two shapes with the same name, the user is asked to rename the new shape. In Edit mode, the user can load a text file, edit it, save it or quit the mode.

The Plot command plots the current diagram onto the selected hardcopy device. The user is prompted if the results are to be put in a file, or sent to a printer through the parallel port or the serial port. Then the user can select the hardcopy device as being a PostScript printer or a HP-GL plotter.

At any time the user can get help pertinent to his current action by typing control-Q. The Help command informs the user of this.

The Quit command asks the user if he means to quit or not.

Program mode commands

When the shape being edited is described by a program, there are seven commands.

The Edit command causes the program to be edited.

The Analyse command 'compiles' the program: it analyses the program to check for syntactical errors and then obeys the program, drawing any line, circle, etc., on the screen and storing such commands so that the shape can be drawn again more rapidly. If an error is detected, it is reported, and the editor invoked at the position of the error.

The File and New commands provide the same options as described above.

The Change command allows the user to specify another shape to be edited, in the same manner as described above.

The Help and Quit commands are the same as above.

The Editor

The Editor is a simple screen editor which allows the user to examine and modify the appropriate text. On the top of the screen is the name of the program, the current cursor position and the state of the 'Insert' or 'OverWrite' mode. Some help is provide in the 'Command' window. To a considerable extent, the editor acts in the same way as the TopSpeed editor (and WordStar and Turbo Pascal, etc.).

Any normal printable character is immediately entered. If the editor is in 'Insert' mode, all characters further up the line are moved to provide space into which the new character is inserted; in 'OverWrite' mode, the new character overwrites the existing character.

Cursor movement is achieved using the cursor keys:

The arrow keys move the cursor by one position up, down, left or right.

PgUp and PgDn move the cursor up or down by one screen's worth.

Home and End move the cursor to the beginning and end of the line.

Ctrl-leftarrow and Ctrl-rightarrow move the cursor one word left or right.

Ctrl-PgUp and Ctrl-PgDn move to the start or end of the program.

Ctrl-Home and *Ctrl-End* move to the top or bottom of the screen.

The *Ins* key toggles between 'Insert' mode and 'OverWrite' mode.

As shown in the 'Command' window, Esc quits the edit, and the function keys F1..F10 are as follows:

F1 is 'Find', that is to search for a specified string of characters: the user is prompted for the string, and then for any options. The options are zero, one or many of the following:

a number, indicating the number of times the search is to occur,

U, meaning that the case of any letter should be ignored,

W, meaning that the search will be for whole words only,

B, meaning that the search will be backwards from the current position.

F2 is 'Find and Replace', that is to search for a string, and if found to replace it with an alternative string. The user is prompted for the 'search' string, the 'replace' string, and then any options. The options are as above, plus:

G, means the search will be global, that is over the whole program,

N, means that the user will not be asked if a replacement is to occur.

F3 is to find the next occurrence (it is F1 without having to specify the search string and the options).

F4 is find and replace the next occurrence.

F5 is to delete the word to the right of the current position.

F6 is to delete the current line.

F7 is to move the cursor to the previous position.

F8 is to restore the last deleted line. Note that deleting a line, moving the cursor to another line, and restoring the line has the effect of moving the line.

F9 is the command to scroll the screen up by one line.

F10 is to scroll the screen down by one line.

3.3 File structure

The data files describing diagrams are stored in files with the name xx.DIG, where xx is any name of up to eight letters. These files are normal text files, so they can be examined easily, using a standard editor, for example. The format of the file is as follows.

The file contains descriptions of all the shapes in the diagram, in order. The first shape is the main diagram, which has the same name as the file. Each shape name is in capital letters. Thus the first line in the file is the name of the diagram. This is followed on successive lines by descriptions of the items that make up the shape, then the next shape is defined.

If a shape is described by a program, a { follows the shape name, then the actual program is written out, as it would appear if it were edited, followed by a }.

Otherwise the items that make up a shape are listed in the form:

For a line:

l colour feature x1 y1 x2 y2

x1, y1, x2, y2 are the x and y coordinates of the end of the line. The colour is the colour of the line, in the range 1 to 8, and the feature is its thickness, in the range 0 to 3.

For a circle:

c colour feature x y r

x and y are the origin, r is the radius.

For an arc:

a colour feature x y r a1 a2

x, y and r, as above, a1 and a2 are the start and end angles, in degrees.

For a rectangle:

r colour feature x1 y1 x2 y2

x1, y1, x2, y2 are the coordinates of two opposite corners of the rectangle.

For a diamond:

d colour feature x1 y1 x2 y2

x1, y1, x2, y2 are coordinates of two points of the diamond.

For a Bezier curve:

b colour feature x1 y1 x2 y2 x3 y3 x4 y4

x1, y1, x4, y4 are the end points of the curve, x2, y2, x3, y3 are the coordinates of the points which together with x1,y1 and x4, y4, respectively form tangents to the curve.

For a string:

s colour feature x y xs ys rot string

x, y defines the base of the string, xs and ys are the string sizes, rot is the angle in degrees of the string from the horizontal.

For a usershape made up of lines, circles, etc:

u colour feature x y xs ys rot shapename

For a usershape described by a program:

g colour feature x y xs ys rot shapename

For both the above, x, y defines the base of the shape, xs and ys the scaling factors in 64ths, rot is the angle of the shape from the horizontal.

The coordinates of a shape are in the range 0..4095. Scaling factors for usershapes are in multiples of 1/64: a factor 32 means that the shape is drawn in half the size in which it is defined. As shapes cannot be included larger than their original size, it is a good idea to define shapes so that they fill the range as much as possible.

3.4 Syntax of the programming language

The programming language used to describe shapes is a very much cutdown version of Modula-2. Most of the 'pruning' has been done to simplify the analysis of the program; thus the description of the analyser is not too complex. However, the language has most of the constructs needed to allow diagrams to be generated easily.

The language has a number of in-built procedures, and the user is allowed to define his own. Nesting of procedures is allowed and the Modula-2 scope rules usually apply as regards local and global variables. The one exception to the rule is that two variables of the same name cannot be in scope at the same time. For example, if a procedure has a procedure local to it, both procedures cannot have a local variable, or be passed a parameter, of the same name. This was done to simplify the analyser.

Identifiers (names of variables and procedures) must begin with a letter, and can be followed by any number of letters or digits. Identifiers are case sensitive.

The variable types allowed are NUMBER (which is a REAL), and ARRAY (which is an array, between limits specified by the user, of NUMBER). When passing parameters to a procedure, ARRAYs are specified without limits (as in Modula-2), a number may be passed as a variable parameter by being called a VARNUMBER instead of NUMBER, and constant STRINGs may be passed. All user defined procedures return a value of type NUMBER. A NUMBER of value 0.0 is considered to be FALSE, a NUMBER of any other value is TRUE.

Variables must be declared before they are used. The format is:

```
VAR name1 : TYPE1, name : TYPE2, etc.
```

A few valid declarations are given below:

```
VAR x : NUMBER
VAR x : NUMBER, y : NUMBER, array : ARRAY [1,9]
VAR anotherarray : ARRAY [1*7, x]      #note dynamic array size#
```

Assignments are of the form:

```
variable := expression
```

where the variable can be a number or an array suitably indexed, and the expression one which returns a value of type NUMBER; or the variable can be an array, and the expression another array, or a series of numerical expressions separated by commas and enclosed with [and]. For example,

```
x := 5 + SIN (y)
array [3] := SQRT (x)
array := [x, x+1, y*y, x*6+7, 1, 56.9, 78.04, 0.5E-7, 0.0]
```

Diagram Package - Introduction 51

Procedure declarations follow the construct one might expect given the form of VAR declarations, and as all procedures return a value of type NUMBER, no return type is declared:

```
PROC name (para1 : TYPE1, para2 : TYPE2, etc)
```

Following the procedure heading, there are a series of statements (which can include VAR declarations, normal statements, other procedures), followed by the word ENDPROC.

All variables and procedures must be declared before they are used. So as to permit mutually recursive procedures (see chapter 20), procedural forward references are needed. This is achieved by a declaration of the form:

```
FORWARDPROC name (para1 : TYPE1, para2 : TYPE2, etc)
```

When the procedure is actually given, its parameter list must be declared in full.

The in-built procedures are mainly those used for drawing lines, circles etc., and for providing some arithmetic functions. They require little explanation. Lines, etc., are drawn in the current colour and with the current feature. The procedures are:

```
DOT (x, y)
LINE (x1, y1, x2, y2)
RECTANGLE (x1, y1, x2, y2)
DIAMOND (x1, y1, x2, y2)
CIRCLE (xorg, yorg, radius)
ARC (xorg, yorg, radius, startangle, endangle)
BEZIER (x1, y1, x2, y2, x3, y3, x4, y4)
USERSHAPE (x, y, xsize, ysize, rotation, shapename)
PLOTSTRING (x, y, xsize, ysize, rotation, string)
PLOTNUMBER (x, y, xsize, ysize, rotation, value, field, precision)
(xsize, ysize are the size of the characters, field and precision
are as used in WrReal, except 0 precision means plot as INTEGER)

COLOUR (value)
(this sets the current colour, and should be in the range 0..8)
FEATURE (value)
(this sets the current feature (thickness or italic): range 0..3)

DEBUG (message, value, wait)
(this prints the message and the value in the 'Prompt' window,
and so allows debugging. If wait is non zero, the user must hit
a key to continue)
RANGE (xmin, ymin, xmax, ymax)
(this specifies the minimum and maximum values which correspond
to the size of the plotting area. The default is 0..4095 in both
x and y directions)
```

The arithmetic procedures are like those in Modula-2:

```
LOW and HIGH which return the low and high limits of the array,
SIN, COS, TAN, ARCTAN, ARCTAN2, LOG, LN, SQRT, ABS, ODD, and
RND (n), which returns a random number in the range 0..n
```

The language has the control statements IF, REPEAT, WHILE, FOR, LOOP, RETURN and EXIT whose syntax are similar to Modula-2, so they are not described in detail. They are shown below:

```
IF <expression> THEN
   action
ELSIF <expression> THEN
   action
ELSE
   action
ENDIF
```

the ELSIF and ELSE parts are optional.

```
REPEAT
   action
UNTIL <expression>


WHILE <expression> DO
   action
ENDWHILE


FOR variable := startvalue TO endvalue BY stepvalue DO
   action
ENDFOR
```

The BY part is optional. startvalue, endvalue and stepvalue can be any arithmetic expression returning a numerical result.

```
LOOP
   action
ENDLOOP
```

The statement EXIT aborts a LOOP, in the same manner as in Modula-2.

Another statement, RETURN, followed by a numerical expression, terminates the procedure and causes it to return with the given value.

In the above, action is any sequence of statements; variable declarations, calls to procedures, assignments, or control statements, like IF, LOOP, etc. <expression> is any arithmetic expression returning a numerical result, which is deemed to be true if its result is non zero.

Comments are enclosed between two #.

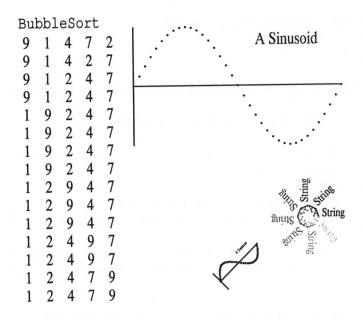

Figure 3.2 Example diagram produced by the package

An example

The following is the contents of a file, EXAMPLES.DIG, which has three shapes defined by program that are called from the main diagram. This shows the format of a file. The first program sorts an array of five numbers using the BubbleSort algorithm and displays the actions around each loop (see chapter 2, or Wirth[1], for more details on BubbleSort). The second program draws eight strings at 45 degree intervals using the 8 different colours, and calls the third shape, which plots a sinusoid. To make the file easier to read some blank lines have been added. The output of the program is given in figure 3.2. Thus the file also shows some of the features of the language in operation.

```
EXAMPLES
g 1 1949 894 33 25 0 SINUSOID
g 1 1411 1789 33 33 0 STRINGS
g 1 128 128 48 56 0 BUBBLE
```

54 Modula-2 Applied

```
BUBBLE {
#This shape shows the action of the BubbleSort algorithm#

VAR Bubble : ARRAY [1, 5], y : NUMBER
Bubble := [9, 1, 4, 7, 2]
y := 3800

#The above define the array to be sorted, and give it values#

PLOTSTRING (400, 4000, 100, 100, 0, 'BubbleSort', 17)

#The following procedure draws the current state of the array#
PROC PlotBubble
VAR ct : NUMBER
  FOR ct := LOW (Bubble) TO HIGH (Bubble) DO
    PLOTNUMBER (200 + ct*250, y, 100, 100, 0, Bubble[ct], 1, 0, 1)
  ENDFOR
  y := y - 180     #y is decremented so that on the next call to
            PlotBubble, the array will be shown on lower line#
ENDPROC

#This procedure swaps the two numbers: note the VARNUMBER
declaration for n1 and n2: both are changed by the procedure.#
PROC Swap (n1 : VARNUMBER, n2 : VARNUMBER)
VAR temp : NUMBER
  temp := n1
  n1 := n2
  n2 := temp
ENDPROC

VAR i : NUMBER, j : NUMBER

PlotBubble    #Plot initial state: then enter the two FOR loops#
FOR i := LOW (Bubble) TO HIGH (Bubble) DO
  FOR j := HIGH (Bubble) TO i+1 BY -1 DO
    IF Bubble[j-1]  Bubble[j] THEN
      Swap (Bubble[j-1], Bubble[j])
    ENDIF
    PlotBubble
  ENDFOR
  PlotBubble
ENDFOR
}
```

Diagram Package - Introduction 55

```
STRINGS {
#This program plots a string eight times at 45 degree intervals#
VAR ct : NUMBER

FOR ct := 0 TO 359 BY 45 DO
   PLOTSTRING (2048, 2048, 100, 100, ct, ' A String', 1 + ct / 45)
ENDFOR

#Now it calls the procedure SINUSOID#
USERSHAPE (2048, 1024, 2048, 2048, 0, 'SINUSOID', 1)
}

SINUSOID {
#This is another shape: it plots a sinusoid#
VAR PI : NUMBER
PI := 3.14159265


PROC XScale (x : NUMBER)
   RETURN 100 + x * 10
ENDPROC

PROC YScale (y : NUMBER)
   RETURN 2048 + 1000 * y
ENDPROC

VAR x : NUMBER
#Note x allowed here, as earlier x in XScale now out of scope#
FOR x := 0 TO 360 BY 10 DO
   DOT (XScale (x), YScale (SIN (x * PI / 180)), 17)
ENDFOR
                                           #Now draw the axes#
LINE (XScale (0), YScale (1), XScale (0), YScale (-1), 2)
LINE (XScale (0), YScale (0), XScale (360), YScale (0), 2)
                                         #And label the graph#
PLOTSTRING (XScale(210), YScale(0.7), 150, 150, 0, 'A Sinusoid', 3)
}
```

3.5 Modules that form the diagram package

The Diagram package is implemented using a number of modules which are provided on the accompanying disk. In this section, a brief description of these modules is given, so as to allow the user to understand and/or modify the program.

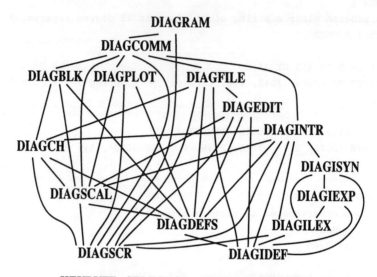

Figure 3.3 Author's modules used in Diagram

The modules are listed below and drawn in figure 3.3, where the interaction between the modules is shown:

DIAGRAM - the main module.

DIAGCOMM - diagram commands

this contains the main loop and all the associated commands.

DIAGBLK - diagram block commands

this contains the block routines, move, copy, etc. and the routine to select an item to be modified (once selected the item is changed by a routine in DIAGCH).

DIAGCH - diagram change

this contains the routines for entering a new Line, Circle, etc and for modifying an existing item. Items are drawn using the DIAGSCAL module.

DIAGFILE - diagram files

this contains routines for loading and saving a diagram in files. For shapes described by a program, this calls the DIAGEDIT module.

DIAGPLOT - diagram plot

this contains the code to draw the diagram on the specified hardcopy device.

DIAGEDIT - diagram edit

this contains the code for organising files so they can be handled by the editor.

DIAGSCAL - diagram scaling

this contains the routines for scaling the shapes and drawing them on the screen.

DIAGINTR - diagram interpreter

this contains the code for interpreting a shape described by a program. It first calls the syntax analyser, then runs the program.

DIAGISYN - diagram syntax analyser

this contains the code needed to check a program for syntactical errors. It calls the expression analyser routine.

DIAGIEXP - diagram expression analyser

this contains a routine which returns the next expression in the program. It calls the lexical analyser.

DIAGILEX - diagram lexical analyser

this analyses the next item in the program, and categorises it as a number, identifier, procedure, operator, etc. It also contains the routine for reporting errors.

DIAGIDEF - diagram interpreter definitions

this module contains definitions of data types needed in the interpreter, and the associated routines for using the heap.

DIAGDEFS - diagram definitions

this module contains definitions of the main data types needed for describing lines, circles, etc, and the associated heap routines.

DIAGSCR - diagram screen

this contains the routines for handling the screen: organising the windows, etc.

All the above modules are specific to the diagram package. However, they also call other general purpose modules written by the author:

GRWINDOW - graphics window

this contains the low level primitives for drawing lines, etc., displaying text and for dividing the screen into windows.

SELECTOR - option selection

this module contains routines for selecting an item from a list of items. This includes routines for forming a list as well as selecting from the list.

KEYBUFF - keyboard buffer

this contains the routines for maintaining a keyboard buffer, so as to allow the user to 'type ahead', and to provide a mechanism for aborting from an unwanted situation.

EDITOR - screen editor

  this contains the routines for editing a program.

LINEEDIT- line editor

  this contains a routine for editing a string.

HELP - give on screen help

  this contains the routines which provide context dependent help.

IDMACHIN - machine identification

  this determines whether the computer has CGA, EGA or VGA graphics.

The program also calls a number of the TopSpeed libraries including IO, Lib, Dos, Storage, Str (see TopSpeed Manual [2]).

Conclusion

This chapter gives a general description of the diagram package, which should help anyone using the package, and provides a basis so as to allow the reader to understand the techniques discussed in the following chapters. To reiterate, the main aim of this book is to describe useful programming techniques in an application: the diagram package. This chapter should have given the reader an overview of the application. The next chapter examines some low level primitives, such as plotting text, circles, etc., which are needed for the package.

References

1 Niklaus Wirth *Algorithms and Data Structures* Prentice-Hall 1986

2 J&P Partners Ltd *TopSpeed Modula-2 Manual* 1989

4 Low Level Primitives

In this chapter techniques for handling the computer screen are described. These include the very lowest level commands for direct control of the hardware (like placing a dot on the screen). Then higher level commands are described (like drawing a circle), which use the routine for drawing a dot. Finally the suitable partitioning of the screen into windows is described. This is used in the diagram package: one window is used for drawing the diagram, another is used to list commands which the user can select, and the third is used to report messages.

The routines which directly control the actual hardware are specific to the IBM PC and compatibles (which are used in the development of the diagram package), and these will need to be rewritten for other machines. However, the higher level routines for using the screen as a character VDU, or for drawing lines and circles, usually call the lower level routines, and so they are more general and can be used with other computers. More powerful computers may provide these routines as a matter of course: some chips used to control graphics systems provide built-in facilities for drawing lines, circles, etc.

In addition, some useful techniques are also described, including the use of Sets, opaque types, absolute memory addressing and look-up tables.

4.1 Screen control on a PC

The original IBM PC had no graphics facility, so no standard was set for graphics. Therefore various manufacturers produced graphics cards to connect to the PC, and these are not directly compatible. Some PCs have CGA graphics, others EGA, VGA, Hercules, etc. Different routines are needed for handling these standards, which means that it cannot be guaranteed that a program written on one PC will work on another. However, there is a tendency to standardise on EGA or VGA, and the routines for handling these two standards are almost identical. Therefore the diagram package, and hence the routines described in this chapter, are designed to use EGA or VGA. See also the technical reference manual of your computer.

VDUs on the PC operate either in text mode or graphics mode: in the former text only can be displayed, but in the latter (for EGA/VGA graphics) both graphics and text can be used. In the Diagram package, graphics mode is used throughout. In graphics mode, the specification for EGA and VGA screens is as follows:

	EGA	VGA
Number of horizontal pixels	640	640
Number of vertical pixels	350	480
Number of colours available	16	16
Number of columns of text	80	80
Number of rows of text	25	30

60 Modula-2 Applied

Controlling the screen is achieved by calling the appropriate routines provided in the operating system, or by accessing the memory and ports which directly affect the graphics hardware. The operating system routines (the software interrupts) are accessed using the Intr and Dos routines provided in the TopSpeed library module Lib: see TopSpeed manual[1]. Addressing the screen memory is achieved by accessing absolute memory addresses, and the ports are accessed using the In and Out procedures provided in the module System. In the following many addresses are specified in hexadecimal (base 16). This is indicated by the H after a number: 10H is 16 in decimal.

To initialise the screen, Interrupt 10H should be called, with register AX containing 12H if VGA mode is required, and 10H for EGA. Using the routine Intr from the TopSpeed module Lib, the definition of Registers from SYSTEM, and assuming the variable Regs is of type Registers, the algorithm is:

```
IF VGA THEN Regs.AX := 12H ELSE Regs.AX := 10H END;
Lib.Intr (Regs, 10H)
```

The data that form the picture are stored in successive bytes starting at address 0A000H: the first row is stored, then the second, etc. The first byte contains the state of the first eight pixels of the top line of the screen. This idea is slightly complicated to allow the 16 different colours; there are in fact 4 sets or planes of memory beginning at address 0A000H. The actual colour of a particular dot is determined by the 4 bits, one from each memory plane, at the given address. To access a particular bit, the appropriate plane must be selected, the correct byte found, and then the appropriate bit of that byte accessed.

Note that it is possible to determine automatically the graphics available on the current computer. This is not so easy as it should be: ideally the program should be able to ask the operating system which graphics facilities (if any) are available. The identification technique uses the fact that some routines are available for VGA, but not for EGA or CGA, and similarly, routines are available for EGA, but not for CGA. Such routines return values associated with the graphics mode if it is provided. The technique is to set the register in which a result is returned to an illegal value, say 0FFH, call the routine using Intr, and see if the register still contains 0FFH. Full details are in the module IdMachin, but the basic algorithm is:

```
WITH Regs DO
  BH := 0FFH; AH := 1AH; AL := 0; Lib.Intr (Regs, 10H);
  IF BH<3 THEN Mode := VGA
  ELSE
    BH := 0FFH; AH := 12H; BL := 10H; Lib.Intr (Regs, 10H);
    IF BH<1 THEN Mode := EGA ELSE Mode := Other END
  END
END
```

4.2 Sets

As the program is to access bits of bytes, a convenient definition in Modula-2 is to define a byte as a series of bits. The mechanism for this is the variable type SET. A set is a series of items, and the associated operations are to put a value into or remove a value from a set, or to test if a value is a member of a set. This is achieved in Modula-2 by having a variable with a bit set in it if the appropriate item is in the set.

Built into the language is the type BITSET, which is a 16-bit value, defined by:

```
BITSET = SET OF {0..15}
```

A variable B of type BITSET can be affected by:

```
B := {};            (* makes it an empty set *)
INCL (B, 13};       (* Include bit 13 into the set *)
B := {1, 13};       (* B is given with bits 1 and 13 set *)
```

One use of BITSET is to allow the logical operations, AND, OR, XOR, to affect numerical types. Between SET types the operators *, + and /, are interpreted as these operations. Thus B1 * B2 means B1 AND B2.

To perform AND of two integers, type coercion is needed. BITSET (i) converts integer i into a variable of type bitset, etc. Thus

```
INTEGER ( BITSET (I1) * BITSET (I2) )
```

converts I1 and I2 from integers to bitset, the * ANDs them together, and the surrounding INTEGER () returns the result to being type integer. Note that the conversion does not change the values, only their types, so that the compiler can tell that the AND operation, rather than multiply, is to be performed.

Sets are not restricted to numbers, but any ordinal type. For the screen memory, which is accessed in bytes, a different set is needed:

```
TYPE ScreenBits = SET OF {0..7};
```

A variable of type ScreenBits is an 8-bit value, and so can be used to represent a location in screen memory and hence can have bits set or reset, which is required for drawing dots on the graphics screen.

4.3 Accessing screen memory

Using this type, the screen can be considered as an array of ScreenBits at a fixed base address. The 8086 family microprocessor in PCs divides its memory into 64K segments, so memory is addressed as some offset relative to a segment (see, for example, Rector and Alexy[2]). The address of the screen memory is at segment A000H, offset by the actual position on the screen.

If ScreenSegment is a constant of value 0A000H, such an address is

```
ScreenSegment : offset
```

This addressing mechanism is not true for all computers, and so is not valid for all Modula-2 compilers. The above is how it is achieved by the TopSpeed compiler.

To access position x,y of the screen, the byte is at offset

```
y * 80 + x DIV 8
```

It is y * 80, because the screen width is 640 dots, or 80 bytes. The bit required is bit number

```
7 - x MOD 8
```

To access absolute memory locations, TopSpeed Modula-2 allows the programmer to define the absolute address of memory. In Modula-2 terms, an address of a variable is a POINTER to the variable. If P is a pointer to a variable, then that variable is P^.

As this construct allows the specification of the address of any type of variable, the user must specify the type. Thus the pointer we require is a POINTER to ScreenBits.

```
ScreenPointer = POINTER TO ScreenBits
```

The instruction to specify the variable at an absolute memory location is:

```
[address ScreenPointer]^
```

Thus, to find if the bit at position x,y is set in the screen memory, the code in TopSpeed Modula-2 is:

```
7 - x MOD 8 IN [ScreenSegment : y * 80 + x DIV 8 ScreenPointer]^
```

Reading colour at specified position

To read the state of the colour at a particular position (x, y), the value of the bits in the four planes is required. The algorithm is:

```
OffsetAddress := y * 80 + x DIV 8;
BitRequired  :=  7 - (x MOD 8);

EnableReading
     (* by accessing appropriate control registers *)
EnablePlane (3);
IF BitRequired IN
    [ScreenSegment : OffsetAddress ScreenPointer]^ THEN
  colour := 8
ELSE
  colour := 0
END;
EnablePlane (2);
IF BitRequired IN
    [ScreenSegment : OffsetAddress ScreenPointer]^ THEN
  colour := colour + 4
END;
EnablePlane (1);
IF BitRequired IN
    [ScreenSegment : OffsetAddress ScreenPointer]^ THEN
  colour := colour + 2
END;
EnablePlane (0);
IF BitRequired IN
    [ScreenSegment : OffsetAddress ScreenPointer]^ THEN
  colour := colour + 1
END;

RETURN colour
```

This is encoded in the module GrWindow as procedure Point.

Plotting a point at the specified position

A similar procedure is needed for plotting a point. However, instead of accessing each plane individually, the user is able to access as many as required. Thus to write a particular colour, all planes are cleared at the given position, then the appropriate planes are set: the required colour determines which planes should be set. The algorithm is essentially:

64 Modula-2 Applied

```
SetMode;
Enable All Planes;
Output (0);    (* This clears all planes at the address *)
Enable Those Planes To Be Set;
Output (1);
TidyUpMode;
```

The above allows the user to plot a point in a given colour and position. However, it is sometimes required that the colour of the position should be inverted: this is needed in the diagram package. This 'exclusive or' mode could be achieved by:

```
Plot (x, y, 15 - Point (x, y) )
```

However, this is slow because of the processing required for the routine Point. Therefore, as the EGA controller supports XOR mode, the above is modified to:

```
IF XOR THEN Set XOR Mode ELSE Set OverWrite Mode END;
Set Other Modes;
Enable All Planes;
IF NOT XOR THEN
  Output (0);
  Enable Required Planes
END;
Output (1);
Tidy Up
```

In the GrWindow module the above is accomplished by the routine Plot. If the colour is greater or equal to 256, then XOR mode is used.

Thick dots

The Plot routine in GrWindow is slightly more sophisticated than the above: it allows 'thick' dots. If the colour is less than 16 a single dot is plotted at point x,y; if the colour is between 16 and 31, a double sized dot is plotted, that is 4 dots are plotted, at points x,y, x+1,y, x,y+1 and x+1,y+1; a colour between 32 and 47 results in 9 dots; and between 48 and 63, 16 dots are plotted.

Plotting horizontal lines

To plot a point, the appropriate address must be found, then the required bit at that address affected. If a horizontal line is drawn, it is possible that all the bits in the byte at that address are affected. By taking this into account, faster line drawing is possible. Hence a routine HLine is provided. The algorithm is:

```
Use Plot for dots in part byte at the left of the line
Use Plot for dots in part byte at the right of the line
Process the complete bytes in the middle of the line.
```

4.4 Text routines

The other routines required which control the screen memory directly are those for handling text. The functions provided are to write a character on the screen, position the cursor, clear areas, etc. It is possible to set the colour of the characters, the foreground colour, and the background colour. Many of these functions are accomplished using the same trap routine used to configure the screen, but with different parameters, that is with different values in the registers. The routines are briefly as follows:

```
PROCEDURE GotoXY (x, y)      (* position cursor at x, y *)
  Remember x, y in global variables
  Load registers: AH := 2; BH := 0; DL := x; DH := y;
  Call interrupt.

PROCEDURE WhereX(),
PROCEDURE WhereY()           (* return X or Y position *)
  Return the value saved in last call to GotoXY.

PROCEDURE ClrScr (* clear screen to background colour *)
  Depending on the background colour, some of the 4 planes
  must be set and the others cleared. The planes to be
  cleared are enabled and filled with 0, then the planes
  to be set are enabled and filled with 255. The Fill
  routine from module Lib is used so the routine is fast.

PROCEDURE ClrEol             (* clear to end of line *)
  This uses a trap which can clear many lines:
  Registers: AH := 6; AL, BH := 0; DH, CH := current y;
  DL := x position at end of line; CL := current x;
  Call interrupt.

PROCEDURE DeleteLine (y) (* scroll up all lines below y *)
  Registers: AH := 6; AL := 1; BH := 0;
  CL := x at start of line; CH := current y;
  DH, DL := x and y at bottom of screen;
  Call interrupt.
```

```
PROCEDURE InsertLine (y)
      (* scroll down line y and those below *)
   As for DeleteLine, except AH := 7.


PROCEDURE PutChar (char, colour)
       (* plots char in particular colour *)
   Registers: AH := 9; BH := 0; CX := 1;
   AL := char; BL := colour;
   Call Interrupt.


PROCEDURE WriteChar (char)
(* write character and move cursor position.
char could be 'normal' or control: the latter
could  specify deletion, cursor movement, etc. *)
   IF the character is a control char THEN
     CASE character OF
        formfeed    : ClrScr |
        return      : GotoXY (1, WhereY()) |
        linefeed    : IF WhereY() < BottomLine THEN
                         GotoXY (WhereX(), WhereY()+1)
                      ELSE
                         DeleteLine (1)
                      END |
        tab         : REPEAT
                         WriteChar (' ')
                      UNTIL WhereX() MOD 8 = 1 |
        CursorUp    : IF WhereY() > 1 THEN
                         GotoXY (WhereX(), WhereY()-1)
                      END |
        CursorDown  : IF WhereY() < BottomLine THEN
                         GotoXY (WhereX(), WhereY()+1)
                      END |
        CursorLeft  : IF WhereX() > 1 THEN
                         GotoXY (WhereX()-1, WhereY())
                      END |
        CursorRight : IF WhereX() < LastColumn THEN
                         GotoXY (WhereX()+1, WhereY())
                      END |
        DeleteToEOL : ClrEol |
        DelLine     : DeleteLine (WhereY()) |
        InsLine     : InsertLine (WhereY())
     END (* of CASE *)
```

```
    ELSE  (* i.e. a normal character *)
      Write character to screen; (see below)
      IF WhereX()=LastColumn THEN
        WriteChar (Return);
        WriteChar (LineFeed)
      ELSE
        GotoXY (WhereX()+1, WhereY())
      END
    END
  END
```

Writing the character to the screen is straightforward if the background colour is 0, all that is needed is

```
PutChar (char, ForeGroundColour)
```

Otherwise the program must fill the space where the character is to be put in the background colour, and write the new character over the top in such a way that it appears to be in the correct colour. The character 0DBH fills the complete character space, so this is plotted in the background colour. Then the new character is written in 'exclusive OR' mode, as opposed to the normal 'overwrite' mode, and its colour is ForeGround XOR BackGround. XOR mode is indicated by the colour of the character having bit 7 set, so the colour required is 128 + ForeGroundColour XOR BackGroundColour. The code is:

```
PutChar (CHAR (0DBH), BackGroundColour);
PutChar (char, 80H + CARDINAL (BITSET (ForeGroundColour) /
                               BITSET (BackGroundColour) ) )
```

Other routines required include those for handling the keyboard:

```
PROCEDURE KeyPressed () (* has a key been pressed ? *)
  Register: AH := 0BH;
  Call operating system: use routine Dos from Lib;
  AL=0FFH if a key has been pressed.

PROCEDURE GetChar() (* get character from the keyboard *)
  Register: AH := 8;
  Call Dos;
  AL is the character.
```

```
PROCEDURE ReadChar
  LOOP (* First wait for keypress, flashing cursor *)
    IF KeyPressed() THEN EXIT END;
    PutChar ('_', 80H + ForeGroundColour);
         (* in XOR mode again *)
    Delay;         (* using routine from module Lib *)
    PutChar (' ', 80H + ForeGroundColour);
    IF KeyPressed() THEN EXIT END;
    Delay
  END;
  RETURN GetChar  (* now get the character *)
```

The detailed implementation of these routines is given in the GrWindow module.

4.5 Higher level graphics

The above routines provide the lowest level functions. These are used by routines for drawing lines, circles, arcs, and plotting graphical text. The Bresenham line drawing algorithm is described in chapter 2, and so is not covered here.

Circles

Bresenham also produced an integer only circle drawing algorithm. This also adopts the philosophy that the position of the next dot is calculated given the current position and using a 'decision' variable. The algorithm calculates points on the 45-degree segment to the right of the point on the circle directly above the origin, the other 7 points are calculated by symmetry: see Foley and VanDam[3]. For this segment, the next dot is at the next x position along and the same y position or the one below. The algorithm, which is derived in[3], is:

```
PROCEDURE DrawCircle (xorigin, yorigin, radius, colour : INTEGER);
VAR d, x, y : INTEGER;

   PROCEDURE PlotEightPoints;
   BEGIN
      Plot (xorigin + x, yorigin + y, colour);
      Plot (xorigin + x, yorigin - y, colour);
      Plot (xorigin - x, yorigin - y, colour);
      Plot (xorigin - x, yorigin + y, colour);
      Plot (xorigin + y, yorigin + x, colour);
      Plot (xorigin + y, yorigin - x, colour);
      Plot (xorigin - y, yorigin - x, colour);
      Plot (xorigin - y, yorigin + x, colour)
   END PlotEightPoints;
```

```
BEGIN
  x := 0;            (* initialise x, y positions and decision *)
  y := radius;
  d := 3 - 2 * radius;
  WHILE x <= y DO                (* for 45 degree segment *)
    PlotEightPoints;
    IF d < 0 THEN                (* update decision variable *)
      INC (d, 4 * x + 6)
    ELSE
      INC (d, 4 * (x - y) + 10);
      DEC (y)
    END;
    INC (x)
  END
END DrawCircle;
```

Arcs

An arc of the circle can be plotted by modifying the above algorithm. Again integer only calculations are used. The idea essentially is to calculate the points around the circumference, using the above, and at the same time to calculate the current angle. For each of the 8 mirror points, if the angle is between those specifying the start and end of the arc, then the dot is drawn. There is a slight problem: how to calculate the angle?

As the algorithm progresses around the segment, it must map out 45 degrees. So each time round the loop, the angle may or may not change. The changes in the angle can be calculated using the algorithm for drawing lines: there the x value is changed each time around the loop, but the y value may not change. As the number of points may be less than 45, the version of the line algorithm used in the area fill routine is used.

The number of points calculated varies with the radius of the circle, but the relationship is non linear: for large radii it tends towards 1.44 * radius. The actual number of points, rct, can be calculated quickly by doing a dummy run around the circle algorithm:

```
x := 0; y := radius; d := 3 - 2 * radius; rct := 0;
WHILE x < y DO
  Update (x, y, d);
  INC (rct)
END;
```

Then preparatory calculations for the line drawing algorithm (for updating the angle) are performed:

```
AngleIncr1 := 2 * (45 MOD rct);
AngleDecision := AngleIncr1 - rct;
AngleIncr2 := AngleDecision - rct;
angle := 0
```

Then the main variables are set and the main loop is entered:

```
x := 0; y := radius; d := 3 - 2 * radius;
WHILE x <= y DO
  PlotEight;
  Update (x, y, d)
    (* Now update angle estimate: using Line drawing scheme *)
  IF AngleDecision < 0 THEN
    INC (AngleDecision, AngleIncr1);
    INC (angle, AlwaysIncr)
  ELSE
    INC (AngleDecision, AngleIncr2);
    INC (angle, AlwaysIncr + 1)
  END;
END;
```

The plot eight points procedure is as follows:

```
PROCEDURE PlotEight;
BEGIN
    IF OkAngle( 90-angle) THEN Plot(xorigin+x,yorigin-y,colour) END;
    IF OkAngle( 90+angle) THEN Plot(xorigin-x,yorigin-y,colour) END;
    IF OkAngle(270+angle) THEN Plot(xorigin+x,yorigin+y,colour) END;
    IF OkAngle(270-angle) THEN Plot(xorigin-x,yorigin+y,colour) END;
    IF x <> y THEN
     IF OkAngle(angle) THEN Plot(xorigin+y,yorigin-x,colour) END;
     IF OkAngle(180-angle) THEN Plot(xorigin-y,yorigin-x,colour) END;
     IF OkAngle(360-angle) THEN Plot(xorigin+y,yorigin+x,colour) END;
     IF OkAngle(180+angle) THEN Plot(xorigin-y,yorigin+x,colour) END
    END
END PlotEight;
```

Where OkAngle determines if the angle specified is between StartAngle and EndAngle:

```
PROCEDURE OkAngle (a :CARDINAL) : BOOLEAN;
BEGIN
  IF StartAngle <= EndAngle THEN
    RETURN (a >= StartAngle) AND (a <= EndAngle)
  ELSE
    RETURN (a >= StartAngle) OR (a <= EndAngle)
  END
END OkAngle;
```

In the implementation in GrWindow, the Circle routine calls the Arc routine with angles 0 and 360, and the Arc routine returns OkAngle is TRUE if the angles are 0 and 360, and does none of the calculations required for determining the angle.

Ellipses

The circle drawing algorithm can also be modified to draw ellipses. There is one major difference, however. In the circle algorithm points were calculated on one 45-degree segment of the circle, and the other seven sets of points were calculated by symmetry. For the ellipse this is not possible, instead points must be calculated on a 90 degree segment, and the other three sets of points generated by symmetry. This is achieved in two stages, generating the points on the top 45 degree segment, then doing the same for the next 45 degree segment.

For each segment, the algorithm is in the same form as that for the circle. However, for an ellipse the decision variable must process values of the order of the square of the radii of the ellipse, whereas for circles the largest values are of the order of the radius; so LONGINTs must be used for ellipses. The algorithm can be derived by a simple extension of the derivation of the circle algorithm, given in Foley and VanDam[3]. The algorithm is:

```
PROCEDURE Ellipse (xorigin, yorigin, aradius, bradius : CARDINAL);
VAR asquared, bsquared, d : LONGINT;
    x, y : CARDINAL;
BEGIN

    (* First initialise variables *)
  asquared := LONGINT (aradius) * LONGINT (aradius);
  bsquared := LONGINT (bradius) * LONGINT (bradius);
  x := 0;
  y := bradius;
  d := 2 * bsquared + asquared - 2 * asquared * LONGINT (bradius);

        (* Now enter loop for first 45 degree segment *)
```

72 Modula-2 Applied

```
      WHILE asquared * LONGINT (y) > bsquared * LONGINT (x) DO
        PlotFourPoints;
        IF d < 0 THEN
          INC (d, 4 * bsquared * LONGINT (x) + 6 * bsquared)
        ELSE
          INC (d, 4 * (bsquared * LONGINT (x) -
                  asquared * LONGINT (y) + asquared) +
                  6 * bsquared);
          DEC (y)
        END;
        INC (x)
      END;
              (* Now do second 45 degree segment *)
      WHILE y > 0 DO
        PlotFourPoints;
        IF d < 0 THEN
          INC (d, 4 * (bsquared * LONGINT (x) -
                       asquared * LONGINT (y) + asquared) +
                  6 * bsquared);
          INC (y)
        ELSE
          INC (d, -4 * asquared * LONGINT (x) + 6 * asquared)
        END;
        DEC (y)
      END
    END Ellipse;
```

Note that if aradius=bradius, and the values by which the decision variable are initialised and changed are divided by aradius, the above reduces to the circle algorithm.

A comprehensive ellipse routine would allow the drawing of ellipses at any angle, and arcs of ellipses. These are more complicated, and left to the reader as an exercise.

Plotting text

The basic text routines described above display characters in a fixed size on the various text lines of the screen. The diagram package requires that characters of various sizes be drawn, at different positions, and at any angle. Thus the GrWindow also contains routines for plotting characters.

These require descriptions of the characters, and a special program was written to produce such a description and store these in a file. The GrWindow module reads this file and stores the contents in memory. How this is achieved is described in chapter 10 on using files.

The description of characters can be in either raster or vector form. In the former, each character is defined by a matrix of dots, with a '1' at a particular location if a dot is to be drawn. This is straightforward but tends to produce relatively unsightly characters when enlarged. A vector character set contains a description of all the lines which make up the character. For example, a K is a vertical line plus two lines at an angle starting at about the middle of the vertical line. It is easy to plot such characters in different sizes and angles, by just amplifying and rotating the lines. Thus a vector character set is used in the diagram package.

The data for the complete set are stored in two arrays. One array contains the commands defining each part of each character in the set, the other specifies the start and end positions of the data for each character. The latter is defined as:

```
PositionArray = ARRAY [' '..177C] OF CARDINAL;
```

the former is

```
DataArray = ARRAY [0..MaxSize] OF BYTE;
```

and the first part of character 'A' is at

```
DataArray [PositionArray['A']]
```

and the last part is at

```
DataArray [PositionArray['B']-1]
```

The algorithm is thus to take each data item in turn and so determine the end coordinates of each vector, and to then draw each vector suitably. This requires processing the coordinates to account for size of character and rotation. If the base of the character is at xbase,ybase, it is scaled by xsize, ysize, and it is to be drawn at angle degrees, then the end of a vector at point x, y is transformed to position:

```
xbase + x * xsize * COS (angle) - y * ysize * SIN (angle)
ybase - x * xsize * SIN (angle) - y * ysize * COS (angle)
```

Having calculated the end points of the lines, they can be drawn using the Line command. In the GrWindow module the actual routine is given. This again allows for 'thick' characters. However, it is defined that the four levels of thickness mean different things:

74 Modula-2 Applied

0 : thin lines
1 : thick lines
2 : thin lines, but italic characters
3 : thick lines, but italic characters.

The italic characters are produced by processing the x value before it is passed to the above calculations:

```
x := x + y DIV 2
```

The above process plots a character. To plot a string the same routine is used:

```
FOR each character in the string DO
  PlotChar at base position;
  move base position to that for next character
END;
```

'move base position' is done using the same transformation routine as that used to determine the coordinates of the lines of the character.

4.6 Look-up tables

The above needs calculations of cosine and sine functions, which require floating point numbers and so slow the plotting routines. To overcome this the values of the functions are calculated earlier and stored as integers in an array, so that when the program runs the calculations are performed by looking up the appropriate value from the table.

The table is an array of numbers and the element at position a in the array is the integer value of 100 * COS (a). This is achieved by:

```
TYPE ACT = ARRAY [0..90] OF INTEGER;
CONST CosArray = ACT (100, 100, 100, 100, 100, 100,  99,  99,
                       99,  99,  98,  98,  98,  97,  97,  97,
                       96,  96,  95,  95,  94,  93,  93,  92,
                       91,  91,  90,  89,  88,  87,  87,  86,
                      etc. )
```

Then a routine to calculate 100 * COS (angle) is:

```
PROCEDURE Cos100 (angle : CARDINAL) : INTEGER;
BEGIN
  angle := angle MOD 360;
  IF angle = 270 THEN RETURN Cos100 (360 - angle)
  ELSIF angle = 180 THEN RETURN -Cos100 (angle - 180)
  ELSIF angle  90 THEN RETURN -Cos100 (180 - angle)
  ELSE RETURN CosArray [angle] END
END Cos100;
```

and 100 * SIN (angle) is calculated by the procedure:

```
PROCEDURE Sin100 (angle : CARDINAL) : INTEGER;
BEGIN
  RETURN Cos100 (angle + 270)
END Sin100;
```

4.7 Windows

The module GrWindow has an extra level of sophistication: it allows the user to divide the screen into separate areas, or windows, such that lines, circles, etc., and the text routines, appear only in a window. There can be many windows on the screen, as is used in the diagram package, and one window is 'active' at any one time. The routines described above (Plot, Line, GotoXY, WriteChar, etc.) all operate within the active window.

A number of variables must be associated with each window, for example, the size and position of the window, the colour of text, the current cursor position. Therefore a RECORD is used to describe the window. The user does not need to know the exact contents of the RECORD, so it is defined in the IMPLEMENTATION module only, but an associated definition is needed in the DEFINITION module so that the rest of the program can refer to the type. Ideally the IMPLEMENTATION module should contain the only procedures which are able to change the contents of the record, so that if the record is corrupted, the error must be in the IMPLEMENTATION module. This requires a method of declaring that the type exists, but not allowing the outside world to know what it is. This can be achieved using an *opaque* type declaration (see Hewitt and Frank[4]).

In the DEFINITION MODULE, there is a statement:

```
TYPE GWindow;
```

which states that the type exists, and its actual definition exists in a type declaration in the IMPLEMENTATION Window. Therefore, a GWindow cannot be accessed directly from the outside, because the outside does not know what a GWindow is.

76 Modula-2 Applied

Thus the contents of a GWindow can be changed only by procedures within the module GrWindow: this is good practice.

The procedures to handle the windows are:

```
PROCEDURE InitialiseWindows;
  (* Identifies the graphics and initialises the window system *)

PROCEDURE CreateWindow (x1, y1, x2, y2 : CARDINAL) : GWindow;
  (* Creates window whose size is determined by the parameters *)

PROCEDURE ActivateWindow (w : GWindow);
  (* Sets the current window: all text and graphics are now
    done within the window w *)
```

When a window is produced, a border is drawn around it, the colour of which can be specified. For text windows, a special 'text' border can be drawn. The background colour and the colour of text (the foreground colour) can also be set. For Text the border around the window prevents characters being written in the whole window area: as the border is written in parts of the character space. However, it is sometimes useful to be able to put a title to the window, so it is possible to access the top line of the window for this purpose. Another feature associated with text allows the user to specify whether the cursor should be moved to the start of the next line when the text reaches the right hand side.

All the routines described above (line, circle, GotoXY, etc.) take into account the current window. Coordinates of lines, etc., are specified relative to point 0,0, and these must be translated to the start of the window. This is easy to do: the Plot routine adds the origin of the window to the x, y coordinates passed to the routine before accessing the screen memory; and the GotoXY routine adds the origin of the window to the x,y position passed to it before calling the operating system.

Also the functions must not affect the screen outside the area of the window. Thus if a line is given which extends outside the window, only that part that falls within the window is drawn. This is easy to achieve. As a line is drawn as a series of dots, all points of the line are calculated, but only those which fall within the window are actually plotted. The Plot routine does this as well: it does not plot a dot at x,y if the dot is outside the window. More sophisticated 'clipping' algorithms are described in chapter 7.

As regards text, the same idea can be used: the GotoXY routine adds the start of the window to the values set in the registers. Also the WriteChar routine does not write characters if the cursor position is outside the window.

The procedures which affect the window contents are as follows (where there are no associated comments, the routine is as described earlier):

```
PROCEDURE GotoXY (x, y : CARDINAL);
PROCEDURE WhereX() : CARDINAL;
PROCEDURE WhereY() : CARDINAL;
PROCEDURE ClrScr;
PROCEDURE ClrEol;
PROCEDURE DeleteLine (y : CARDINAL);
PROCEDURE InsertLine (y : CARDINAL);
PROCEDURE WindowColumns() : CARDINAL;
   (* Returns number of Columns of Text in the current window *)
PROCEDURE WindowRows() : CARDINAL;
   (* Returns number of Rows of Text in the current window *)
PROCEDURE Colour (colour : CARDINAL);
   (* Set colour of text *)
PROCEDURE BackGround (colour : CARDINAL);
   (* Set backgound colour *)
PROCEDURE Border (colour : CARDINAL);
   (* Set colour of border *)
PROCEDURE TextWrap (on : BOOLEAN);
   (* Set whether text wraps on to next line at end of current *)
PROCEDURE TextBorder (on : BOOLEAN);
   (* Is the border a 'text' border or single graphics line ? *)
PROCEDURE InTextHeader (in : BOOLEAN);
   (* Is text to be written in the header line of the window *)
PROCEDURE PlotChar (x, y, Colour, XSize, YSize,
                    Orientation : CARDINAL; ch : CHAR);
PROCEDURE PlotString (x, y, Colour, XSize, YSize,
                      Orientation : CARDINAL; S : ARRAY OF CHAR);
PROCEDURE WindowWidth () : CARDINAL;
   (* Returns width of the current window *)
PROCEDURE WindowDepth () : CARDINAL;
   (* Returns depth of the current window *)
PROCEDURE Plot( x,y,c : CARDINAL);
PROCEDURE Point(x,y:CARDINAL) : CARDINAL;
PROCEDURE HLine ( x,y,x2 : CARDINAL; c:CARDINAL );
PROCEDURE Line(x1,y1,x2,y2: CARDINAL; c: CARDINAL);
PROCEDURE Rect (x1, y1, x2, y2, col : CARDINAL);
PROCEDURE Circle(x0,y0,r, c: CARDINAL);
PROCEDURE Arc (x0, y0, r, SAngle, EAngle, c: CARDINAL);
PROCEDURE Ellipse (xo, yo, a, b, c : CARDINAL);
PROCEDURE WriteChar (c : CHAR);
PROCEDURE ReadChar() : CHAR;
PROCEDURE KeyPressed() : BOOLEAN;
PROCEDURE Cos100 (angle : CARDINAL) : INTEGER;
PROCEDURE Sin100 (angle : CARDINAL) : INTEGER;
```

78 Modula-2 Applied

For storing and retrieving the contents of the screen three routines are used:

```
PROCEDURE StoreWindowSize (w : GWindow) : LONGCARD;
  (* Returns the number of bytes needed to save a window *)
PROCEDURE SaveWindow (w : GWindow; VAR M : ARRAY OF BYTE);
  (* Saves the window into the array M *)
PROCEDURE RestoreWindow (w : GWindow; VAR M : ARRAY OF BYTE);
  (* Loads the window from the array M *)
```

The first is used to decide how much memory is needed. The second then stores the contents of the screen memory into the array. The third copies the array contents into the screen memory. These routines are used in the help facility (see chapter 12).

Conclusion

In this chapter a series of useful low level techniques have been described. At the lowest level are text and graphics routines for direct control of the VDU screen. Then a series of higher level commands are provided for drawing lines, circles, etc. Finally a windowing system is described for dividing the screen suitably. These routines provide a good basis on which to build the diagram package, and a variety of other applications.

Also described are some useful programming techniques: sets, opaque types, look-up tables and absolute memory addressing. These may be useful in a number of different applications.

References

1 J&P Partners Ltd *TopSpeed Modula-2 Manual* 1989

2 Russell Rector and George Alexy *The 8086 Book* Osbourne/McGraw-Hill 1980

3 J.D.Foley and A.Van Dam *Fundamentals of Interactive Computer Graphics* Addison-Wesley 1983

4 J.A.Hewitt and R.J.Frank *Software Engineering in Modula-2* Macmillan Education 1989

5 Array Used for a Keyboard Buffer

In the diagram package the user can press keys more quickly than the package can respond. These keypresses must be stored suitably. Another problem occurs when the user instigates a command which causes the program to loop continually; some means is required whereby the user can interrupt the program and so return to a safe state. This facility is also useful when the user makes a wrong command, and so wishes to abort. The techniques described here address these problems.

A general purpose library module, called KEYBUFF, was written by the author to implement the buffer and allow the aborting of a program to a safe state. The module is not specific to the diagram package, and so can be used in other applications. Note, however, that this module uses facilities provided in TopSpeed Modula-2, which are not available in standard Modula-2. See reference[1].

5.1 Keyboard buffer

A keyboard buffer is simply an area of memory in which the values of keypresses are stored. When a keypress is detected, the key is read and it is added to the buffer. When the program is ready to process keyboard input, it reads the next value from the buffer. Care is needed to ensure that the buffer is not overfilled: if the buffer is full no new characters are added. However, when the end of the buffer is reached, if values have already been read from the beginning of the buffer, the program can store new values at the beginning of the buffer. This is termed a circular buffer.

A buffer requires an area of memory to hold the values and pointers indicating where the next value should be stored when a key is pressed, and indicating from which position the next character should be read. It is also useful to have a count of the number of characters in the buffer. Suitable data types and variables are:

```
CONST BuffMax = 256;
VAR   Buffer : ARRAY [1..BuffMax] OF CHAR;
      ReadPointer, WritePointer, NumInBuffer : CARDINAL;
```

The buffer is initialised by:

```
ReadPointer := 1;
WritePointer := 1;
NumInBuffer := 0;
```

To test if there is a key to be read from the buffer the code is:

```
RETURN NumInbuffer > 0
```

80 Modula-2 Applied

If a character is there it can be read from the buffer by:

```
NextChar := Buffer [ReadPointer];
DEC (NumInBuffer);
IF ReadPointer = BuffMax THEN
  ReadPointer := 1
ELSE
  INC (ReadPointer)
END;
RETURN NextChar
```

Any new character, ch, is added to the buffer by:

```
IF NumInBuffer <= BuffMax THEN
  INC (NumInBuffer);
  Buffer [WritePointer] := ch;
  IF WritePointer=BuffMax THEN
    WritePointer := 1
  ELSE
    INC (WritePointer)
  END
END;
```

It is sometimes useful to be able to look at the next character in the buffer to see if it is needed immediately, but be able to leave it there if not. This can be done by:

```
RETURN Buffer[ReadPointer]
```

If the key is needed, the read key routine should be called to update ReadPointer.

An alternative method is for the key to be read in the normal way, but its value is returned to the buffer if it is not needed immediately. This can be achieved by:

```
IF NumInBuffer <= BuffMax THEN
  IF ReadPointer = 1 THEN
    ReadPointer := BuffMax
  ELSE
    DEC (ReadPointer)
  END;
  INC (NumInBuffer)
END;
```

One problem with this method is that between the key being read and then put back, another keypress may occur which fills the buffer, so there is no room for the character to be returned. Thus the first method is better.

5.2 Interrupts and polling

Ideally, whenever the user presses a key, the program should immediately read it and store it in a buffer. That is, the current action of the program should be interrupted. When an interrupt occurs, the current state of the program is remembered, a special routine is then obeyed to service the interrupt, then the program reloads its saved state and carries on.

In this case, the action of the interrupt service routine should be to read the value of the key pressed, and store it suitably in the buffer. This simple idea is complicated by the operating system on the PC, and so in the diagram package an alternative system is used, called polling.

Polling is the process where the program periodically looks to see if there is any data (in this case whether a key has been pressed), and if so the program acts appropriately (here the value of the key is read and stored in the buffer). Therefore, at appropriate points in the package, a call to a procedure CheckKey is made which uses the routines to access the TopSpeed module Dos given in the last chapter. The action of CheckKey is:

```
IF ActualKeyPressed() THEN
   ch := ActualReadChar)()
   then store in a buffer
END;
```

Apart from periodic calls to CheckKey, the user program uses routines in the same form as those provided in the TopSpeed libraries. The algorithms are:

```
PROCEDURE ReadChar() : CHAR;   (* Wait for and read a key *)
VAR ans : CHAR;
BEGIN
  REPEAT UNTIL KeyPressed();
  ans := Buffer [ReadPointer];
  DEC (NumInBuffer);
  IF ReadPointer = BuffMax THEN
    ReadPointer := 1
  ELSE
    INC (ReadPointer)
  END;
  RETURN ans
END ReadChar;
```

```
PROCEDURE KeyPressed() : BOOLEAN;(* Has a key been pressed ? *)
BEGIN
  CheckKey;
  RETURN NumInBuffer > 0
END KeyPressed;
```

5.3 Aborting and returning to a safe state

If the user causes a program to loop continually it must be possible to abort the action and return to a safe state. A safe state is one where the user can carry on using the program. In the diagram package an abort should return the program to the main command loop.

One way in which the program can loop continually is when a usershape calls itself at the same size. Here the diagram is recursive, but each time it recurses it does not act on a smaller version, so the program does not terminate. This could be detected relatively easily, but a more difficult problem to detect is where one usershape calls another, which calls the first one again. Here the diagram is mutually recursive.

Thus, rather than specifically testing for loops, a more general abort mechanism is provided. This is achieved using the low level keyboard handling routines. A special character is defined as being an abort character. If the routine CheckKey detects the character, the program aborts by jumping to a safe state, which is normally the main command loop of the program.

GOTO statements, and why they should not be used

To return to the main command loop the program must jump to the address of the code at the safe state. In a language like BASIC this can be achieved by a GOTO statement. GOTOs are rightly frowned upon by good programmers, as they encourage programs which are difficult to understand and debug: if a program jumps around greatly, it is difficult to determine how it got to a particular piece of code, hence it is difficult to see which part of the program caused an error. Some people have seriously suggested that there should be a COMEFROM statement so as to be able to determine the path that the program followed!

Another problem with GOTO statements occurs whenever they are used to jump between subroutines (or procedures): the stack may be corrupted. For example, subroutine A may normally be called from the main program, whereas subroutine C may be called from subroutine B which is called from the main program. When subroutine A is called, the stack will have moved down by one level, but for subroutine C, the stack will have moved down by two levels, one when B was called and the second when C was called from B. If the program jumps from C to A, on return from A the stack will be moved back up by only one level, and so overall it will have moved down by one. This will often not cause the program any immediate problem. However, each time it occurs, the stack will move down, and eventually cause a problem, the debugging of which may take time.

Thus when any form of jump is done it is essential that the stack is balanced as well. In TopSpeed Modula-2, suitable facilities are provided by two routines called SetJmp and LongJmp from the Lib module.

SetJmp and LongJmp

Essentially the action of SetJmp is to store the current state of the program, primarily its stack pointer and program counter. A call to SetJmp is therefore put at the 'safe' place.

A call to LongJmp transfers the program to the place set by SetJmp, and correctly aligns the stack. The system must know where to go, so there needs to be an associated variable of type LongLabel (as defined in Lib).

When SetJmp is called it sets the LongLabel and returns the value 0. When the LongJmp is called it is passed the LongLabel and a suitable result so that the program can tell from where the jump has come (shades of COMEFROM statement). The action of the LongJmp is effectively to return to the correct place by returning, with the stack correctly set, from the SetJmp procedure, with the result value. In practice this can be used as follows.

In the 'safe state', directly before the main command loop:

```
IF SetJmp (label) = 0 THEN  do any initialisation  END;
```

When a call to LongJmp is made, the program returns to the SetJmp, but as the result returned is other than zero, the initialisation will not be performed.

In the CheckKey routine, the code is:

```
IF ActualKeyPressed() THEN
  ch := ActualReadChar();
  IF AbortOn AND (ch=AbortChar) THEN
    LongJmp (AbortLabel, AbortRes)
  ELSIF NumInBuffer < BuffMax THEN
    < put ch in buffer, as described above >
  END
END      (* AbortOn, AbortChar, etc., are defined below *)
```

As was mentioned at the start of the chapter, the keyboard buffer routines were written so as not to be specific to the diagram package. Therefore a routine was provided in the package to specify the character which causes the LongJmp, the location of the jump and the result. This routine sets the following variables local to the module:

```
VAR AbortOn   : BOOLEAN;      (* whether aborts are allowed *)
    AbortChar : CHAR;         (* the abort character *)
    AbortRes  : CARDINAL;     (* result returned with abort *)
    AbortJump : LongLabel;    (* where the jump should go *)
```

The routine is :

```
PROCEDURE SetAbort (l : LongLabel; ach : CHAR; ares : CARDINAL);
BEGIN
   AbortOn := ach <> 0C;
   AbortChar := ach;
   AbortJump := l;
   AbortRes := ares
END SetAbort;
```

Thus, once again, a module is provided which has its own local variables, and these can only be affected by calling the procedure in the module; they cannot be corrupted by any other part of the program.

A convenient time to call SetAbort is with SetJmp:

```
IF SetJmp (Label) = 0 THEN SetAbort (Label, 1C, 1) END;
```

1C is control-A, the abort character. One point to note is that a LongJmp causes the program to jump to the subroutine in which the SetJmp was called, and restores the stack to the correct value. However, the compiler sometimes keeps local variables in registers not on the stack. Such variables will not still be in the registers when the LongJmp is called. Therefore it is important that the variables must be kept on the stack, in memory. This can be ensured using the compiler directive in TopSpeed: (*$W+*) before the procedure heading.

Conclusion

In this chapter some simple techniques are described for using an array as a circular buffer, and for using the special TopSpeed procedures SetJmp and LongJmp. Once again it is worth stressing that jumping around in a program is not good practice. However, one of the few times when it is permissible is when aborting.

Reference

1 J&P Partners Ltd *Top Speed Modula-2 Manual* 1989

6 Arrays for Selecting Commands

In this chapter an algorithm is described for selecting one of a list of commands. This was used in the early development of the diagram package for selecting commands, though it has now been superseded by a more powerful, but more complicated, technique. This shows how part of the program can be quickly developed and then replaced by a better method, when time permits.

The algorithm displays in the command window a list of commands which can be selected, and the user is able to select the right command either by inputting the character associated with the command, or by using cursor keys or the mouse to move up and down the commands until the correct item is specified. The algorithm, therefore, shows how mouse movements can be handled. This processing is also used later on for modifying shapes.

In this chapter the code for the algorithms is given in full, as this module has been superseded by the more advanced method, and so is not included on the disk.

6.1 Commands

The commands listed in the appropriate window are as follows:

```
Line        Circle      Arc         beZier      Rectangle
Diamond     String      Usershape   Modify      moVe
copY        mIrror      deleTe      Block       Editshape
Options     eXamine     Grid        New         File
Plot        Help        Quit
```

The user is able to select the appropriate command by positioning the cursor over the correct item or by entering the character associated with the command. That character is the one for each shape with a capital letter: L would select Line, V would select moVe, etc.

When the user is moving the cursor up and down the list, the cursor position is specified by having the command at that position highlighted: this technique is used by the TopSpeed compiler and many other packages.

Data types

A simple data type was chosen for implementing the algorithm: the commands are stored as a list of strings. The relevant data types are as follows:

```
CONST MaxCommand = 22;
      CommWidth = 14;
```

```
VAR Command : CARDINAL;
    CommandList : ARRAY [0..MaxCommand] OF
                  ARRAY [0..CommWidth] OF CHAR;
```

A string is an ARRAY OF CHAR, so the CommandList is an ARRAY OF strings. This is an example of a two dimensional array. The variable Command indicates the current command in the list.

As it is required that a command can be selected by its associated character, the first position in the string is used to store that character.

The arrays are thus initialised as follows:

```
CommandList [0]  := 'LLine';
CommandList [1]  := 'CCircle';
CommandList [2]  := 'AArc';
CommandList [3]  := 'ZbeZier';
CommandList [4]  := 'RRectangle';
CommandList [5]  := 'DDiamond';
CommandList [6]  := 'SString';
CommandList [7]  := 'UUsershape';
CommandList [8]  := 'MModify';
CommandList [9]  := 'VmoVe';
CommandList [10] := 'YcopY';
CommandList [11] := 'ImIrror';
CommandList [12] := 'TdeleTe';
CommandList [13] := 'BBlock';
CommandList [14] := 'PPlot';
CommandList [15] := 'EEditshape';
CommandList [16] := 'OOptions';
CommandList [17] := 'XeXamine';
CommandList [18] := 'GGrid';
CommandList [19] := 'NNew';
CommandList [20] := 'FFile';
CommandList [21] := 'HHelp';
CommandList [22] := 'QQuit';
```

Displaying the commands

The commands are written in the window initially by first activating the 'Commands' window, then listing each item in the array. The algorithm is shown below:

```
ActivateWindow (Commands);
    (* ensure output is to Command window *)
FOR ct := 0 TO MaxCommand DO
  ListCommand (ct, ct=Command)
END;
```

Where ListCommand is passed the number of the command to be displayed and if it is to be displayed in inverse (highlighted). The command currently selected, as denoted by the variable Command, is inverted. ListCommand is:

```
PROCEDURE ListCommand (n : CARDINAL; InInverse : BOOLEAN);
VAR ct : CARDINAL;
BEGIN
  IF InInverse THEN BackGround (7) ELSE BackGround (0) END;
  Colour (14);
  GotoXY (1, n+1);
  ct := 1;
  WHILE CommandList[n] [ct] <> 0C DO
    WriteChar (CommandList [n] [ct]);
    INC (ct)
  END
END ListCommand;
```

The procedure uses the BackGround, Colour and GotoXY routines from the GrWindow module, and then writes out the command string. Note that the string to be displayed starts at position 1, not position 0: position 0 contains the command character. The CommandList is a two dimensional array, hence two indices are needed, the first specifies which string, the second the position in the string. The end of the string is marked by the character 0C. More detail on strings is given in chapter 8.

6.2 Keyboard handling

The main routine described in the chapter is the one which allows the user to select the appropriate command. This requires the processing of the cursor keys and handling the mouse. On the PC used by the author, the mouse has been set up so that any mouse movement has the same effect as pressing the corresponding arrow cursor key. For example, moving the mouse to the left is the same as pressing the left arrow key. When the right button is pressed, the ESC character is returned, for the left button, ENTER is returned. For other computers the same effect could be obtained by modifying the keyboard buffer routines to insert characters into the buffer whenever mouse movement is detected.

When using a PC, the 'normal' characters (letters, digits and punctuation) are returned as a single byte. However, the function keys and the cursor keys return

88 Modula-2 Applied

two bytes: the first is 0, the second determines the key. The following table shows the values of the second byte returned by these keys: the values are given in decimal and octal (the latter because characters are specified in TopSpeed Modula-2 using the octal notation), and three columns are shown, one for when the key is pressed alone, the others for when the Ctrl or the Alt key is pressed as well.

```
Key             alone          With Ctrl       With Alt

F1              59,   73C      94,   136C      104,  150C
F2              60,   74C      95,   137C      105,  151C
F3              61,   75C      96,   140C      106,  152C
F4              62,   76C      97,   141C      107,  153C
F5              63,   77C      98,   142C      108,  154C
F6              64,   100C     99,   143C      109,  155C
F7              65,   101C     100,  144C      110,  156C
F8              66,   102C     101,  145C      111,  157C
F9              67,   103C     102,  146C      112,  160C
F10             68,   104C     103,  147C      113,  161C

Home            71,   107C     119,  167C
UpArrow         72,   110C
PgUp            73,   111C     132,  204C
LeftArrow       75,   113C     115,  163C
RightArrow      77,   115C     116,  164C
End             79,   117C     117,  165C
DownArrow       80,   120C
PgDn            81,   121C     118,  166C

Ins             82,   122C
Del             83,   123C
```

6.3 Command selection algorithm

The basic selection algorithm is straightforward; the program should loop continually, displaying the current cursor position (by listing the appropriate command highlighted), moving the cursor up or down in response to the arrows keys, until ENTER is pressed or the appropriate character is entered. When the cursor moves, the current command should be redrawn not highlighted, and the new position drawn in highlight. However, when the mouse is used to move the cursor, the movement commands are sometimes entered more quickly than the command can be listed. Thus a command is shown highlighted, and then immediately it must be 'dehighlighted', which is a waste of effort. Worse still, because the program is responding too slowly compared with the input, it can cause the user to move the cursor too far and so select the wrong command, and certainly does not provide a good user interface. The action of the program should appear to the user to be instantaneous.

The solution to this problem, which is simple and is used later in the package when items are entered interactively in the diagram, is not to write the command highlighted if another key has been entered. Consequently, when the command position is moved again, the command is rewritten dehighlighted only if had already been shown highlighted. A boolean variable, HaveDrawn, indicates this. The algorithm for handling cursor keys is:

```
ListCommand (Command, TRUE);
HaveDrawn := TRUE;
LOOP
   AChar := ReadChar();
   CASE AChar OF
      CursorUp   : IF NOT at top THEN GoUp END |
      CursorDown : IF NOT at bottom THEN GoDown END |
      Home       : GoToFirstCommand |
      End        : GotoLastCommand |
      Enter      : EXIT
   END;
   IF HaveMoved AND HaveDrawn THEN
      ListCommand (OldPosition, FALSE)
      HaveDrawn := FALSE
   END;
   IF NOT HaveDrawn AND NOT KeyPressed() THEN
      ListCommand (Command, TRUE);
      HaveDrawn := TRUE
   END
END;
IF NOT HaveDrawn THEN
   ListCommand (Command, TRUE)
END
```

The final version of the algorithm also allows the user to specify a command by entering the appropriate letter, L for Line, V for moVe, etc. This is handled by comparing the character entered with the first character of each command: if the letters match, then the command has been specified, the previously selected command is dehighlighted, and the main loop is exited. The complete procedure is shown in program 6.1.

```
PROCEDURE GetCommand;
CONST UpArrow = 110C;
      Home = 107C;
      DownArrow = 120C;
      End = 117C;
      Enter = 15C;
VAR ch : CHAR;
    CommandWas : CARDINAL;
    HaveDrawn : BOOLEAN;

  PROCEDURE IsCommandLetter() : BOOLEAN;
  BEGIN   (* check if is character associated with a command *)
    Command := 0;
    WHILE (Command <= MaxCommand) AND
          (CommandList[Command][0]CAP(ch) ) DO
      INC (Command)
    END;
    RETURN Command <= MaxCommand (* yes, is such a character *)
  END IsCommandLetter;

BEGIN (* GetCommand *)
  ActivateWindow (Commands);
  ListCommand (Command, TRUE);
  HaveDrawn := TRUE;
  LOOP
    CommandWas := Command;
    ch := ReadChar();
    IF ch=0C THEN
      CASE ReadChar() OF
        UpArrow   : IF Command > 0 THEN DEC (Command) END |
        Home      : Command := 0 |
        DownArrow : IF Command < MaxCommand THEN INC (Command) END |
        End       : Command := MaxCommand
      END
    ELSIF (ch=Enter) OR IsCommandLetter() THEN
      EXIT
    ELSE
      Command := CommandWas
    END;

    IF (Command <> CommandWas) AND HaveDrawn THEN
      ListCommand (CommandWas, FALSE);
      HaveDrawn := FALSE
    END;
```

```
    IF NOT (HaveDrawn) AND NOT (KeyPressed() ) THEN
      ListCommand (Command, TRUE);
      HaveDrawn := TRUE
    END
  END; (* of LOOP *)

  IF (Command<>CommandWas) AND HaveDrawn THEN
    ListCommand(CWas, FALSE);
    HaveDrawn := FALSE
  END;
  IF NOT HaveDrawn THEN ListCommand (Command, TRUE) END
END GetCommand;
```

Program 6.1 GetCommand procedure

Conclusion

In this chapter a few simple points have been described. First a simple use of two dimensional arrays is given. Second, character handling of the PC keyboard is described. Finally a useful technique for user interfaces is given, here applied to displaying commands, but equally applicable elsewhere in the diagram package for modifying shapes.

7 Transformations and Clipping

The diagram package allows the user to enter a diagram interactively. A diagram consists of standard items, such as lines and circles, and other shapes defined by the user, called usershapes, which can be made up of the standard items and other usershapes. An item can be entered anywhere in the diagram, hence it must be possible to position a usershape at any position, size or rotation. If a usershape which contains another shape drawn at 45 degrees, is itself drawn at 90 degrees, then the 'inner' shape must be drawn at 135 degrees. This is best acheived using transformation matrices, which are the first topic of the chapter.

Another important requirement of the package is to allow the user to examine parts of the picture in more detail, that is to zoom into the picture. This requires careful considerations of the scaling of the picture.

When the user zooms into part of the diagram, some of the picture will be outside the window, and so should not be drawn. The graphics window handling routines will prevent such items appearing, because a dot is not drawn if it is not within the window. However, if a line is completely outside the window, the program will calculate the position of each dot, and none will be plotted. This is clearly ineffinect. Hence an algorithm is required which only calls the appropriate drawing routine if any part of the line, circle, etc., is in the window. An even better algorithm would pass to the drawing routine only that part of the line which is in the window. This is achieved using *clipping*.

7.1 Transformations

Transformations are required so that an item may be drawn at any position, in any size and at any angle (see Foley and VanDam[1]). The transformations required are translation, scaling and rotation, and they must be defined in such a way that they may be concatenated. The operations in two dimensions are as follows:

```
translation:    x' := x + Tx
                y' := y + Ty
scaling:        x' := x * Sx
                y' := y * Sy
rotation:       x' :=  x * COS (A) + y * SIN (A)
                y' := -x * SIN (A) + y * COS (A)
```

These operations can be expressed in the form of matrix operations:

$$[x'\ y'\ 1] := [x\ y\ 1] * \begin{matrix} 1 & 0 & 0 \\ 0 & 1 & 0 \\ Tx & Ty & 1 \end{matrix}$$

$$[x'\ y'\ 1] := [x\ y\ 1] * \begin{matrix} Sx & 0 & 0 \\ 0 & Sy & 0 \\ 0 & 0 & 1 \end{matrix}$$

$$[x'\ y'\ 1] := [x\ y\ 1] * \begin{matrix} COS\ (A) & SIN\ (A) & 0 \\ -SIN\ (A) & COS\ (A) & 0 \\ 0 & 0 & 1 \end{matrix}$$

In this form, the transformation matrices have been padded with redundant terms so that they are square, and thus they can be multiplied together. This is required for concatenation of transformations, which is simply achieved by multiplying the transformation matrices together. Thus it is possible to generate a matrix which has the right amounts of scaling, rotation and translation by generating a scaling matrix, a rotation matrix and a translation matrix, and multiplying them together. Once a suitable matrix is produced it can then be used to process each item in the diagram.

As stated above, redundant information is added so that the matrices are made square so as to allow concatenation by matrix multiplication. However, this requires extra processing, which is unnecessary as the last column of each matrix always contains 0 0 1. Therefore, these matrices can be achieved using 3 * 2 matrices, and processed by special matrix manipulation routines. The considerable savings in processing achieved by this, described below, justify this approach.

Using transformations in a diagram

The main diagram consists of a list of items (standard items like lines and circles, or usershapes). A usershape also consists of a list of items. Therefore the same procedure can be used for drawing the main diagram as for a usershape. Both require that the items be suitably transformed and drawn.

Initially, the 3*2 transformation matrix is set as:

```
Const   0
  0   Const
  0     0
```

where Const is a value suitably chosen: this is discussed below. Then each standard item to be drawn is processed by the matrix. If, however, the item to be drawn is a usershape it should be drawn based at the given position, with the specified scaling and rotation. Thus all the items that make up that shape should be drawn relative to the base position of the shape, suitably scaled and rotated. This is achieved by processing the current transformation matrix (by multiplying it by suitable transformation matrices) and then drawing each item processed by this new matrix. Where an item of the usershape also calls a usershape, the current matrix should also be transformed, etc. Thus these actions are best done using a recursive procedure, shown below. This procedure draws an item, where an item can be a line, circle, etc., or a 'head' which is the start of the list of items. The procedure is passed the current scaling matrix and the item to be drawn.

```
PROCEDURE DrawItem (S : ScaleMatrix;  item : ItemType);
VAR Snew : ScaleMatrix;
BEGIN
  CASE type of item OF
    head       : FOR all items in the list DO
                   DrawItem (S, eachitem)
                 END |
    line       : Scale end coordinates of line, and draw |
    circle     : Scale origin and radius, and draw |
etc.
    string     : Scale origin, size and rotation of string
                 and draw |
    usershape  : Generate Snew, by processing S with the
                 specified scaling, rotation & translation;
                 DrawItem (Snew, head of usershape)
  END
END DrawItem;
```

A ScaleMatrix could be implemented in Modula-2 as a two dimensional array:

```
ScaleMatrix = ARRAY [0..2], [0..1] OF number;
```

where number is INTEGER, LONGINT, REAL, etc., whatever is appropriate. In this case LONGINTs are used, as explaining in the next section. Given a ScaleMatrix, any coordinate X, Y, can be transformed using the procedures

```
PROCEDURE XScale (S : ScaleMatrix; X, Y : number) : number;
BEGIN
  RETURN X * S[0,0] + Y * S[1,0] + S[2,0]
END XScale;

PROCEDURE YScale (S : ScaleMatrix; X, Y : number) : number;
BEGIN
  RETURN X * S[0,1] + Y * S[1,1] + S[2,1]
END YScale;
```

Transformations and Clipping

If 'proper' 3*3 matrices were used, the above two procedures would be replaced with code in which the X,Y coordinate was stored in a 3*1 matrix, and this was then multiplied by the 3*3 ScaleMatrix, generating a 3*1 matrix the first two elements of which contain the transformed X,Y coordinates. That would require 9 multiplications and 6 additions, as compared with the above 4 multiplications and 4 additions.

The new ScaleMatrix can be calculated by:

```
PROCEDURE NewScaleMatrix (VAR New:ScaleMatrix; Old:ScaleMatrix;
                         XScal, YScal, Rot, Xoff, Yoff:number);
BEGIN
       (* the new offset is calculated by using the current scale
       matrix to transform the position in Xoff,Yoff *)
   New [2,0] := XScale (Old, Xoff, Yoff);
   New [2,1] := YScale (Old, Xoff, Yoff);
   (* scaling and rotation parts of the transformation are done
   using the first four elements in the matrix. In the following
   the old matrix is multiplied by a matrix with the scaling and
   a matrix with the rotation, all combined *)
   New [0,0] := Old [0,0] * XScal * Cos (Rot) -
                Old [0,1] * YScal * Sin (Rot);
   New [0,1] := Old [0,0] * XScal * Sin (Rot) +
                Old [0,1] * YScal * Cos (Rot);
   New [1,0] := Old [1,0] * XScal * Cos (Rot) -
                Old [1,1] * YScal * Sin (Rot);
   New [1,1] := Old [1,0] * XScal * Sin (Rot) +
                Old [1,1] * YScal * Cos (Rot)
END NewScaleMatrix;
```

Again if 'proper' matrices were used, the above would be done by generating three 3*3 matrices (one each for the translation, rotation and scaling), multiplying them together and then multiplying the result by the Old matrix. The code given above is much more efficient.

Implementation considerations

In this section considerations for dimensioning and scaling the points in the diagram are given. The relevant points are as follows. The size of the digram must be such that the user can provide sufficient detail. Scaling of usershapes must be possible. The program must allow the user to zoom into part of the picture. To ensure fast operation, the coordinates of lines, etc., should be INTEGERs or LONGINTs, rather than REALs.

For the first point, the resolution of the diagram, considerations should be given not just to the size of the screen, but also to any hardcopy device used, which may have a greater resolution than the screen. The highest resolution device used by the author is an A4 size laser printer, so this was used for calculating scaling requirements.

An A4 page is about 300mm long, and it should be possible to resolve at least 0.1mm. Therefore the maximum size of a diagram should be at least 3000 points. As integer calculations are used, it is a good idea to make the maximum size a power of two. Thus the maximum size chosen was 4096. The coordinates of the main diagram, and all usershapes, are thus in the range 0..4095.

Scaling of usershapes affects the initial value of the ScaleMatrix. It must be possible to draw a usershape in the maximum size, and at various smaller sizes. Drawing at smaller sizes is achieved by reducing the values in the scaling matrix (elements 0,0, 0,1, 1,0 and 1,1). Again using powers of two, it was decided that the smallest a usershape should be is 1/64th of the current size. Therefore all scaling of usershapes is in multiples of 64ths. The initial value of the scaling matrix must be greater than 64, to allow for some arithmetic errors, so the initial value of the ScaleMatrix is

```
256    0
  0  256
  0    0
```

Using these values, lines, circles, etc., will be suitably transformed so they can appear in the correct position. However, one further calculation is needed so that these items actual appear on the screen (or on a printer). This calculation should bear in mind that the diagram is conceived to be square, whereas the screen is not (the width of the screen is greater than the depth). This calculation can also be used to allow zooming into the picture. The calculation needed can be derived as follows:

Coordinates are processed by procedures XScale and YScale, so

```
0,0           ->      0,0
4096,4096     ->      1048576, 1048576
                      (* 4096 * 256 = 1048576 *)
```

If the graphics window were square, 0,0 should be the bottom left corner of the main graphics window, at coordinate 0,WindowDepth(), (or the bottom left of the printed page); and 1048756,1048756 should be the top right corner of the window, at point WindowWidth(),0. As the width of the screen is greater than its depth, a y-coordinate of 4096 should be transformed to the top of the screen, and x-coordinates should be transformed so that the midpoint, of value 2048, becomes the middle of the screen. Thus the transformation of point X,Y to point x,y on the screen is achieved by the procedure:

Transformations and Clipping 97

```
PROCEDURE XYScale (S : ScaleMatrix; X, Y : number;
                   VAR x, y : number);
BEGIN
  x := XScale (S, X, Y) * WindowDepth() DIV Scale + XOffset;
  y := WindowDepth() -
       YScale (S, X, Y) * WindowDepth() DIV Scale + YOffset
END XYScale;
```

Where the values Scale, XOffset and YOffset are calculated beforehand:

```
Scale := 4096 * 256;
XOffset := (WindowWidth() - WindowDepth()) DIV 2;
YOffset := 0;
```

The above calculations allow the complete diagram to appear on the screen. However, a simple change to the above, which again can be calculated once and then used often subsequently, allows zooming in. Zooming in is achieved by having a smaller value for Scale: if Scale has half the value given above, the procedure XYScale will ensure that position 2048,2048 will be transformed to the top right of the screen. This thus allows the user to examine the bottom left of the diagram in more detail. Obviously the user must be able to examine any part of the diagram in more detail, that is to zoom in at any point. This is achieved both by reducing Scale and by changing XOffset and YOffset. The following procedure, SetZoom, achieves this:

```
PROCEDURE SetZoom (X, Y, ZoomFactor : number);
VAR x, y : number;
BEGIN
  Scale := 4096 * 256 DIV ZoomFactor;
  IF ZoomFactor=1 THEN
    XOffset := (WindowWidth() - WindowDepth() ) DIV 2;
    YOffset := 0
  ELSE
    XOffset := 0; YOffset := 0;
    XYScale (MainScalematrix, X, Y, x, y);
    XOffset := WindowWidth() DIV 2 - x;
    YOffset := WindowDepth() DIV 2 - y
  END
END SetZoom;
```

98 Modula-2 Applied

The above procedure does the necessary calculations to allow zooming into the diagram with the particular point, X,Y being the centre of interest. It works as follows. If the ZoomFactor is 1, the above calculations are used for generating the offsets. Otherwise, the calculations should ensure that point X,Y is the middle of the screen, and this is achieved by setting the offsets to 0, calculating the position to where point X,Y is transformed, and the offset required is the difference between the middle of the screen and this calculated position. Note, as 4096 and 256 are powers of two, to avoid arithmetic errors, the ZoomFactor is also a power of two.

Practical points

In the above, the coordinates are of type number. What that type is needs to be specified. REALs are not to be used, as processing them is relatively slow. Ideally INTEGERs would be used. However, 4096*256 is greater than the integer range. Thus all coordinates are stored as LONGINTs, and the final transformation generates INTEGERs as these are required by the primitive routines.

The transformation matrices process coordinates suitably, but they also must handle angles and radii of circles. As regards angles: if the current transformation matrix is such that the object is rotated by n degrees, any angle m, must be transformed to m + n degrees. This is achieved by having an extra element in the matrix containing the current amount of rotation. Thus a ScaleMatrix is in fact defined as:

```
ScaleMatrix : ARRAY [0..3], [0..1] OF LONGINT;
```

and the angle is processed by:

```
a := a + S [3, 1];
WHILE a>360 DO a := a - 360 END;
WHILE a<0 DO a := a + 360 END;
```

The above ensures that the angle is in the range 0..360 inclusive. And there is an extra line in NewScaleMatrix:

```
New [3, 1] := (Old [3, 1] + Rot) MOD 360;
```

Radii must be suitably scaled. Element [3,0] of the ScaleMatrix is used for this purpose. It effectively contains the overall scale value. Radii are scaled by:

```
Radius := Radius * S [3, 0];
```

and in NewScaleMatrix it is updated by:

New [3, 0] := (Old [3, 0] * XScal) DIV 64;

The DIV 64 is used because XScal is in multiples of 64ths. This must also be considered in the actual updating of other elements in the scale matrix. The calculations of Cos and Sin are achieved using the routines Cos100 and Sin100, from the module GrWindow described in chapter 4, which return 100 times the Cosine or Sine of the angle. Thus, the elements [0,0], [0,1], [1,0] and [1,1] in the transformation matrix are actually updated by code of the form:

```
New [0,0] := ( Old [0,0] * XScal * LONGINT (Cos100(INTEGER(Rot)))
             - Old [0,1] * YScal * LONGINT (Sin100(INTEGER(Rot))))
             DIV 6400;
```

etc. The numbers are divided by 64 * 100, the 64 to account for scaling in multiples of 64ths, and 100 because of Cos100 and Sin100.

7.2 Clipping

Clipping is required when the user zooms into part of the diagram. It is the process of determining which part, if any, of an item will be visible in the window, and calling the low level primitive routine with the coordinates of the visible part of the item. Clipping of lines will be considered first, then clipping of circles and other items. For more information, see Foley and VanDam[1] or Angell[2].

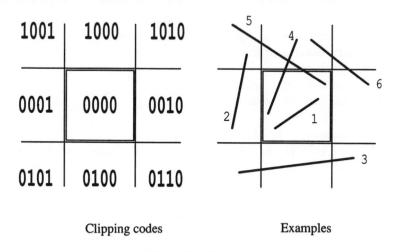

Clipping codes   Examples

Figure 7.1 Clipping

The line clipping algorithm presented here is based on the Sutherland-Cohen algorithm, and it uses Clipping Codes. The action of the algorithm is straightforward. For each line, the end points are assigned clipping codes as shown in figure 7.1a: these codes are binary numbers. In the figure there are nine areas, the middle one represents the visible screen, and the others indicate the areas above, below, to the left and/or to the right of the screen. The code given to an endpoint is the code of the area in which the endpoint is situated.

If both clipping codes are zero (for line 1 of figure 7.1b), then all the line is in the window, therefore all the line should be drawn. If the two codes ANDed together give a non-zero answer (line 2 or 3), no part of the line is in the window, so nothing should be drawn. Otherwise, part of the line may be in the window. Thus at least one endpoint has a nonzero code value. That one (or one of the two) is processed and replaced with the coordinates of the point where the line intersects the screen boundary, its clipping code is established, and the process is repeated. For example, if the point is above the window (line 4), the endpoint is replaced with the intersection of the line with the top of the window. If the point is above and to the left of the window, either the intersection with the top, or the intersection with the left is calculated (line 5). It is possible that after the intersection has been found all of the remainder of the line is outside the window (line 6), all is now inside (line 4), or further processing is required (line 5).

Note that the algorithm finds lines which are within the window or completely outside the window very quickly, which is required. Those lines partially within the window need more processing, but in general these will be in the minority.

The clipping codes, being binary numbers which are to be ANDed together, are best implemented with the type BITSET (see chapter 4 on the use of BITSET and the AND operation). The algorithm can be implemented using three procedures.

```
PROCEDURE ClipLine (x1, y1, x2, y2 : INTEGER);
VAR code1, code2 : BITSET;
BEGIN
  ClipCode (x1, y1, code1);
  ClipCode (x2, y2, code2);
  LOOP
    IF (code1={}) AND (code2={}) THEN
      Line (x1, y1, x2, y2);        (* all in window, so draw *)
      EXIT
    ELSIF code1 * code2 <> {} THEN
      EXIT                          (* none in window, so stop *)
    ELSIF code1<>{} THEN (* x1,y1 offscreen, calc intersect *)
      CalcIntersect (x1, y1, x2, y2, code1)
    ELSE
      CalcIntersect (x2, y2, x1, y1, code2)
    END
  END
END ClipLine;
```

The ClipCode is calculated as follows:

```
PROCEDURE ClipCode (x, y : INTEGER; VAR c : BITSET);
BEGIN
  c := {};
  IF x < WindowLeft THEN
    INCL (c, 0)
  ELSIF x > WindowRight THEN
    INCL (c, 1)
  END;
  IF y < WindowBottom THEN
    INCL (c, 2)
  ELSIF y > WindowTop THEN
    INCL (c, 3)
  END;
END ClipCode;
```

The intersection can be calculated in various ways. The following uses the midpoint subdivision algorithm. Here the intersection of the line with the boundary is found by repeatedly finding the middle of the line, and from its position determining in which half of the line the intersection will be, and then looking in that half.

```
PROCEDURE CalcIntersect (VAR xf, yf : INTEGER; xn, yn : INTEGER;
       VAR c : BITSET);
VAR xm, ym : INTEGER;
BEGIN
  LOOP
    xm := (xf + xn) DIV 2;  ym := (yf + yn) DIV 2;
    IF xm,ym on the Window boundary THEN (* intersection found *)
      xf := xm; yf := ym; ClipCode (xf, yf, c);
      EXIT
    ELSIF xm,ym within the Window THEN
      xn := xm; yn := ym;
    ELSE
      xf := xm; yf := ym
    END;
  END
END CalcIntersect;
```

The midpoint of the line between xf,yf and xn,yn is found as xm,ym. If it is on the edge of the window, the intersection is found, it is at point xm,ym. Otherwise,

102 Modula-2 Applied

if the midpoint is in the window, the intersection is in that part of the line between xm,ym and xf,yf, so xn,yn is replaced by xm,ym, and the search repeated. If the midpoint is outside the window, the intersection must be between xn,yn and xm,ym, so xf,yf is replaced by xm,ym.

Figure 7.2 Approximation to a circle

As regards clipping of circles and arcs; if any part of the circle or arc is visible, the primitive needs to calculate all the points around the item, and plot only those which are visible. Therefore the clipping algorithm need only report if any of the circle is visible. A simple test for this is to approximate the circle as 8 lines (as shown in figure 7.2) and test if any of those lines are visible, using a modified version of the line clipping routine which reports if any of the line is visible, but does not draw it:

```
rad2 := (radius * 7) DIV 10;     (* radius / SQRT (2) *)
AnyPartVisible :=
LineInWindow(xorigin+radius,yorigin,xorigin+rad2,yorigin+rad2) OR
LineInWindow(xorigin+rad2,yorigin+rad2,xorigin,yorigin+radius) OR
LineInWindow(xorigin,yorigin+radius,xorigin-rad2,yorigin+rad2) OR
LineInWindow(xorigin-rad2,yorigin+rad2,xorigin-radius,yorigin) OR
LineInWindow(xorigin-radius,yorigin,xorigin-rad2,yorigin-rad2) OR
LineInWindow(xorigin-rad2,yorigin-rad2,xorigin,yorigin-radius) OR
LineInWindow(xorigin,yorigin-radius,xorigin+rad2,yorigin-rad2) OR
LineInWindow(xorigin+rad2,yorigin-rad2,xorigin+radius,yorigin);
```

The other elements in a diagram are rectangles, diamonds and Bezier curves, which consist of lines and so can be clipped as such, and strings and usershapes, whose elements are drawn if any part of the shape is visible. Strings and usershapes consist of items which exist in a particular rectangular area. Therefore, the string or usershape need not be drawn if the whole of that area is outside the window. If the four corners of this window are at positions x1,y1, x2,y2, x3,y3, x4,y4, then some element may be in the window if the following expression is true:

```
LineInWindow (x1,y1, x2,y2) OR
LineInWindow (x2,y1, x3,y3) OR
LineInWindow (x3,y3, x4,y4) OR
LineInWindow (x4,y4, x1,y1) OR
LineInWindow (x1,y1, x3,y3)
```

The last condition is needed for the case when the object completely surrounds the window: none of the outside lines is in the window, but the diagonal may well be. The test is not foolproof, but gives a good approximation.

7.3 Bezier curves

It is convenient at this point to mention Bezier curves, as these are used in the package, they can be implemented using arrays, and their coding can also be done more efficiently than at first sight. Again see Foley and VanDam[1] for more details.

Bezier curves were developed by the French engineer Bezier for use in the design of some Renault cars, and they are used in many applications. Essentially a curve is defined by a set of control points. If there are k+1 such points, x_0,y_0, x_1,y_1, .., x_k,y_k, a point on the corresponding Bezier curve can be described by a series of points X_t,Y_t, where t is on the range 0..1:

$$X_t = \sum_{r=0}^{k} x_r \frac{k!}{k!(k-r)!} t^r (1-t)^{k-r}$$

$$Y_t = \sum_{r=0}^{k} y_r \frac{k!}{k!(k-r)!} t^r (1-t)^{k-r}$$

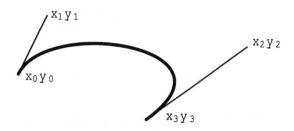

Figure 7.3 Four point Bezier curve

For a four point curve, as is used in the diagram package, the end control points are the coordinates of the end of the curve, and the line from each endpoint to the nearest control point forms a tangent to the curve: this is shown in figure 7.3. Each point X_t, Y_t is given by:

$$X_t = x_0 (1-t)^3 + 3 x_1 t (1-t)^2 + 3 x_2 t^2 (1-t) + x_3 t^3$$
$$Y_t = y_0 (1-t)^3 + 3 y_1 t (1-t)^2 + 3 y_2 t^2 (1-t) + y_3 t^3$$

For any curve, the values x_0, $3 x_1$, etc. are constant and can be calculated before the curve is drawn. The curve can then be approximated by a series of line segments. The following algorithm draws a curve in this way, using a procedure Calculate which finds the appropriate x,y values for the given value of the parameter t.

```
t := 0.0;
Calculate (xp, yp);
WHILE t<=1.0 DO
   Calculate (x, y);
   Line (xp, yp, x, y);
   xp := x;
   yp := y;
   t := t + somefac
               (* somefac is some number, say 0.03 *)
END;
```

However, the above requires the use of floating point arithmetic. The algorithm can be made faster by using LONGINTs, and by varying the integer parameter t in steps of 1 from 0 to Tmax (where Tmax is, say, 30). Then

$$X_t = (x_0 (Tmax-t)^3 + 3 x_1 t (Tmax-t)^2 + 3 x_2 t^2 (Tmax-t) + x_3 t^3) \text{ DIV } Tmax^3$$

$$Y_t = (y_0 (Tmax-t)^3 + 3 y_1 t (Tmax-t)^2 + 3 y_2 t^2 (Tmax-t) + y_3 t^3) \text{ DIV } Tmax^3$$

The parameters x_0, $3x_1$, $3x_2$ and x_3 (and similarly for y) can be calculated once before the curve is drawn, and stored in two arrays, one for X and one for Y, and $Tmax^3$ can also be found. Then each point X or Y can be calculated using a procedure of the form:

```
PROCEDURE Bezier (Para : ARRAY OF LONGINT; T : LONGINT) : INTEGER;
VAR TmaxMinusT : LONGINT;
BEGIN
   TmaxMinusT := Tmax - T;
   RETURN INTEGER ( (Para[0] * TmaxMinusT * TmaxMinusT * TmaxMinusT
                  + Para[1] * T * TmaxMinusT * TmaxMinusT
                  + Para[2] * T * T * TmaxMinusT
                  + Para[3] * T * T * T) DIV TmaxCubed)
END Bezier;
```

Conclusion

In this chapter some useful matrix techniques have been introduced. Their use in the diagram package is specialised, so some efficent coding of matrix operations is possible. In general, however, such simplifications are not possible, so general purpose matrix routines are needed. Exercise 3 below provides such routines.

Exercises

1) Write a procedure to draw a Bezier curve of any order.

2) The procedure to draw a Bezier curve with fixed increments of T is simple but not optimal. Sometimes the increment is too small and many points are calculated very close to one another, and sometimes the increment is too large. Optimally the increment should vary as the curve is drawn. Devise and implement a scheme for varying T suitably.

3) Write a series of matrix handling routines. These should allow any size matrix (within limits). It should be possible to mulitply a 3*2 matrix by a 2 * 4 matrix, for example. The routines should, however, report any attempt to process matrices of incompatible sizes: a 3*2 matrix cannot be multiplied by a 1*1 matrix for example. A matrix may be defined by the following:

```
CONST MaxSize = 4;    (* Changeable by user for the application *)
TYPE Matrix = RECORD
        NumberRows, NumberColumns : CARDINAL;
        Actual : ARRAY [1..MaxSize], [1..MaxSize] OF REAL;
     END;
```

This allows the user to define a maximum size for the matrix, but also allow smaller versions of the matrix within that size. Then a procedure to add two matrices together is:

```
PROCEDURE MatrixAdd (m1, m2 : Matrix; VAR m : Matrix) : BOOLEAN;
VAR row, col : CARDINAL;
BEGIN
  IF (m1.NumberRows = m2.NumberRows) AND
     (m1.NumberColumns = m2.NumberColumns) THEN
    m.NumberRows := m1.NumberRows;
    m.NumberColumns := m1.NumberColumns;
    FOR row := 1 TO m.NumberRows DO
      FOR col := 1 TO m.NumberColumns DO
        m.Actual [row] [col] :=
          m1.Actual [row] [col] + m2.Actual [row] [col]
      END
    END;
    RETURN TRUE
  ELSE
    RETURN FALSE
  END
END MatrixAdd;
```

Write and test routines to:

a) input and output such matrices.

b) multiply two matrices (use the above as a basis).

c) generate the transpose of a matrix.

d) calculate the determinant, D, of a matrix. This can be done using a recursive algorithm.

For a 1*1 matrix, A, its determinant $D := A[1,1]$

For a n*n matrix, $D := A[1,1]*D'1,1 - A[2,1]*D'1,2 + A[3,1]*D'1,3 - ..$

where D'a,b is the determinant of Matrix A excluding row a and column b

e.g D (of matrix $\begin{smallmatrix} a & b \\ c & d \end{smallmatrix}$) is a * D(d) - b * D (c) = ad - bc

Reference

1 J.D.Foley & A.Van Dam *Fundamentals of Interactive Computer Graphics* Addison-Wesley, 1983

2 Ian O. Angell *High-resolution Computer Graphics Using C* Macmillan Education 1990

8 String Handling

A string is another data structure much used in programming. In this chapter a number of useful simple string processing algorithms are given. Also provided is a routine which allows the user to enter a string or edit an existing one. Although this routine was written for the diagram package, and works within the window system, it was written in such a way that it could be used in other programs which do not use windows. This requires the use of procedure variables, which is another topic described in the chapter.

8.1 Strings

A string is a series of characters stored in successive memory locations. In Modula-2 it is stored in an array of the form:

```
ARRAY [0..MaxNumber] OF CHAR;
```

where MaxNumber is chosen as appropriate. The characters which form the string need not fill the whole array, but they are stored in the first few locations in the array, and normally the end of the string is marked by the character with ordinal value 0, denoted in Modula-2 by 0C. For the string 'FRED', element 0 in the array will contain 'F', element 1 will have 'R', etc., and element 4 will contain 0C. This is shown in figure 8.1. However, if the string fills the array, there is no room for the end of string character. Thus the end of the string is found by calculating the maximum size of the array: the HIGH function provides this. Thus if the string is an ARRAY [0..3] OF CHAR, then the four characters of the string 'FRED' would occupy the array and there would be no 0C. See also figure 8.1.

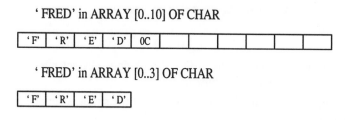

Figure 8.1 Memory allocation for strings

Note, in the fourth edition of Wirth's book on Modula-2[1], there is always space for the terminating character in a string.

108 Modula-2 Applied

Strings of various sizes can be declared, but these different sized arrays can be processed by the same procedures. This is achieved by passing them to procedures as just ARRAY OF CHAR, rather than a specific sized array of characters. The procedure can then determine the array size using the HIGH function. For example, the routine to print a string is:

```
PROCEDURE WrStr (S : ARRAY OF CHAR);
VAR ct : CARDINAL;
BEGIN
  ct := 0;
  WHILE (ct<=HIGH (S)) AND (S[ct]<>0C) DO
    WriteChar (S[ct]);
    INC (ct)
  END
END WrStr;
```

This use of 'open array' parameters is not just restricted to strings, but can be used on arrays of any type.

8.2 Simple processing

In this section a few simple string processing routines are provided. As these often process the nth element in the string, and sometimes n can be greater than the size of the array, the following routine is often used:

```
PROCEDURE GetCh (S : ARRAY OF CHAR; n : CARDINAL) : CHAR;
BEGIN
  IF n>HIGH (S) THEN RETURN 0C ELSE RETURN S[n] END;
END GetCh;
```

If n is outside the range of the string, the obvious character to return is 0C, otherwise the nth character is returned.

Using this, a procedure to find the length of the string is simple; it scans the string until 0C is found:

```
PROCEDURE Length (S : ARRAY OF CHAR) : CARDINAL;
VAR ct : CARDINAL;
BEGIN
  ct := 0;
  WHILE GetCh (S, ct)<>0C DO INC (ct) END;
  RETURN ct
END Length;
```

Capitalising a string is simple, each element in the string is processed by the CAP function:

```
PROCEDURE CapS (VAR S : ARRAY OF CHAR);
VAR ct : CARDINAL;
BEGIN
   ct := 0;
   WHILE GetCh (S, ct) <> 0C DO
     S [ct] := CAP (S [ct]);
     INC (ct)
   END
END CapS;
```

Comparing strings lexicographically is also quite simple. The following returns -1, 0 or 1 depending on whether the first string is less than, equal to or greater than the other. Starting from the beginning the procedure examines the nth character of each. If they differ then the strings are different and -1 or +1 is returned. If both of the characters are 0C, the strings are identical. Otherwise the search continues.

```
PROCEDURE Compare (S1, S2 : ARRAY OF CHAR) : INTEGER;
VAR c1, c2 : CHAR;
    ct : CARDINAL;
BEGIN
   ct := 0;
   LOOP
      c1 := GetCh (S1, ct);   (* get next chars of each string *)
      c2 := GetCh (S2, ct);
      IF c1<c2 THEN
         RETURN -1          (* chars different, so are strings *)
      ELSIF c1>c2 THEN
         RETURN 1
      ELSIF c1=0C THEN
         RETURN 0    (* end of string on both, so strings same *)
      ELSE
         INC (ct)                       (* carry on searching *)
      END
   END
END Compare;
```

The above is an example where there are multiple returns from the procedure, which in general is not good practice. Here, however, the author feels justified in its use as the above is a direct implementation of the algorithm: the procedure ends with the correct result as soon as that result is determined. A 'proper' method would be to store the result and set a flag indicating the result, and use the flag to determine if the loop should continue: that is considered to be clumsy.

The next routine tests if one string is within the another, returning its position if the string is there, or MAX (CARDINAL) otherwise. The first string is scanned and at each point a routine is performed, similar to Compare, to see if the next few characters are the same as the other string.

```
PROCEDURE Pos (S1, S2 : ARRAY OF CHAR) : CARDINAL;
VAR ct : CARDINAL;

  PROCEDURE PartCompare() : BOOLEAN;
  VAR ct2 : CARDINAL;
    c1, ch2 : CHAR;
  BEGIN
    ct2 := 0;
    LOOP
      ch1 := GetCh (S1, ct+ct2);
      ch2 := GetCh (S2, ct2);
      IF ch2=0C THEN
        RETURN TRUE       (* end of second string, so found it *)
      ELSIF ch1=0C THEN
        RETURN FALSE  (* end of first string, second not found *)
      ELSIF ch1<>ch2 THEN
        RETURN FALSE           (* strings different, not found *)
      ELSE
        INC (ct2)                    (* carry on searching *)
      END
    END
  END PartCompare;

BEGIN
  ct := 0;
  LOOP
    IF ct>HIGH (S1) THEN
      RETURN MAX (CARDINAL)  (* string end, thus S2 not in S1 *)
    ELSIF PartCompare() THEN
      RETURN ct                         (* part string found *)
    ELSE
      INC (ct)                        (* carry on searching *)
    END
  END
END Pos;
```

The following routine is used by other procedures. It copies part of one string into another: the first positions in the source string and the destination string, putpos and getpos, are passed also:

```
PROCEDURE StrAdd (VAR R : ARRAY OF CHAR; S : ARRAY OF CHAR;
                  putpos, getpos : CARDINAL);
VAR ch : CHAR;
BEGIN
  LOOP
    IF putpos>HIGH (R) THEN   (* no more space in result, stop *)
      EXIT
    ELSE
      ch := GetCh (S, getpos);   (* get next char from source *)
      R [putpos] := ch;                    (* put in result *)
      IF ch=0C THEN EXIT END;   (* end of source reached, stop *)
      INC (putpos);                      (* move pointers on *)
      INC (getpos)
    END
  END
END StrAdd;
```

Having defined these, a routine to copy from one string to another is just:

```
PROCEDURE Copy (VAR R : ARRAY OF CHAR; S : ARRAY OF CHAR);
BEGIN
  StrAdd (R, S, 0, 0)
END Copy;
```

And to concatenate one string onto the end of another, the first string is copied to the result, then the second is copied onto the end, thus:

```
PROCEDURE Concat (VAR R : ARRAY OF CHAR; S1, S2 : ARRAY OF CHAR);
BEGIN
  StrAdd (R, S1, 0, 0);
  StrAdd (R, S2, Length (S1), 0)
END Concat;
```

The following takes a specified number of characters from one string starting at a given position and puts them into the start of another:

```
PROCEDURE Slice (VAR R : ARRAY OF CHAR; S : ARRAY OF CHAR;
       Pos, len : CARDINAL);
BEGIN
  StrAdd (R, S, 0, Pos);
  IF Length (R) > len THEN R[len] := 0C END
END Slice;
```

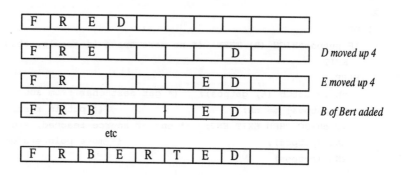

Figure 8.2 BERT inserted into FRED at position 2

The next routine inserts one string into another at a given position. Its action is in two parts: first space is made for the insert string by moving all elements further up the result string. This is done by starting at the end of the string and working backwards, not going forwards. If the search were forward, the first character moved would be copied into each position further up the string. The substring is then copied into the place provided. This is illustrated in figure 8.2.

```
PROCEDURE Insert (VAR R : ARRAY OF CHAR;
                      S : ARRAY OF CHAR; P : CARDINAL);
VAR ct, len : CARDINAL;
BEGIN
  len := Length (S);
  FOR ct := Length(R) TO P BY -1 DO
    IF ct+len<=HIGH(R) THEN R[ct+len] := R[ct] END
  END;
  FOR ct := 0 TO len-1 DO
    IF P+ct<=HIGH(R) THEN R[P+ct] := GetCh (S, ct) END
  END
END Insert;
```

The next routine deletes a number of characters from a string starting at the specified position. This is done by copying characters from further up the string so as to overwrite the deleted characters. The end of the string is then marked.

```
PROCEDURE Delete (VAR S : ARRAY OF CHAR; pos, num : CARDINAL);
VAR ct, len : CARDINAL;
BEGIN
   len := Length (S);
   ct := pos + num;
   WHILE ct<len DO
     S[pos] := S[ct];
     INC (pos);
     INC (ct)
   END;
   IF pos<=HIGH (S) THEN S[pos] := 0C END
END Delete;
```

8.3 Numerical conversion routines

Another useful set of routines converts numerical values into strings, and back again. These are used by the procedures for reading and writing REALs, INTEGERs, etc. The following routine converts a string to a cardinal. Starting from the beginning of the string, the routine skips over any leading spaces. Then each new decimal character is added into the result. The routine stops when a non-decimal character is found.

```
PROCEDURE StrToCard (S : ARRAY OF CHAR; VAR c : CARDINAL);
VAR ct : CARDINAL;
    ch : CHAR;
BEGIN
   c := 0;
   ct := 0;
   WHILE GetCh (S, ct) = ' ' DO INC (ct) END;   (* skip spaces *)
   LOOP
      ch := GetCh (S, ct);
      IF (ch>='0') AND (ch<='9') THEN
         c := c * 10 + (ORD (ch) - ORD ('0') );
         INC (ct)
      ELSE
         EXIT
      END
   END
END StrToCard;
```

114 Modula-2 Applied

The following routine converts a CARDINAL to a string. Essentially the routine is straightforward: the number of 10000s, 1000s, 100s, 10s and units must be printed. This could be achieved with an algorithm like:

```
PowerOfTen := 10000;
WHILE PowerOfTen<>0 DO
  Add Character of (c DIV PowerOfTen);
  c := c MOD PowerOfTen;
  PowerOfTen := PowerOfTen DIV 10
END
```

However, the above is not quite right because, for example, the number 506 would be printed as 00506: the leading zeros are not wanted. Thus if the number divided by PowerOfTen is 0 it should not be printed if it is the first character to be added to the string. The exception to this is if the PowerOfTen is 1, then a zero should be printed. The complete procedure is:

```
PROCEDURE CardToStr (VAR S : ARRAY OF CHAR; c : CARDINAL);
VAR ct, PowerOfTen, Mod : CARDINAL;
BEGIN
  PowerOfTen := 10000;
  ct := 0;
  WHILE PowerOfTen>0 DO
    Mod := c DIV PowerOfTen;
    IF (Mod<>0) OR (ct<>0) OR (PowerOfTen=1) THEN
      IF ct<=HIGH(S) THEN S[ct] := CHR (Mod + ORD('0') ) END;
      INC (ct)
    END;
    c := c MOD PowerOfTen;
    PowerOfTen := PowerOfTen DIV 10
  END;
  IF ct<=HIGH(S) THEN S[ct] := 0C END
END CardToStr;
```

Conversion of other number types is achieved by extending the above. See the examples at the end of the chapter.

8.4 String edit routine

The string edit procedure is used in the diagram package whenever a string is to be entered, for example the name of a diagram or a new shape. It is also used for entering numbers, by converting a number to a string, editing the string and then converting back again. The associated routines are stored in a self-contained module, LineEdit. The specification for the edit routine is as follows:

The current value of the string is displayed.

The user can just hit Enter or Esc to leave the string unchanged.

Any normal character immediately entered is the first of a new string.

Otherwise the user can move around the string and change it. 'Normal' characters are inserted into the string at the current position (if insert mode is on the characters further up the string are moved up to make space for the new character, but in overwrite mode the new character replaces the previous value). The Ins key toggles the mode. Two keys are used for deletion: Del deletes the character at the current position, DeleteBackwards deletes the previous character. The left and right arrow keys allow movement within the string, and the Home and End keys move the cursor to the start and end of the string, respectively. The algorithm is:

```
x := WhereX();       (* remember start position of string *)
WriteString;   ct := 0;    firstChar := TRUE;
LOOP
  GotoXY (x+ct, WhereY());(* put cursor at current char *)
  ch := ReadChar();
  IF ch = 'normal' character THEN
    IF firstChar THEN delete string END;
    IF InsertMode AND ct < length of string THEN
       insert character into string and display
    ELSE
       add character to string at position ct
    END
  ELSE
    CASE ch OF
     Esc, Enter : EXIT |
     DeleteBackwards : IF ct>0 THEN Delete Character END |
     Home : ct := 0 |
     LeftArrow : IF ct>0 THEN DEC (ct) END |
     RightArrow : IF ct<length of string THEN INC (ct) END |
     End : ct := length of string |
     Ins : InsertMode := NOT InsertMode |
     Del : IF ct < length of string THEN
              INC (ct); Delete Character
           END
    END
  END;
  firstChar := FALSE
END
```

116 Modula-2 Applied

Then, for example, a routine to allow the user to edit an integer is:

```
IntToStr (TempString, I);
EditString (TempString);
StrToInt (TempString, I);
```

8.5 Procedure variables

The edit string routine is used in the diagram package and hence is used with the graphics window routines. It requires the ReadChar, WriteChar, GotoXY, WhereX and WhereY procedures which are part of this windows module. However, the edit string routine may be required in a program which does not use the graphics windows, for example it may be used in a text only program and so use the text window module, WINDOW, provided with the TopSpeed compiler. Therefore a mechanism is needed so that the EditString routine uses the appropriate procedures. This is best achieved using procedure variables.

A procedure variable is simply a variable whose contents define a procedure. If that variable name is then stated in a program, the procedure stored in the variable is run. As Modula-2 is a strongly typed language, so its procedure variables must be rigidly defined. Thus a procedure variable is defined as a procedure, having certain types of parameters passed to it and returning a specific result.

For example, a procedure variable to describe the ReadChar procedure, that is one which returns a CHAR, is defined as having the type:

```
TYPE RdCharProc = PROCEDURE() : CHAR;
```

whereas procedure WriteChar is just passed a CHAR as a parameter, so:

```
TYPE WrCharProc = PROCEDURE (CHAR);
```

Built into the language is the procedure type PROC, which is simply a parameter-less procedure returning no result.

For the edit string module, the types needed are:

```
TYPE RdCharProc : PROCEDURE() : CHAR;
     WrCharProc : PROCEDURE (CHAR);
     GotoXYProc : PROCEDURE (CARDINAL, CARDINAL);
     WhereProc  : PROCEDURE() : CARDINAL;
```

And the local variables are:

```
VAR ReadChar : RdCharProc;
    WriteChar : WrCharProc;
    GotoXY : GotoXYProc;
    WhereX, WhereY : WhereProc;
```

Then, assuming that the variables have been initialised (so that they contain a reference to a procedure), to write a character, the code is simply:

```
WriteChar (ch);
```

Initialising the variables can be achieved by a procedure SetUp which is passed the actual procedures to be used:

```
PROCEDURE SetUp (R : RdCharProc; W : WrCharProc;
                 G : GotoXYProc; WX, WY : WhereProc);
BEGIN
  ReadChar := R;
  WriteChar := W;
  GotoXY := G;
  WhereX := WX;
  WhereY := WY
END SetUp;
```

This is called from the main part of the diagram package:

```
SetUp (GrWindow.ReadChar, GrWindow.WriteChar, GrWindow.GotoXY,
       GrWindow.WhereX, GrWindow.WhereY);
```

but a program which uses, say, the cursor routines from the TopSpeed module WINDOW, and the character routines from module IO, might call

```
SetUp (IO.RdKey, IO.WrChar, Window.GotoXY,
       Window.WhereX, Window.WhereY);
```

Note that, as well as being variables, procedures can also be passed as parameters to procedures. An example of this is given in the exercises.

One restriction on the use of procedures as variables and parameters is that the procedures so passed cannot be local procedures, they must be procedures at the highest scope level.

Conclusion

The algorithms presented in this chapter provide useful string processing operations. The topic of procedure variables has also been covered which is a useful advanced feature of the language, and which is used in many parts of the diagram package. As used here it provides a good method of allowing the programmer to write a library module which can be used in a great variety of programs.

Exercises

1) Using the CardToStr and StrToCard routines as a basis, write routines to convert INTEGERs and REALs to strings and vv.

2) Modify the INTEGER and CARDINAL procedures to work in hexadecimal numbers (base 16), octal numbers (base 8) as well as decimal (base 10).

3) Write a procedure to reverse the contents of a string.

4) Write a procedure to draw a graph of either a SIN wave, a COS wave or a square wave, by passing the appropriate function as a parameter. The procedure should calculate the points, and automatically scale them so that the graph fits in the screen. Assuming the type

```
RProc = PROCEDURE (REAL) : REAL;
```

which is applicable to SIN and COS, your procedure should be defined as:

```
PROCEDURE DrawGraph (CalcProc : RProc);
```

Reference

1 Niklaus Wirth *Programming in Modula-2* Fourth Edition. Springer-Verlag 1988

9 Variant Records

Programs written in a high level language, as opposed to machine code or assembly language, are written in terms of the problem being solved, not in terms of the machine. When programming in machine code the instructions specify registers, memory addresses, etc., which are divorced from the problem being solved. Thus, for example, in a high level language, the programmer is able to specify and define a data type for days of the week if the program being written is concerned with days of the week. Similarly, if the program is dealing with data which have associated parts, the programmer is able to define a record which includes these parts, and so is able to process the elements as a whole. The use of records is encouraged, and various examples given earlier in the book use them.

9.1 Records

A record consists of a number of fields, which may have the same or different types. In the hex problem of chapter 2, a piece was defined by

```
Piece = RECORD
          Colours : CArray;
          Rotation : CARDINAL;
          BeenUsed : BOOLEAN;
        END;
```

A program which is used to store data about a collection of CDs may hold the composer's name, the title of the music and its opus number, the orchestra, the data of recording, and whether it was a digital recording. Thus each CD could be defined by a record of the form:

```
CD = RECORD
       Composer, Title, Orchestra : ARRAY [0..30] OF CHAR;
       OpusNumber : CARDINAL;
       RecordingDate : DateRecord;
       RecordingType : (AAD, ADD, DDD)
     END;
```

where a DateRecord could be defined as

```
DateRecord = RECORD
               Day, Month, Year : CARDINAL;
             END;
```

120 Modula-2 Applied

In all these records the fields are fixed: for each CD there are three strings, a CARDINAL, a DateRecord and a RecordingType. However, for some data, the actual types required in a record will vary depending upon some of the contents of the record. This can be achieved using variant records.

Requirement in diagram package

A diagram consists of a series of items, where an item is a head of a list of items, the beginning of a program describing items, a line, circle, arc, rectangle, diamond, Bezier curve, string or usershape. These require various associated types, some of which are common, others are different:

A line is defined by the endpoints of the line, 4 numbers.

A circle requires the origin and radius, 3 numbers.

An arc requires the origin, radius, the start and end angle, 5 numbers.

A rectangle needs the coordinates of opposite corners, 4 numbers.

A diamond is defined by coordinates of two corners, 4 numbers.

A Bezier curve is defined by 4 coordinates, 8 numbers.

A string needs its size, position and rotation and the actual string.

A usershape needs its size, position and rotation, and the usershape.

The types which are common include the colour and the feature.

Therefore, to define an item, a data structure is needed which contains different fields depending upon the contents.

9.2 Variant records

A variant record contains a number of fields. Some fields are fixed and so are common to all versions of the record, others vary and so their contents will depend upon the context of the variable. The variants are declared in the form of a case statement within the record declaration. This is best shown by example. Consider the following:

```
AudioType = (Record, Cassette, CompactDisc);
MusicItem = RECORD
            Title, Composer, Orchestra : ARRAY [0..30] OF CHAR;
            OpusNumber : CARDINAL;
            DateRecorded : DateRecord;
            CASE Atype : AudioType OF
               Record      : RecordSize : (LP, Single) |
               Cassette    : CassetteSize : (C45,C60,C90,C120);
                             CassetteType : (D, AD, SD) |
               CompactDisc : CDtype : (AAD, ADD, DDD)
            END;
            END;
```

The above definitions could apply to a music collection consisting of cassettes, records and compact discs. For these certain parts are common (for each the name of the recording is needed), but others vary (for example the size of the cassette, or the record, etc.).

The fields Title, Composer, Orchestra, OpusNumber, DateRecorded and Atype are fixed fields. The others are variant fields, the ones actually being used are determined by the value stored in the field Atype. For each variant there can any number of fields, of any type.

Having defined the record, the elements in the record can be accessed in the normal way, using the dot notation or WITH statements. Thus if M is a variable of type MusicItem, the following are legal:

```
WrStr (M.Title);
M.type := Record;
WITH M DO OpusNumber := 45 END;
M.RecordSize := LP;
```

However, having defined M.type as a Record, it does not make sense to say:

```
M.CDtype := DDD;
```

because here the variable M is defining a Record, and as such it does not contain a field specifying its CDtype. The compiler will not object to the statement, as it is syntactically correct, but the program will be in error.

It is likely that the RecordSize and the CDtype fields will use the same location in memory, but the programmer should not assume this.

Another important point to note about variant records is that the size of the record is as large as necessary such that the complete record will fit into the memory whatever the variant. Thus in the following

```
fred = RECORD
    CASE b : BOOLEAN OF
      FALSE : ch : CHAR |
      TRUE  : data : ARRAY [0..67] OF INTEGER
    END
  END;
```

each variable of type fred will take enough memory for a boolean and 68 integers, even though only one boolean and one char may be stored there.

9.3 Variant record in the diagram package

The main data structures used to represent items in the diagram package are:

```
GCommandType = (head, program, line, circle, arc, rectangle,
        diamond, bezier, string, usershape, pselect, wselect);
```

(* A head is the start of a list of shapes. A program indicates a shape described by a program. pselect and wselect are items used to specify a position or a window. The rest are the standard items. *)

```
GCommand = RECORD
    Marked, MarkedPrev : BOOLEAN;
    colour, feature : CARDINAL;
    Next : GCommandLink;
    CASE Gtype : GCommandType OF
        head,
        program   : first : GCommandLink;
                    name : GStringLink;
                    programptr : ProgramLink |
        line      : xl1, yl1, xl2, yl2 : INTEGER |
        circle    : xc, yc, rc : INTEGER |
        arc       : xa, ya, ra, a1, a2 : INTEGER |
        rectangle : xr1, yr1, xr2, yr2 : INTEGER |
        diamond   : xd1, yd1, xd2, yd2 : INTEGER |
        bezier    : xb1, yb1, xb2, yb2,
                    xb3, yb3, xb4, yb4 : INTEGER |
        string    : xs1, ys1, xs2, ys2, rs : INTEGER;
                    str : GStringLink |
        usershape : xu1, yu1, xu2, yu2, ru : INTEGER;
                    shape : GCommandLink |
        select,
        wselect   : xsl1, ysl1, xsl2, ysl2 : INTEGER
    END
END;
```

The above are mainly straightforward, though some explanation is needed. Each item is defined by a GCommand, and each has a specific colour, feature, Gtype and two booleans, Marked and MarkedPrev, used for searching. Then, depending upon the type of the item, different data are stored; for a line 4 integers are needed, for a string, 5 integers are needed and the string, etc.

The main diagram and all usershapes consist of a list of items. The program needs to know about the next item in the list. Thus for each item there is a field indicating the next item. How this is achieved is explained in chapter 12 on linked lists. At this stage all that needs to be known is that a GCommandLink indicates the next item in the list.

For a string, the record must store its position, size, angle and the actual string. The string could contain up to say 80 characters; therefore space is required in the record for them. Such a record would therefore need about 100 bytes, whereas for others, like a line, less than 20 bytes are required. As all variant records must be large enough to hold the largest variant, this is clearly wasteful. Therefore, rather than storing a string inside the record, that string is stored elsewhere, and in the record there is only a pointer to the string. A GStringLink indicates the position of the string.

A GStringLink contains the address of the string, therefore it is a pointer to a string:

```
String = ARRAY [0..80] OF CHAR;
GStringLink = POINTER TO String;
```

If G is a variable of type GCommand, and G.Gtype = string, the string is that variable pointed to by G.str, that is, G.str^. G.str is an address and that which is at the address is G.str^. Thus, to print the string the code is:

```
WrStr (G.str^);
```

The head of a list, the start of a usershape, also requires a name: that of the shape. This is also true of a shape described by a program. Both also require an indication of the start of the shape, a GCommandLink, and a program also needs data structures to store and analyse the program: this is achieved using a Program-Link. As a head and a program are very similar, both have the same variants, though a head does not use a ProgramLink.

Variant record in action

In this section one use of this variant record is described. This is the procedure Edit which allows the user to modify an item. For example, if the item is a line, the user is able to move the end coordinates of the line. As described in chapter 3, this is achieved by allowing the user to move one aspect of the item, using the mouse or cursor keys, and then move on to the next aspect, etc., with the ability to return to the first aspect. Only when the item is correctly entered will the user press the enter key or the left mouse button. For a line, the aspects are the coordinates of the two end points, and for a string, the aspects are the string itself, its origin, its size and finally the angle at which it is drawn.

The basic algorithm is similar to that described in chapter 6 for selecting commands. The object is drawn in XOR mode. Then in a loop, when a cursor

124 Modula-2 Applied

movement key is entered, the object is redrawn in XOR mode (to erase it but leave unchanged any other item that was there), the aspect of the item is changed, and then the item is redrawn in XOR mode. Again, as in the earlier routine, the item is not generally redrawn in XOR mode if the next key has been pressed. However, if the mouse is used to move the item, an almost continuous set of movement keys can be entered, so nothing is drawn. This can be distracting to the user. So the new version is drawn if either a key has not been pressed, or if 16 successive cursor movements have been detected. Note that, in the loop of the procedure, the first aspect of a string, editing of the string, is a special case. The procedure is:

```
PROCEDURE Edit (VAR Item : GCommand);
VAR HaveDrawn : BOOLEAN;
    NumNotDrawn,            (* number of successive cursor moves *)
    Para : CARDINAL;        (* used to indicate which aspect *)
BEGIN
  NumNotDrawn := 0; Para := 0; DrawItem (XOR); HaveDrawn := TRUE;
  LOOP
    IF (Para=0) AND (Item.Gtype=string) THEN
      IF HaveDrawn THEN DrawItem (XOR); HaveDrawn := FALSE END;
      EditString (Item.str^);
      Delta (0, 0, 1)   (* move on to next aspect *)
    END;
    REPEAT UNTIL KeyPressed();
    CASE ReadChar() OF
      UpArrow     : Delta (0, 1, 1) |
      LeftArrow   : Delta (-1, 0, 1) |
      RightArrow  : Delta (1, 0, 1) |
      DownArrrow  : Delta (0, -1, 1) |
(* For Home, PgUp, End, PgDn, as above but third parameter is 8 *)
(* For Ctrl-Home, Ctrl-PgUp, etc., the third parameter is 64 *)
      Ins         : ZoomIn |
      Del         : ZoomOut |
      '*'         : RecentrePicture |
      '+'         : INC (Snap) |
      '-'         : DEC (Snap) |
      Enter       : EXIT |
      Esc, ' '    : Delta (0, 0, 1)
    END
  END; (* LOOP *)
  IF HaveDrawn THEN DrawItem (XOR) END;     (* erase item *)
  DrawItem (Normal)                          (* draw in final form *)
END Edit;
```

The procedure terminates whenever Enter is entered, and moves on to the next aspect whenever space or Esc is pressed. Other characters have special effects. The Ins key allows the user to zoom into the picture, Del allows zooming out and * recentres the picture around the current position. + and - increment and decrement the 'snap' value: this is the smallest amount that an aspect can be moved, varying it allows fine and coarse movement. The arrow keys, PgUp, End, etc., specify movements of the item.

The procedure uses a sub-procedure, Delta, which causes the current aspect to be moved by the amount passed to the routine. This is passed the amount to be moved in both the x and y directions, dx and dy, and a scaling factor: dx and dy are both 0 if the program should move on to the next aspect. Generally, it is in this subprocedure that the actions are taken which are specific to the item: the exception is for modification of the text of a string.

For the procedure Delta, if dx=dy, the system should move on to the next aspect, otherwise the specified aspect of the item should be changed. For a line, going on to the next aspect means changing Para from 0 to 1, or from 1 to 0, which can be achieved by, *Para := 1 - Para*. For an arc, which has three aspects, the action is to move from 0 to 1, 1 to 2 or 2 to 0, whichever is approproriate, etc. The procedure has two subprocedures, one for changing an x,y coordinate and one for changing an angle. For the latter, if the Factor is 1, the angle is changed by 1 degree, otherwise it is changed by 45 degrees.

```
PROCEDURE Delta (dx, dy, Factor : INTEGER);

  PROCEDURE Change (VAR x, y : INTEGER);
  BEGIN
    INC (x, dx * Snap * Factor);
    INC (y, dy * Snap * Factor)
  END Change;

  PROCEDURE AngleInc (VAR a : INTEGER; amount : INTEGER);
  BEGIN
    IF Factor=1 THEN INC (a, amount) ELSE INC (a, amount * 45) END;
    WHILE a>360 DO DEC (a, 360) END;
    WHILE a<0 DO INC (a, 360) END
  END AngleInc;

BEGIN
  WITH Item DO
    IF HaveDrawn THEN
       DrawItem (XOR);     (* to erase item *)
       HaveDrawn := FALSE
    END;
```

```
      CASE Gtype OF
      line   : IF dx=dy THEN Para := 1 - Para  (* next aspect *)
               ELSIF Para=0 THEN Change (xl1, yl1)
               ELSE Change (xl2, yl2)
               END |
(* for rectange or diamond, much the same, except xr1,yr1 or
xd1,yd1, etc. changed, for a circle either xc,yc are changed,
or the radius rc *)
      arc    : IF dx=dy THEN
                    IF Para=2 THEN Para := 0 ELSE INC (Para) END;
                ELSIF Para=0 THEN Change (xa, ya)
                ELSIF Para=1 THEN INC (ra, (dx + dy) * snap * factor)
                ELSE AngleInc (a1, dx); AngleInc (a2, dy)
                END |
      bezier : IF dx=dy THEN
                    IF Para=3 THEN Para := 0 ELSE INC (Para) END
                ELSIF Para=0 THEN Change (xb1, yb1)
                ELSIF Para=1 THEN Change (xb2, yb2)
                ELSIF Para=2 THEN Change (xb3, yb3)
                ELSE Change (xb4, yb4)
                END |
      string : IF dx=dy THEN
                    IF Para=3 THEN Para := 0 ELSE INC (Para) END
                ELSIF Para=1 THEN Change (xs1, ys1)
                ELSIF Para=2 THEN Change (xs2, ys2)
                ELSE AngleInc (rs)
                END |    (* similarly for usershape *)
         (* code for pselect and wselect is similar *)
      END;
      IF NOT HaveDrawn THEN
        IF NOT KeyPressed() OR (NumNotDrawn=16) THEN
          DrawItem (XOR);
          HaveDrawn := TRUE;
          NumNotDrawn := 0
        ELSE
          INC (NumNotDrawn)
        END
      END
   END
END Delta;
```

9.4 Location of an item

Another time where the variant record is used is when the user is selecting an item to be modified. Here the user moves the cursor around the screen until it is nearest the item he wishes to change, then hits the Enter key or presses the left mouse button. The system then searches through the diagram to see which item is nearest to the point. It does this by calculating the shortest distance between the specified point and each item in the diagram.

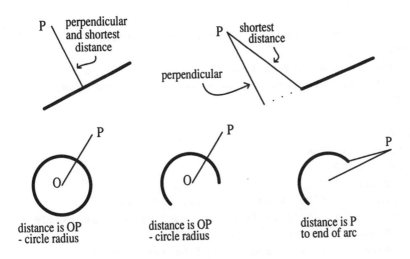

Figure 9.1 Shortest distances

This is achieved by the procedure DiffCalculate which finds the distance between a point and the specified item. The action of the procedure is shown by figure 9.1 and the following description. For a line, the shortest distance is found as follows: the intersection of the perpendicular to the line going through the point is found; if this is within the limits of the line then the shortest distance is that between the point and the intersection, otherwise it is the distance between the point and the nearest endpoint of the line. For a rectangle, diamond or Bezier curve, the distance between the point and each line which forms the item is found. For a circle, the distance is that between the point and the origin minus the radius. For an arc, if the angle of the point from the origin is within the limits of the arc, then the calculation used for circles gives the shortest distance, otherwise the nearer of the endpoints of the arc is used. For a string, the distance between the point and the lines which form the notional boundary around the string is used. For a usershape, a new scale matrix is calculated and the procedure called on all the items which form the shape. The algorithm is:

```
    PROCEDURE DiffCalculate (S : ScaleMatrix; x, y : INTEGER;
                             Item : GCommand) : REAL;
    VAR Diff : REAL;

      PROCEDURE TestDiff (new : REAL);
    (* new, latest distance from point, is it smallest yet? *)
      BEGIN
        IF new<Diff THEN Diff := new END
      END TestDiff;

      PROCEDURE TestLine (x1, y1, x2, y2 : INTEGER);
      BEGIN
        ScaleLine according to S;
        TestDiff (Shortest distance between x,y and line)
      END TestLine;

    BEGIN
     Diff := MAX (REAL);
     WITH Item DO
      CASE Gtype OF
        line       : TestLine (x11, y11, x12, y12) |
        rectangle  : call TestLine on   each line of rectangle |
        diamond    : test each line of diamond |
        bezier     : test each line of bezier curve |
        circle     : TestDiff (ABS (CalcDiff (xc, yc) - rc) ) |
    (* Diff is difference between x,y and origin, - radius *)
        arc        : IF angle of x,y & origin in a1..a2 THEN
                        TestDiff (ABS (CalcDiff (xa, ya) - ra) )
                     ELSE
                        TestDiff (CalcDiff (one end of arc) );
                        TestDiff (CalcDiff (other end of arc) )
                     END |
        string     : test the 4 lines surrounding the string |
        usershape  : CalcNewScaleMatrix;
                     FOR each item in the usershape DO
                        TestDiff (DiffCalculate)
                     END
      END
     END;
     RETURN Diff
    END DiffCalculate;
```

Conclusion

This chapter has described another useful facility in the Modula-2, variant records, which can be used to store data about similar items that contain different types of data depending upon the item. Some processing of such records has also been described.

Exercises

1) Write a routine to calculate the distance between a point and a line.

2) Assuming that the contents of a music collection have been stored in an array of variant records as described earlier, write procedures to

    a) print the array

    b) sort the array using the QuickSort algorithm, so that all Cassettes are given first, then all CDs, then all Records, and each category is sorted in alphabetical order of composer, and for each composer the data are sorted by opus number. This requires a routine to compare two records: if their categories are different, then whichever comes first is decided by the category, otherwise the composer is tested, etc.

10 Use of Files

A file is a structure in which data can be stored, and is usually associated with disks. This allows a program to store information so that it can be retrieved on a subsequent occasion. The actual handling of the disks is done by the operating system of the computer, and this varies between machines. However, in general the user does not have to worry particularly, but just uses some standard facilities provided in the library.

Essentially, to read a file the user opens it, reads each item in turn and then closes the file at the end. To write a file, it is created, then each item of data is written to it, and the file is closed. Thus most accesses to a file are sequential, the first item is found, then the second, etc. However, random access, the process of accessing items in any order, can also be possible.

In this chapter some simple routines for accessing files are given. These include the use of both text files and binary files, and also routines for listing the files on a disk, that is, providing a directory. All these routines use the TopSpeed library module FIO. It should be noted, however, that the TopSpeed routines are not in the same form as 'standard' Modula-2, though that can also be said of many implementations of Modula-2. See the TopSpeed manual[1].

10.1 Files

The file names allowable on a computer are determined by its operating system. On PCs the filenames have two parts, the first of up to 8 characters, followed by a '.', then a string of upto 3 characters, the extension. The extension is usually used to classify the type of file. EXE means executable files, that is files containing programs that can be run. MOD means a Modula-2 source file, OBJ its object code, etc. For the diagram package, all data files have a filename with extension DIG.

Text files and binary files

All files, like computers, contain binary data. However, a file is called a text file, as opposed to a binary file, if its contents are characters that can be read by a normal editor, that is if the binary codes in the file are normal printable characters (letters, digits, punctuation and the control characters return and linefeed). In a text file, the 16-bit integer 263 would be stored as three bytes, the character codes for 2, 6 and 3. In a binary file, however, the number would be stored as the binary equivalent of that number, in two bytes, one containing 1 and the other containing 7.

The file routines provided with the compiler allow both text and binary files. The advantage of a text file is that it can be readily examined by an editor. The problem with text files is that they are relatively slow: to read an integer, the characters that form the integer must be read into a string and then converted to the actual integer (using a procedure like StrToInt), whereas for a binary file, the two bytes can be read in directly and stored in the integer variable unchanged.

Error handling

Various errors can occur with files. For example, it is wrong to attempt to open a file which does not exist. If the disk is full, there is no space for any more data, so creating a new file will cause an error. Such errors should not cause the program to abort, the program should report the error and return to a safe state. This is achieved in FIO by using the boolean IOcheck and the procedure IOresult.

If IOcheck is TRUE, any file error is reported and the program aborts. If IOcheck is FALSE, this does not happen and the user program should check the result after each file operation. This can be achieved by noting any value returned (for example the Open routine returns a legal file handle if the operation was correct, or MAX(CARDINAL) if the file was not opened). Alternatively, the procedure IOresult can be called: this returns zero if the operation was successful, otherwise an error has occurred which the program can report to the user and any appropriate action taken.

Handling text files

The routines described here show the use of text files. Using files requires a file handle, which is a data structure which identifies the file. When a file is opened, the file handle is returned. All subsequent operations on the file use the handle. In FIO the handle is of type File.

To read a text file, it must first be opened, then each item can be read until the end of the file is reached, and the file is then closed. The end of the file is detected by the boolean EOF which is set true if after a read operation the end of the file has been reached. The following procedure reads a text file and displays it on the screen.

```
PROCEDURE ReadFile (name : ARRAY OF CHAR);
VAR F : File;
    ch : CHAR;
BEGIN
  F := Open (name);
  IF F=MAX(CARDINAL) THEN
    WrStr ('Sorry, file does not exist')
  ELSE
    LOOP
      ch := RdChar (F);
      IF EOF THEN EXIT ELSE WrChar (ch) END;
    END;
    Close (F);
  END
END ReadFile;
```

132 Modula-2 Applied

To write a file, the action is similar. The procedure Create is used instead of Open, data are written to the file instead of being read from it, and at the end the file is also closed.

In the above example, characters were read from the file. However, numbers can be read from or written to text files: TopSpeed routines RdInt, WrInt, RdCard, WrReal, etc., all work with files, and WrStr and RdStr can be used with strings in files. All these routines are like those used in the IO library except in FIO a file variable is also specified. In IO the routines are like:

```
WrStr ('String')          and          i := RdInt()
```

but in FIO the equivalent routines are (if F is a variable of type File):

```
WrStr (F, 'String');      and          i := RdInt (F);
```

10.2 Saving a diagram into a file

As the process of saving a diagram is simpler than loading a diagram from a file, the saving process is described first. The format of the file is described in chapter 3, but a few brief comments are made here. The file contains a list of each shape in order: the main shape first (which has the same name as that of the file), then any user defined shapes. Each shape consists of its name followed by the items that make up the shape: if the shape is a program, then that is listed, otherwise all the lines, circles, etc., are given. The names of shapes are given in capital letters, with a { after the name if the shape is a program. Items like lines are listed in the form:

```
l colour feature x1 y1 x2 y2
```

that is, the first letter identifies the type (it is always in lower case to distinguish it from a shape name) followed by its parameters. The algorithm to save a diagram to file with the given name is given below:

```
IF Create (F, FileName) THEN
   SaveShape (FirstShape, FileName);
   FOR each usershape DO
      SaveShape (shape, name of shape)
   END;
   Close (F)
ELSE
   Report that cannot create file
END;
```

and procedure SaveShape is effectively:

```
WrStr (F, ShapeName);
IF Shape is described by program THEN
  WrStr (F, ' {');
  WrLn (F);
  Save Program;
  (* by storing each character which forms the program *)
  WrChar (F, '}');
  WrLn (F);
ELSE
  WrLn (F);
  FOR all items in the shape DO
    CASE item type OF
      line : WrChar (F, 'l');
             WrChar (F, ' '); WrInt (F, colour, 0);
             WrChar (F, ' '); WrInt (F, feature, 0);
             WrChar (F, ' '); WrInt (F, xl1, 0);
             WrChar (F, ' '); WrInt (F, yl1, 0);
             WrChar (F, ' '); WrInt (F, xl2, 0);
             WrChar (F, ' '); WrInt (F, yl2, 0);
             WrLn (F) |
    etc: with similar routines for other items
      END
    END
END
```

Note that it is necessary to write a space character so as to separate the numbers that form the items. The above might produce a line in the file of the form:

1 1 0 100 100 3000 4000

without the spaces it would appear as:

11010010030004000

and the routine which read that in could not correctly separate the numbers.

10.3 Loading a diagram

The routine used to load a diagram is more complicated as it must decide how to store the data that make up the shapes. Also, there are two forms of loading a file: either loading a complete new diagram, or inserting another file into the current diagram, where there is the potential problem of two shapes, one from each file, having the same name. Ignoring this latter problem, the read file algorithm is:

```
Get file name and Open file;
Keep Reading until end of file or read a capital letter;
LOOP
  IF end of file THEN
    EXIT
  ELSIF char is a capital letter THEN
    Read Shape
  ELSE
    Report error : illegal file;
    EXIT
  END
END;
Close file
```

where ReadShape is effectively:

```
Read shape name
IF read { THEN
 Read a program
ELSE
 LOOP
  CASE next char OF
    'l' : ReadCommand (line) |
    'r' : ReadCommand (rectangle) |
    'd' : ReadCommand (diamond) |
    'c' : ReadCommand (circle) |
    'a' : ReadCommand (arc) |
    'b' : ReadCommand (bezier) |
    's' : ReadCommand (string) |
    'g' : ReadCommand (usershape) |  ( * program start *)
    'u' : ReadCommand (usershape) | (* usershape start *)
    'A'..'Z' : EXIT   (* it is first char of next shape *)
  END
 END
END
```

where ReadCommand stores the data of the given type in a GCommand:

```
WITH GCommand DO
   Gtype := type;
   colour := RdInt (F);
   feature := RdInt (F);
   CASE Gtype OF
      line : x11 := RdInt (F); y11 := RdInt (F);
             x12 := RdInt (F); y12 := RdInt (F); RdLn (F) |
         < similar routines for other types >.
   END
END
```

When a call to a usershape is made, the associated GCommand must store a reference to the actual shape. Thus the program looks to see if that shape has already been loaded, in which case its position is known. Otherwise a new position for the shape is needed. Thus when a shape is read in, the program must look to see if it has already been referenced, and store the shape there if so, or whether a new position must be found, in which case the data are stored in this new position.

When a file is inserted into a diagram, there is the problem that two shapes, one from the diagram already installed and the other from the file, may have the same name. This could cause problems. It must be ensured that all usershapes in the 'insert' file refer to shapes in that file, and not in the existing diagram. Thus when a file is inserted all searches for the name of a usershape are confined to the shapes that make up the insert diagram. Then when the file has been loaded the following check is made:

```
FOR all shapes from the 'insert' file DO
   IF shape of that name is in the main diagram THEN
      get user to rename shape
   END
END
```

10.4 Filenames, paths and directories

The names of all the files used for storing diagrams are of the form xx.DIG, where xx is the name of the diagram, and is up to 8 letters. Thus when a file is opened or created the program takes the name of the diagram, checks that it is legal and adds the '.DIG' on to the end.

Computers which can store a great number of files on their disks usually allow the user to partition the disk into separate areas. If this were not permitted a user searching for a particular file would have to look through a large number of files.

On PCs the partitions are called directories, and the user is encouraged to divide the disk into a series of directories each containing associated files. It is conceivable therefore that a user may assign a number of different directories for his diagrams: the author for example keeps the diagrams for this book in one directory, those for his previous book in another, etc. Thus when entering diagrams the diagram package must know in which directory they are stored. This is achieved by specifying a path: this is a string describing the position of the directory. The actual complete file name is the path name followed by the file name. Typical paths are shown below:

    A: *(* just on the A disk *)*
    C:\DIAGRAMS\MOD2BOOK\
    (* in the directory MOD2BOOK off directory DIAGRAMS on drive C *)

A routine which opens or creates a file must specify the complete file name including the path, and the DIG extension. In the package the following procedure is used to open or create a file:

```
PROCEDURE GetDIGFile (create : BOOLEAN;
                     Name : ARRAY OF CHAR) : File;
VAR LegalName : ARRAY [0..80] OF CHAR;
BEGIN
  Copy the main part of Name (up to '.') into LegalName;
  Concat (LegalName, LegalName, '.DIG');
  Concat (LegalName, Path, LegalName);
  IF create THEN
    RETURN Create (LegalName)
  ELSE
    RETURN Open (LegalName)
  END
END GetDIGFile;
```

When the user wishes to load a file, a list of the files in the given directory is presented. This requires a routine which gets all those files with extension DIG in the directory specified by Path. This is accomplished using the routines ReadFirstEntry and ReadNextEntry provided in FIO (see the TopSpeed manual[1]). The first procedure is called to get the first name matching the specification (in this case the Path then '*.DIG'), and this sets up data in a variable of type DirEntry (defined in FIO) and returns the name of the first file matching the specification, if one exists. Getting subsequent files is achieved by calling the second procedure which is passed the DirEntry variable. In FIO, the procedure Directory returns the name of a file. Its algorithm is:

```
PROCEDURE Directory (First : BOOLEAN;
VAR FileName : ARRAY OF CHAR) : BOOLEAN;
(* if First, a search for the first file should be made *)
(* the procedure returns true if any file is found *)
BEGIN
  IF First THEN
    Concat (FileName, Path, '*.DIG');
    IF NOT ReadFirstEntry (FileName, FileAttr({}), D) THEN
      RETURN FALSE
    END
  ELSIF NOT ReadNextEntry (D) THEN
    RETURN FALSE
  END;
  Copy file name from D.Name, up to '.', into FileName;
  RETURN TRUE
END Directory;
```

The variable, D of type DirEntry, must of course be global, as it must continue to exist between successive calls to Directory. The name found by ReadFirstEntry or ReadNextEntry is in the field D.Name. The second parameter passed to ReadFirstEntry is any file attribute, like system files, read only files, etc., and these are specified by a set variable of type FileAttr. In this case no such attributes are specified so the empty set is passed.

The above procedure is used to generate a list of files to be loaded, by an algorithm of the form:

```
Empty list;
First := TRUE;
WHILE Directory (First, name) DO
  Add name to list;
  First := FALSE
END;
```

10.5 Binary files

The above routines access text files. Similar algorithms can be used for binary files: the file is opened or created, data are read from or written into the file, and then the file is closed. However, instead of using routines like RdChar, WrInt, WrStr, etc., the TopSpeed routines RdBin and WrBin are used.

```
RdBin (F : File; VAR Buf : ARRAY OF BYTE;
       Count : CARDINAL): CARDINAL;
```

reads Count bytes from file F into array Buf, returning the number of bytes actually read.

```
WrBin (F : File; Buf : ARRAY OF BYTE; Count : CARDINAL);
```

writes Count bytes from array Buf into file F.

In the diagram package binary files are used for storing the data which define the character set. As explained in chapter 4, the characters are defined by two arrays:

```
PositionArray : ARRAY [' '..177C] OF CARDINAL;
DataArray : ARRAY [0..MaxSize] OF BYTE;
```

the latter contains the data about all the characters, and the former specifies the start positions in the latter of each character. Thus the first byte defining the character '0' is at DataArray[PositionArray['0']] and the last byte of '0' is at DataArray[PositionArray['1']-1]. Note that the last character defined is '~', and 177C is the character after '~'. Therefore PositionArray[177C]-1 defines the last byte of character '~'.

The following routine (from the graphics window module, GrWindow) reads in the character set:

```
CFile := Open ('GRWINDOW.VCH');
IF CFile <> MAX (CARDINAL) THEN
   dummy := RdBin (CFile, PositionArray, SIZE (PositionArray) );
   dummy := RdBin (CFile, CharPtrArray, PositionArray[177C]);
   Close (CFile)
END;
```

First the position array is read in and then the actual character data are read. The number of bytes to be read in are determined by the position of the last byte of character '~', which is stored in PositionArray[177C].

The character set itself was defined in a separate program. This took a text file with descriptions of the characters, converted these so as to position them in the arrays defined above, and then wrote them into a file, using code similar to that given above (except that Create was used instead of Open, and WrBin used instead of RdBin).

10.6 Random access

In the above, sequential access to files is provided, that is, the first item is read or written, then the second, then the third, etc. The alternative to this, where an arbitrary item is accessed, is termed random access. This is achieved in the Top-Speed FIO module using the procedure Seek.

```
Seek (FileHandle, Position)
```

specifies that the next item of data read from or written to the given file will be at the given Position. Position is a variable of type LONGCARD.

An associated routine is GetPos (File), where File is the file handle, which returns the current position (again as a LONGCARD) in the file. The size of the file can be found using the routine Size (File) which also returns a LONGCARD.

One use of these routines is given in chapter 13.

Buffers

When data are read from the disk, they are not read singly, but in groups. These are called sectors and they are arranged in radial tracks on the disk, with many sectors in any track. To read a particular sector, the computer waits for the disk to revolve so that the start of the sector appears, then the sector is read. The disks revolve continually, and if the computer just misses the start of a sector it must wait one revolution time. Thus file operation can be made faster if many successive sectors are read at once: then the main overhead is waiting for the start of the first sector. Reading many sectors is achieved in FIO by providing a large enough area of memory, which is done by assigning a large area of memory to a file variable. The procedure AssignBuffer is used:

```
AssignBuffer (F : File; VAR Buf : ARRAY OF BYTE);
```

For efficient use, the size of the buffer should be N*512+BufferOverHead, where N is at least 2 and BufferOverHead is defined in FIO. Once this procedure has been called, the other file routines can be used as normal.

10.7 Simple database

One use of variant records, binary files and random access is in files used for databases. Essentially, the database contains a number of items of data, and the user is able to add more items, remove them, etc. This is best achieved in a binary file, where complete items can be read from or written to the file.

Thus reading the nth item in the file is achieved by code of the form:

```
Seek (File, n*itemsize);
RdBin (File, item, itemsize);
```

A similar routine is used for writing. When an item is deleted it must be marked so, by writing a record with the deleted mark in it. It should be arranged that when an item is added to the file, it is inserted in any deleted area, or it is inserted at the end if no items have been deleted. This requires remembering the positions of all the deleted items, and can be achieved by remembering the number of the first deleted item, and the number of the n+1th deleted item is stored in the actual nth deleted item. Thus if an item is deleted, it needs a reference to the next deleted one, otherwise the item contains the actual data of an item. This is a use of variant records. Also, the first record should contain the number of the first deleted item, the number of items in the file, and any other pertinent information. Thus,

```
FileItem = RECORD
    CASE ItemType : (Firstitem, Deleted, NotDeleted) OF
      FirstItem : FirstDeleted : LONGCARD;
                  NumberOfEntries : LONGCARD;
                  < any other pertinent data >|
      Deleted : NextDeleted : LONGCARD |
      NotDeleted : appropriate data
    END
  END
```

The following describe in general terms some useful routines which could be used in a database. The first starts the program: if the database file exists, then appropriate data are read from the first record, otherwise the file is created.

```
IF Open File successfully THEN
  Read First Record;
  NumFirstDelete := Record.FirstDeleted;
  NumRecords := Record.NumberOfEntries
ELSE
  Create File;
  NumFirstDelete := 0;
  NumRecords := 0
END
```

Note that NumFirstDelete and NumRecords are kept in memory not on disk, otherwise the program would continually have to access the first record, which would slow the program.

Adding a new item to the file is achieved by:

```
    Load FileRecord with pertinent data
    IF NumFirstDelete=0 THEN
            (* no deleted items, so add to end of file *)
       INC (NumRecords);
       Write Record at Position NumRecords
    ELSE
       Read Record (D) at Position NumFirstDelete;
       Write New Record at Position NumFirstDelete;
       NumFirstDelete := Record (D).NextDeleted
    END
```

Deleting item N is achieved by:

```
    Record.ItemType := Deleted
    Record.NextDeleted := NumFirstDelete;
    Write this Record to Position N;
    NumFirstDelete := N
```

At the end of the program, the first record is set as appropriate, and then the file should be closed:

```
    Record.ItemType := FirstItem;
    Record.FirstDeleted := NumFirstDelete
    Record.NumberOfEntries := NumRecords
    Write Record to position 0
    Close File
```

Note that more efficient use of the disk is made if the size of an item is some power of two. This is because the size of sectors on the PC is a power of two. Therefore each item will always be within a minimum number of sectors, so the fewest number of accesses to the disk will be needed to read or write each item.

Conclusion

In this chapter some useful file handling routines have been described. These allow the user to process text files and binary files, accessing them sequentially and randomly.

Exercises

1) Question 2 of the last chapter described a problem to sort data about a music collection. Create a text file containing such data and write a program to read the data in, store them in an array and then sort them using the QuickSort algorithm.

2) A database is required to store information about the contents of a shop. The information on each item to be stored is as follows:

Name of item

Manufacturer

Supplier's order code

Price

Quantity normally ordered.

Define suitable data types for the problem and implement the routines given above for opening and closing the file, and adding and deleting items.

Reference

1 J&P Partners Ltd *TopSpeed Modula-2 Manual* 1989

11 Plotting the Diagram

An important requirement of the package is the ability to obtain hardcopy of a diagram, that is, to plot the diagram on a plotter or print it on a printer. In the package two such devices are supported, though others could be added. These devices are a PostScript printer[1] and a plotter which can understand HP-GL, the graphics language defined by Hewlett-Packard for their plotters[2]. The acquiring of hardcopy is thus the main topic of the chapter, and this includes methods of using the printer ports on the PC.

The handling of the different output devices is achieved by a series of suitable procedures, and these are stored in modules local to the plot diagram module, DIAGPLOT. Thus this chapter describes an application of local modules.

PostScript is a language which describes a page of text or graphics, and is therefore very suitable for displaying a diagram. One interesting aspect of the language is that it uses postfix or reverse Polish notation. Thus this provides an opportunity to discuss the notation, and some suitable exercises are given.

11.1 Plotting requirements

The diagram package generates the necessary code so that a diagram can be drawn on a hardcopy device. There are many hardcopy devices, so to handle them all would be difficult. Thus two different devices were chosen, their choice reflecting the devices available to the author. Any reader wishing to obtain hardcopy on another machine can extend the plot module.

The module generates the appropriate code for the plotter or printer. This code can then be directed to the printer or plotter through the serial or parallel ports on the computer, or the code can be written into a file. This last option allows the user to run the package on a machine not connected to the hardcopy device and then port the code to a machine which does have the hardcopy facilities.

Generating the hardcopy codes: another use of procedure variables

To plot a diagram on the hardcopy device, the package must draw the diagram and send the codes to the device rather than to the graphics screen. This is easily achieved by the use of procedure variables. The DIAGSCAL module takes each item, scales it appropriately and then calls the relevant routine in the GrWindow module. The relevant routine is in fact stored in a procedure variable. Thus, when plotting is to be done, these procedure variables are changed from the screen routines to those which handle the hardcopy device.

For example, normally the procedure variable Line references the procedure Line from GrWindow. However, when the diagram is to be drawn on the PostScript printer, the variable is given the reference to the procedure which generates code to draw a line on the printer. Similarly, when the diagram is drawn on the plotter,

144 Modula-2 Applied

the program loads the Line procedure variable with the procedure which generates the commands for the plotter.

The procedure variables used are Line, Circle, Arc, PlotString and DrawBezier which draw the relevant items; SetColour which sets the colour and feature of an item; and the procedures WindowWidth and WindowDepth for determining the size of the output device. These variables and their default procedures are in DIAGSCAL. The hardcopy drivers emulate these routines.

11.2 Accessing the printer through the ports or writing to file

The code generated to draw each item is either written to a file, or sent directly to the hardcopy device via the parallel or serial port. This is easy to do. When an item is drawn suitable command strings and numbers must be sent to the device. Sending a number is achieved by converting a number to a string and sending the string. Sending a string is done by outputting each character in the string. Thus ultimately a character must be sent to the appropriate device. If a file is used, then the character is written to a file, otherwise it is sent out through either the parallel or serial port.

Thus, whatever the hardcopy device is, the following routines are used:

```
PROCEDURE InitPlot;
  IF sending to file THEN Open file END;

PROCEDURE SendChar (ch : CHAR);
  CASE where sending OF
    File : Write char to file |
    Parallel Port : Output Char to parallel port |
    Serial Port : Output to serial port
  END;

PROCEDURE SendString (S : ARRAY OF CHAR);
  FOR each char in S DO SendChar (S[n]) END;

PROCEDURE SendCard (c : CARDINAL);
VAR S : ARRAY [0..10] OF CHAR;
  CardToStr (S, c);
  SendString (S);

PROCEDURE SendLn;
  SendChar (Return);
  SendChar (LineFeed);

PROCEDURE EndPlot
  IF sending to file THEN Close File END;
```

Sending to ports

There are various ways of outputting characters to the serial and parallel ports. One method is to access the ports directly, using the procedures In and Out from the SYSTEM module, checking the appropriate status registers to see that the device is ready, and then sending the character. Another method is to use the operating system on the PC. It turns out that controlling the parallel printer is best done using the operating system, and the serial printer is best controlled by accessing the ports.

When using the operating system, the control of the port is achieved by considering it to be a file. Associated with a file is a file handle, and one has been predefined for the parallel port and another for the serial port. Thus writing a character to the parallel port is

```
WrChar (PrinterDevice, ch)
```

and to the serial device, the code is

```
WrChar (AuxDevice, ch)
```

The 'files' for these two devices are defined in the FIO module, and they are already open, so the user program does not need to open them or close them.

However, using the above for the serial port has problems. When accessing a device which is not ready, whether it is a printer port or disk drive, the operating system will automatically write to the screen

Device not ready:
Abort, Retry, Ignore ?

after the 'time out' period. This is not wanted, but appears often in serial communication because the data transfer rate is slow: the package generates characters to be output more quickly than the communications link can send. One way to avoid this message is to access the port directly. Another reason for so doing is to allow the user to configure the serial port. Thus in the diagram package, the control of the port is achieved using a general purpose serial control module. This module is called SERIAL.

When the user wishes to obtain hardcopy, he is given the choice of sending to a file, to the printer port, to the serial port or to configure the serial port before the plot and then send to the serial port. If the last is chosen, the user is asked to specify a series of parameters for the port before the plotting occurs.

146 Modula-2 Applied

The serial control module has procedures to configure the port, to test if the port is able to send a data byte, to send a byte, to test if the port has received data and to receive the data.

The actual port on a PC is controlled by a serial communications controller chip, the 8250, and the program controls it by reading from or writing to the device. For more detail on the controller, see the appropriate data sheet, and for serial communication see the reference[3].

Controlling the chip is achieved by accessing one of eight addresses. These addresses are all relative to a base address, and the base address of the main serial port, COM1, is at address 3F8H. Some computers have another serial port, COM2, whose base address is 2F8H. Addresses 3E8H and 2E8H are also sometimes used for COM3 or COM4. For more information see[4].

The serial output port is ready, that is a byte can be sent, if bit 5 at address base+5 and bit 4 at address base+6 are set. This is tested by:

```
BITSET (In (PortBase+5) ) * BITSET (20H) <> {} ) AND
BITSET (In (PortBase+6) ) * BITSET (10H) <> {} )
```

using the In routine from the SYSTEM module. A character c is output by:

```
Out (PortBase, SHORTCARD (c) );
```

In the plot module, the following code is used:

```
REPEAT
  CheckKey
UNTIL SerialCanSend();
SerialSend (ch);
```

By calling the CheckKey (see chapter 5) routine, the user is able to abort the plotting if the communications link stops.

The parameters of the port to be configured are the baud rate; whether the data sent has parity added, and if so is the parity even or odd; the length of each data item (5 bits..8 bits); and whether 1 or 2 stop bits are set. The baud rate is a measure of the speed at which the data are sent. Associated with the controller is a timing signal, and this is slowed down by a factor to give the correct baud rate. The factor is a 16-bit number sent to the controller in two parts. This is achieved by:

```
Out (PortBase+3, 80H);    (* to allow baud rate to be set *)
Out (PortBase+1, Least sig. byte of baud rate factor);
Out (PortBase, Most sig. byte of baud rate factor);
Out (PortBase+3, OptionsParameter)   (* see below *)
```

The baud rate factor is 12 for a speed of 9600 baud, 24 for 4800 baud, etc. The *OptionsParameter* is a byte whose bits are determined as follows:

bit 7 set to allow the baud rate to be set, clear for normal operation
bit 6 set to send the 'break' character
bit 5 set for 'stick' parity
bit 4 set if even parity, clear if odd parity (valid if bit 3 set)
bit 3 set if even or odd parity, clear if no parity
bit 2 set if 2 stop bits, clear if 1 stop bit
bits 1,0 specify number of data bits (00 = 5, 01=6, 10=7 and 11=8)

Normally no parity is set, and 2 stop bits and 8 data bits are used. These parameters are all set by the Configure procedure. The procedure also allows the user to specify whether COM1 or COM2 is used. Full details of the procedure are in the module SERIAL.

11.3 Local modules used as drivers

The drivers for the two hardcopy devices, that is, the routines for drawing lines, circles, etc., for the plotter and printer, are contained in two modules local to the DIAGPLOT module. This is an appropriate use of local modules as the drivers for each are self contained, with their own associated variables, types and procedures. Drivers for other devices should be written in other modules.

A local module, like a library module, must specify which items within it are visible from the outside, and which items outside the module it can see. For library modules, a DEFINITION module is used for the former and IMPORT statements are used for the latter which specify the module from which the outside items are found. Local modules are different. They explicitly EXPORT those items which are visible to the outside, and IMPORT specifically those items outside the module which are visible from within. Note that anything IMPORTed must be directly available outside. This is made clearer by example, and in introductory Modula-2 books, for example Beidler and Jackowitz[5].

The start of the PostScript plot module is as follows:

148 *Modula-2 Applied*

```
MODULE PostScript;

IMPORT InitPlot, FinishPlot, SendChar, SendString, SendCard,
  SendLn, Line, Circle, Arc, PlotString, DrawBezier,
  SetColour, WindowWidth, WindowDepth;

EXPORT PlotPostScript
```

That is, the only item within the module which can be 'seen' from outside is the procedure PlotPostScript. Also the module needs to see the routines InitPlot, FinishPlot, etc., so these are imported. InitPlot, and others, are in the DIAGPLOT module, but the procedure variables Line, Circle, etc., come from the DIAGSCAL module. In order for the PostScript module to be able to IMPORT them, they must be visible in the main part of DIAGPLOT, so DIAGPLOT should import them. Thus even though Line, Circle, etc., are not used in the main part of DIAGPLOT, the following declaration is needed:

```
FROM DIAGSCAL IMPORT Line, Circle, Arc, PlotString  etc.
```

The start of the Plotter module is much the same as for the PostScript module. Then each has any local variables needed and the various procedures used to generate the code to draw lines, etc., on the appropriate device.

11.4 Reverse Polish notation

The language PostScript is used to describe the contents of a page of text and/or graphics, and an increasing number of devices can understand the language. One interesting aspect of the language is that it uses postfix or reverse Polish notation, as opposed to the normal infix notation. In fact there are three types of notation, prefix, infix and postfix: prefix notation was invented by the Polish logician Lukasiewicz, and would be known as Lukasiewicz notation if the word was easily spelt or pronounced, so instead it is often termed Polish notation. For more information, see Graham[6].

In infix notation, an operation on numbers is specified in the order:

number operator number   e.g 5 + 78

but in prefix notation, the operator is specified first:

operator number number   e.g + 5 78

and in postfix notation, the operator is last (the reverse of prefix, hence the term reverse Polish notation).

number number operator   e.g 5 78 +

One reason why postfix notation is used is that processing of such expressions is easy on stack based machines. Also both prefix and postfix notations do not need brackets or operator precedence to determine the order in which the operations are performed: the notations are unambiguous. For example, the infix expression

*3 + 4 * 5*

is potentially ambiguous. It is usually interpreted as 3 added to the product of 4 and 5, that is, 23, and not as 35. This is because the multiply operator binds more tightly than the add operator. The multiply operator is said to have a greater *precedence* than the add operator.

The equivalent prefix expression is

*+ 3 * 4 5*

which is unambiguous, as is the equivalent postfix expression

*3 4 5 * +*

Evaluation of a postfix expression is very easy: the process is to scan the expression from left to right, noting each item (as either a number or operator). If it is a number, it is remembered. If it is an operator, the previous two numbers are operated upon suitably, and the result remembered. This is best achieved using a stack. A stack is a simple data structure like a stack of cards: a card added to the stack is put on the top of the stack, and the one removed from the stack is the one at the top: it is the last one added. Thus a postfix expression can be evaluated by an algorithm like:

```
Initialise Stack;
FOR each item in the expression DO
   IF number THEN
      Push Number on to stack
   ELSIF operator THEN
      Pop Top Two Numbers off the stack;
      Operate on them suitably;
      Push Result back on to the stack
   END
END;
Pop Result off the stack
```

For example, the expression 3 4 5 * + is evaluated as follows:

Expression	*Stack*
3 4 5 * +	
4 5 * +	3
5 * +	3 4
* +	3 4 5
+	3 20
	23

150 *Modula-2 Applied*

whereas 3 4 * 5 + is processed as:

Expression	Stack
3 4 * 5 +	
4 * 5 +	3
* 5 +	3 4
5 +	12
+	12 5
	17

Thus evaluation of postfix expressions is easy. Another advantage is that errors such as not having enough operators, or having too many operators, can be detected. Not having enough operators results in the stack having more than one number on it at the end, which is easily detected.

*The stack after 3 4 * 5 is processed is 20 5*

If there are too many operators, then the algorithm will want to pop two numbers off the stack when there is only one there.

*When processing 3 4 * +, the + will operate on the stack containing only 12.*

An implementation of this is given in the exercises at the end of the chapter.

People tend to find it easier to use infix notation rather than postfix. Thus algorithms have been developed to convert from expressions in infix to their postfix equivalent. One such algorithm, Dijkstra's stacking method, is described in an exercise in chapter 13.

11.5 PostScript

More detail on the language PostScript can be found in the various books on the subject (see [1], [6]). Here a few brief comments will be given as regards those parts of the language used in the diagram package.

Expressions are specified in postfix notation as described above, though the operators are given in words, not symbols. Thus

    3 4 mul 5 add

means 3 multiplied by 4 and the result added to 5, with the final result left on the stack. The other basic operators are sub, div, mod and idiv (the last being integer division). Functions like sin and cos are also provided.

There are various graphics commands. These allow the user to specify a series of continuous items, called a path, which are then drawn. They all begin by specifying the start of the items, with the command 'newpath', then a series of positions and commands are given (like drawing line segments or circles) and then a command to draw is given: this is 'stroke' to draw the items, or 'fill' to fill the area specified ('fill' also automatically closes the path, that is, it joins the last point to the first one).

To draw a line from x1,y1 to x2,y2 the command is:

```
newpath x1 y1 moveto x2 y2 lineto stroke
```

Multiple lines (like x1,y1 to x2y2 to x3,y3) are done by:

```
newpath x1 y1 moveto x2 y2 lineto x3 y3 lineto stroke
```

The commands 'moveto' and 'lineto' use the two values at the top of the stack to specify absolute positions. The commands 'rmoveto' and 'rlineto' do the same except that the positions are relative to the current position.

To draw an arc of a circle, origin x,y, radius r, between angles a1 and a2 (in an anticlockwise direction), the command is:

```
newpath x y r a1 a2 arc stroke
```

Drawing a circle is achieved using the above with angles 0 and 360.

A Bezier curve is drawn using the 'curveto' operator. The four points specified are those used in the diagram package. The command is then:

```
newpath x1 y1 moveto x2 y2 x3 y3 x4 y4 curveto stroke
```

'curveto' takes the three coordinates on the stack and forms a Bezier curve with them and the previous position, which in this case is specified by the 'moveto'.

All the above routines draw or fill the specified shapes in the current shade of grey selected, and use the current choice of line thickness and other parameters. The grey level is set by

```
num setgray
```

where num is in the range 0 to 1, 0 being black, 1 is white.

The line thickness is set by:

```
num setlinewidth
```

where num is how wide the line is in multiples of the size of a dot.

The end of a line can be specifed:

```
num setlinecap
```

if num is 0, the line is squared off at the ends

if num is 1, the end of the line is semicircular

if num is 2, the end is square but projects by half the line width from the end of the line.

In order that a dot is drawn, that is a, line of zero length actually appears, the semi-circular end should be chosen.

As regards text, the user can specify the character font used, and the size of the font. Then a string of text can be printed by positioning it and then sending the string enclosed in brackets followed by the command show.

```
x y moveto ( <the string> ) show
```

This presents the problem of how to print a (or) within a string. This is easily achieved by sending a \ before the particular (or). To print a \ in the string, it is also preceded by a \.

Specifying a font and its size consists of:

 /<font name> findfont <size> scalefont setfont

The four fonts used in the diagram package (providing normal, bold, italic and bold and italic characters) are Courier, Courier-Bold, Courier-Oblique and Courier-BoldOblique, though the printer used by the author has other fonts as well. These were chosen as the width of each character is constant (it is not a proportional font), and the characters used in the graphics window routines have constant width also.

All text and graphics are drawn suitably scaled, translated and rotated. Thus, built into the language are commands to specify the necessary transformations. These commands specify extra transformations on top of the existing transformation: that is, the current matrix is multiplied by another specified by the appropriate command. These commands are:

 x y scale

adds extra scaling in the x and y directions.

 x y translate

shifts the origin by an amount x y (suitable scaled and rotated).

 angle rotation

specifies the extra rotation.

Two other useful commands are 'gsave' and 'grestore' which save and restore the current transformation matrix and other associated parameters. These are used to allow the program to remember the current state, then allow further transformations, and then return to the previous state.

It is also possible to define procedures. One use of these is to reduce the amount of text needed in the file. An operator like 'moveto' or 'newpath' contains many characters, and any command to draw a line requires these and other multi letter commands. If, however, at the start of the PostScript program definitions like the following were made:

 /N {newpath} def /M {moveto} def
 /L {lineto} def /S {stroke} def

which define four procedures, N, M, L and S, whose actions are newpath, moveto, lineto and stroke, respectively, then a command to draw a line is reduced to:

 N x1 y1 M x2 y2 L S

which is significantly shorter than the full length command. By using the above technique, the author was able to reduce the size of the PostScript file for figure 20.9 from 167K bytes to 98Kbytes.

There is much more to PostScript, including FOR loops and IF statements, conditional operators, etc. For more information, the reader should consult the references Thomas [1] and Adobe [7].

11.6 The PostScript module

The basic routines in the module are straightforward. However, a few points should be noted. The diagram is perceived to be square, whereas a page is normally of size A4. Thus the diagram is drawn so that its midpoint is in the middle of the paper. Also, the printer has a greater resolution than the screen, so the size of the page is set to 2000 by 2000 suitably centred. In fact, in the printer's units, an A4 sheet is 850*600, but the printer can resolve to fractions of a unit. Thus before the diagram is drawn, the following initialisation is done:

    50 150 translate 0.25 0.25 scale

which means that the diagram will appear in the middle of the page and it will fit on the page. Also the end of lines is specified by the command

    1 setlinecap

so that dots appear (as explained above). The other initialisation is to define single character procedures for the commands like 'newpath', 'moveto', etc.

Lines, etc., are drawn in the current colour and thickness. Rather than specifying these each time, the printer is only told them when they change. The same applies for the fonts for text: the font is only specified when it changes or a different size is used. Thus the module remembers the current FontSize, FontType, GreyLevel and Thickness. Then, for example, the procedure to draw a line is:

```
PROCEDURE PSLine (x1, y1, x2, y2, colour : CARDINAL);
BEGIN
  CheckGreyThick (colour);
  SendString ('N ');              (* N is newpath *)
  SendXY (x1, y1);
  SendString ('M ');              (* M is moveto *)
  SendXY (x2, y2);
  SendString ('L S');  (* L is lineto, S is stroke *)
  SendLn
END PSLine;
```

The value of colour MOD 16 is the grey level in the range 1..8, 1 is black, 8 is very light grey (0 is white). The value of colour DIV 16 is the line thickness (0..3).

CheckGreyThick sets a new value of Grey if the current GreyLevel does not equal colour MOD 16, and sets a new linewidth if Thickness differs from colour DIV 16. Note that, because the scale is 0.25 (a quarter), a line thickness of 1 is specified by setting the line width to be 4.

Plotting rectangles and diamonds is done by drawing lines. Circles, arcs and Bezier curves are plotted with routines similar to the above.

The handling of text, however, is different. PostScript allows the user to specify the size of the text, but does not directly allow the X and Y sizes to differ. However, they can be scaled differently using the scale command. Thus the X-scaling size is used to select the text size and then the text is scaled by (1, YSize / XSize). Transformations are also used to rotate the text. Thus the routine calls gsave, changes the transformation, plots the text and then calls grestore. The routine is:

```
PROCEDURE PSPlotString (XPos, YPos, Colour, XSize, YSize, Angle :
                        CARDINAL; S : ARRAY OF CHAR);
BEGIN
   CheckGrey (Colour);
   IF (XSize<>FontSize) OR (Colour DIV 16<>FontType) THEN
           (* Colour DIV 16 is the feature *)
      SetFontAndSize (XSize, Colour DIV 16)
   END;
   SendString ('gsave');
   SendXY (XPos, YPos); SendString (' translate');
   IF XSize<>YSize THEN
      SendString ('1 '); SendCard (YSize);
      SendCard (XSize); SendString (' div scale')
   END;
   IF Angle<>0 THEN SendCard (Angle); SendString (' rotate') END;
   SendChar ('(');
   SendTheString (S);
   SendString (') show grestore');
   SendLn
END PSPlotString;
```

The font to be selected is determined by the feature, which is the specified colour DIV 16. The text size is not directly the same size used in the graphics, but needs to be scaled by a factor 1.66 (which was determined experimentally). Thus selecting the font is:

```
PROCEDURE SetFontAndSize (Size, Font : CARDINAL);
BEGIN
   CASE Font OF
      0 : SendString ('/Courier') |
      1 : SendString ('/Courier-Bold') |
      2 : SendString ('/Courier-Oblique') |
      3 : SendString ('/Courier-BoldOblique')
   END;
   SendString (' findfont ');
   SendCard (Size); SendString (' 1.66 mul scalefont setfont')
END SetFontAndSize;
```

The string itself is sent in the following manner, with extra '\'s inserted as appropriate (as explained earlier):

```
PROCEDURE SendTheStrng (S : ARRAY OF CHAR);
VAR ct : CARDINAL;
BEGIN
  ct := 0;
  WHILE (ct <= HIGH(S) AND (S[ct] <> 0C) DO
    IF (S[ct] = '(') OR (S[ct] = ')') OR (S[ct] = '\') THEN
      SendChar ('\')
    END;
    SendChar (S[ct];
    INC (ct)
  END
END SendTheString;
```

11.7 The HP-GL plotter module

The commands for the Hewlett-Packard graphics language are relatively straightforward. This language is much simpler than PostScript, and less powerful. The commands are two letters followed by any parameters separated by commas and a suitable terminator, which is normally a semicolon. The commands are as follows.

A line from x1,y1 to x2, y2 is specified by a command of the form:

   PU x1,y1; PD x2,y2;

that is the pen is lifted up (PU), moved to point x1,y1, the pen is put down (PD) and moved to point x2,y2.

A circle of origin x,y and radius r is drawn by moving to the origin and then specifying a circle of the requisite radius:

   PU x,y; CI r;

Circles are drawn by calculating points separated by a given angle. The default value is 5 degrees, but a second parameter to CI can be sent to specify the angle separation. For small circles, 5 degree separation is too small, but for larger circles the value should be reduced.

Drawing an arc is more complicated. The AA command draws an arc of a circle whose origin is specified: the current position is the start of the arc, and the number of degrees of the arc is specified. Thus, to draw an arc whose origin is x,y and radius r, between angles a1 and a2, the command is:

   *PU x+r*COS(a1),y+r*SIN(a1); PD; AA x,y,a2-a1;*

The program should calculate the value for x+r*COS(a1), etc., and send that. Again, an extra parameter for AA specifies an angle separation.

Bezier curves are not supported directly, so the curve is divided into suitable line segments, as is done in the GrWindow module for the screen, and these

156 Modula-2 Applied

segments are drawn. Early plotters did not have circle or arc drawing commands, thus for these the program must also send suitable line segments.

As regards text, the following are used:

```
LB <the string> and then control-C.
```

plots the given string

```
SI xsize,ysize;
```

specifies the size of the characters

```
SL tan(angle);
```

specifies the slant of characters: this is used for italic characters

```
DI Cos(a), Sin(a);
```

specifies that the text is to be drawn at angle a.

Different colours are specified by selecting different pens:

```
PU; SP 1;
```

lifts the pen (a sensible precaution) and selects pen 1.

```
PU; SP;
```

puts the pen away, which is done at the end of the diagram.

The size of an A4 plotter is 10800 by 7680 units, so the coordinates need to be scaled suitably. Using all these commands, the diagram can be drawn easily.

Conclusion

This chapter has introduced various useful points: using printer ports, local modules, postfix notation, the PostScript language and control of HP plotters. Also, another application of procedure variables has been given.

Exercises

1) One way of simulating a stack is to consider it as an array of numbers and index into the array suitably: the index is effectively the stack pointer. Thus pushing a number on the stack is achieved by moving the stack pointer and writing the number into the array at the position specified by the stack pointer. Popping a result is reading the value from the array and then moving the stack pointer back.

Write routines to push a number on to the stack and pop one off it.

2) Write a procedure to scan a postfix expression containing single letter numbers and the operators + - * /, and evaluate it. Any errors detected should be reported.

3) Most operators are binary, that is they act on two numbers, and in the evaluation routine this is achieved by popping two numbers off the stack, processing them, and pushing the result back. A unary operator, like the minus in -1, acts on one

number only, so its evaluation consists of popping only one number, processing it suitably and pushing the result back.

Using m to signify the unary - operator and p the unary + operator, modify the routine in exercise 2 to account for these operators as well.

4) Write a routine to draw an arc of a circle by drawing a series of line segments whose end points are 5 degrees apart.

References

1 Barry Thomas *A PostScript Cookbook* Macmillan Education 1988

2 Hewlett-Packard *HPGL manual*

3 R.J.Mitchell *Microcomputer Systems using the STE bus* Macmillan Education 1989

4. J.P.Royer *Handbook of software and hardware interfacing for IBM-PCs* Prentice-Hall 1987

5. John Beidler and Paul Jackowitz *Modula-2* PWS Publishers 1986

6. Neill Graham *Introduction to Computer Science* West 1982

7. Adobe *PostScript Reference Manual* Adobe-Systems 1982

12 The Heap and One-way Linked Lists

In the diagram package the user can create a diagram made up of a series of shapes, each of which contains a number of items. Each shape can consist of any number of items, and there can be any number of shapes. Thus, when the program is written, it is not known how many items are required, or how many shapes are needed. This can be determined only when the program is being run. However, space is needed in which these items and shapes are stored. It would be possible to predeclare this using VAR statements of the form:

```
VAR Shapes : ARRAY [0..ShapeMax] OF Items;
    Items  : ARRAY [0..ItemMax] OF GCommand;
```

where ShapeMax and ItemMax are suitable constants, and GCommand is a record defining an item (see chapter 9). This is limiting, as the user is restricted as to the number of GCommands that can make up a shape, and the number of shapes. It is also wasteful of memory, as some shapes may require very few GCommands. A much better solution is one where the memory for a new GCommand is acquired as and when it is needed, that is, when the program is run. This is achieved using the heap (see Wirth[1]).

12.1 The heap

A computer has an area of memory which can be used for programs. That area is used for various parts: the program is stored in one part, its variables are stored in another, and a third is used for the stack. The rest can be used for the heap.

The heap is an area of memory initially unused. If, however, a program needs some extra memory to store data, it can obtain some from the heap. That area of memory is then passed to the program. If more space is needed, the heap is called again, and the next area of memory is returned. This is termed dynamic storage allocation. There is the potential problem that all the memory will have been used, so no more can be obtained from the heap. The program should thus check that enough space is available before trying to get memory from the heap. Careful consideration is needed to decide what to do in such a case.

In some applications, the program may subsequently have no further use for the memory, and so will return it to the heap. Then, if another part of the program requires memory, that discarded part of the heap may be reused.

In the diagram package, memory will be required whenever a new item is added to the diagram: the heap will be called and the memory returned will be filled with the data that make up a GCommand. If an item is deleted, it is then returned to the heap.

Pointers

When the program is allocated memory, it must know the address of the memory that has been allocated, so that it can put the data into the memory. The data type which specifies an address is called a pointer. A pointer is a data variable which contains the address of memory.

In Modula-2, a strongly typed language, the type of the variable pointed to by the pointer must be specified. Therefore types of pointers are defined by the type of variable that they address. This is achieved by declaring a pointer as a POINTER TO a type. For example,

```
TYPE RealPointer = POINTER TO REAL;
     CharPointer = POINTER TO CHAR;
     GCommandLink = POINTER TO GCommand;
```

In use, a pointer variable is given the address of a variable (possibly using the heap), then the object addressed by the pointer can be accessed by dereferencing using the symbol ^. For example, if R is a variable of type RealPointer, the object pointed to by R is R^. Thus the following are legal:

```
R^ := 3.5;
WrReal (SIN (R^), 10, 5);
```

A pointer which does not point to any memory should be given the constant value NIL. Pointers, like all other variables, should be given suitable initial values. Care is required with pointers: if they have incorrect values they may address unwanted memory, like the operating system of the computer, and create havoc.

Using the heap

The basic operations of the heap are to get memory from it, and to return memory to it. These operations are variously called New and Dispose, or Allocate and DeAllocate. Both operations need pointers to specify the address of memory, and the amount of memory required. The amount of memory needed can be calculated using the operators TSIZE and SIZE:

```
TSIZE (REAL)
```
returns the size of a type, in this case a REAL

```
SIZE (R^)
```
returns the size of a variable, here an item pointed to by R.

Before attempting to allocate memory it is a good idea to check that there is enough space on the heap. Thus the following procedure will get space for a REAL number from the heap:

160 Modula-2 Applied

```
PROCEDURE GetReal (VAR R : RealPointer) : BOOLEAN;
BEGIN
  IF Available (SIZE (R^) ) THEN
    ALLOCATE (R, SIZE (R^) );
    RETURN TRUE
  ELSE
    RETURN FALSE
  END
END GetReal;
```

Procedure Available checks that there is enough space, and if there is, memory is acquired by procedure ALLOCATE, and the address of the space is returned in variable R. These routines are in the TopSpeed module Storage. Note that, in earlier editions of Modula-2, the built-in procedure New was used for allocation. This is now obsolete in version 4 (see Wirth[2]).

It should be remembered that when the memory is allocated its contents are undefined. The user should initialise the memory appropriately.

To dispose of that space, the procedure is:

```
DEALLOCATE (R, SIZE (R^) )
```

Once it has been deallocated, the user must not attempt to use the memory. The routine Dispose was formerly used for deallocation, but is also now obsolete.

12.2 Allocating and deallocating GCommands in the diagram package

In the diagram package special routines have been written to allocate and deallocate memory for GCommands. The allocation is achieved by a procedure which is passed a pointer and the type of GCommand. Its operation requires the definitions given in chapter 9, and the following:

```
GCommandLink = POINTER TO GCommand;
```

The allocation procedure gets the memory from the heap, and initialises it appropriately. For example, if space for a line is required, then the memory is obtained and the coordinates of the line are set suitably. For a string and a head, space for the string is not made within the GCommand (because that would make the size of a GCommand unnecessarily large, as explained in chapter 9), instead a pointer to the string is included in the record, which references the memory where the string is actually stored. Thus the allocation procedure must also acquire space for the string as well. The GCommand allocation procedure is:

```
PROCEDURE GCommandAllocate (VAR Link : GCommandLink;
                            GCType : GCommandType) : BOOLEAN;
BEGIN
  IF Available (SIZE (Link^) ) THEN
    ALLOCATE (Link, SIZE (LINK^) );
    WITH Link^ DO
      Gtype := GCType;
      colour := 1;
      feature := 0;
      Marked := FALSE;
      MarkedPrev := FALSE;
      Next := NIL;
      CASE Gtype  OF
        head       : first := NIL; programptr := NIL;
                     RETURN StrAllocate (name) |
        program    : first := NIL; name := NIL;
                     RETURN ProgramAllocate (programptr) |
        line       : xl1 := 0; yl1 := 0; xl2 := 0; yl2 := 0 |
        circle     : xc := 0; yc := 0; rc := 0 |
        arc        : xa := 0; ya := 0; ra := 0; a1 := 0; a2 := 0 |
        rectangle  : xr1 := 0; yr1 := 0; xr2 := 0; yr2 := 0 |
        diamond    : xd1 := 0; yd1 := 0; xd2 := 0; yd2 := 0 |
        bezier     : xb1 := 0; yb1 := 0; xb2 := 0; yb2 := 0;
                     xb3 := 0; yb3 := 0; xb4 := 0; yb4 := 0 |
        string     : xs1 := 0; ys1 := 0; xs2 := 0; ys2 := 0;
                     rs := 0;  RETURN StrAllocate (str) |
        usershape  : xu1 := 0; yu1 := 0; xu2 := 0; yu2 := 0;
                     ru := 0;  shape := NIL
      END
    END;
    RETURN TRUE
  ELSE
    RETURN FALSE
  END
END GCommandAllocate;
```

The above acquires memory for the GCommand if there is space. For a string and a head, memory is then also required for the actual string. For a program, space for a program is acquired by a similar procedure called ProgramAllocate. The string allocation procedure is as follows:

```
PROCEDURE StrAllocate (VAR SLink : GStringLink) : BOOLEAN;
BEGIN
  IF Available (SIZE (SLink^) ) THEN
    ALLOCATE (SLink, SIZE (SLink^) );
    SLink^[0] := 0C;      (* initialise string to '' *)
    RETURN TRUE
  ELSE
    RETURN FALSE
  END
END StrAllocate;
```

In the above, a check is made to see that memory is available, and only if it is does the procedure call the heap. The memory thus obtained, space for a string, is then initialised by putting the null string there.

12.3 Linked lists

A shape consists of a list of GCommands. Space for each GCommand is obtained as and when it is needed. Clearly some means is required for connecting these items together: there must be a link between one GCommand and the next. That link need only indicate the position of the next item, that is the address of the next item. Thus the link is simply a pointer to the next item. A list of items which are so connected is called a linked list (see Wirth [1]).

A list is a sequential collection of data. To access an element of the list, its address must be found. This is achieved by searching the list from the start and then examining each item in turn: if the current one is the item required, the search stops; otherwise if the item is not at the end of the list, the search moves to the next position, but if the end has been reached the search is unsuccessful.

Therefore a list needs a start point, a series of items which are linked together, and some means of indicating the end of the list. The start point is simply a pointer to the first item in the list, the links are pointers to the next item, and the end of the list is marked by a pointer whose value is NIL.

Linked lists have many applications and varieties, and in this chapter a simple one way list is given. Some more complicated lists, including two way lists, are described in later chapters.

Operations on a list

The simple operations on a list are to scan through a list, to add items to the list and to delete items from a list. These will be described with reference to the diagram package. In each record for a GCommand, there is a field called Next, of type GCommandLink. This is a pointer variable which indicates the position of the next item in the list. A GCommandLink is thus:

```
GCommandLink = POINTER TO GCommand;
```

For a head of the shape, there is also a pointer called first. This points to the first GCommand in that shape.

To draw a shape, each item in that shape must be drawn. This is achieved in the procedure DrawItem, given in chapter 7, which draws the item passed to it. As given earlier, if the item is of type head, the code is:

```
FOR all items in the list DO
   DrawItem (S, eachitem)
END
```

In practice this is achieved using Ptr, a variable of type GCommandLink:

```
Ptr := item.first;
WHILE Ptr <> NIL DO
   DrawItem (S, Ptr);
   Ptr := Ptr^.Next
END
```

Initially Ptr is given the address of the first element in the list. It then scans the list until the end is reached, drawing each item in turn and then moving onto the next, by *Ptr := Ptr^.Next*. As the list may contain nothing, this is done using a WHILE loop and not a REPEAT UNTIL loop.

Adding a new item is also simple. Conventionally, the obvious thing to do would be to add a new item to the end of the list. However, this requires searching through to the end and then processing the end. In this case there is no reason why the new item should not be added to the beginning of the list, and as that is easier, this is what is done. The operation is thus:

```
Get memory for new item
Next part of the new item := the current start of the list
Make new memory the start of the list.
```

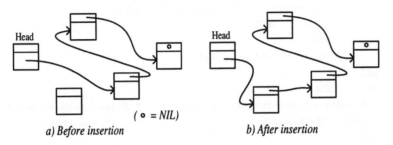

a) Before insertion   (○ = NIL)   b) After insertion

Figure 12.1 Insertion into a linked list

The action of this is illustrated in figure 12.1. The state of the list before the insertion is shown in figure 12.1a), and 12.1b) shows the list after the insertion.

Inserting in the list is done when the user specifies that a new line, circle, etc., is to be added. A procedure Insert is called which is passed the type of the item to be added. This is added into the shape currently being edited: the global variable CurrentShape, of type GCommandLink, points to the head of this shape. The procedure, which uses the GCommandAllocate procedure given earlier, is:

```
PROCEDURE Insert (type : GCommandType);
VAR NewUn : GCommandLink;
BEGIN
  IF GCommandAllocate (NewUn, type) THEN
    NewUn^.Next := CurrentShape^.first;
    CurrentShape^.first := NewUn
      (* then Edit item, using routine Edit from chapter 9 *)
  END
END Insert;
```

Adding new items to the start of the list has another advantage. When the user wants to modify an item, he can select an item by moving a crosshair over the item, select the last item added to the list, or use the previous choice. Determining the last item added is easy: it is the first item in the list. Remembering the previous choice simply requires storing a pointer, MoveLink, to any choice made. The Modify procedure is thus:

```
PROCEDURE Modify;
VAR x, y : INTEGER; ok : BOOLEAN;
BEGIN
  ok := FALSE;
  CASE Select (Specify, Last, Previous) OF
    'S' : GetPoint (x, y);
          ok := Locate (x, y, MoveLink) |
    'L' : IF CurrentShape^.first<>NIL THEN
             MoveLink := CurrentShape^.first;
             ok := TRUE
          END |
    'P' : ok := MoveLink <> NIL
  END;
  IF ok THEN
    DrawItem (MoveLink, EraseColour);   (* delete from screen *)
    Edit (MoveLink)                     (* and change it *)
  END
END Modify;
```

The Heap and One-way Linked Lists 165

The procedure Select allows the user to select an item from a list (the topic of the next chapter), GetPoint allows the user to specify a position, and Locate finds the nearest item to that position. The algorithm for Locate also uses pointers, and calls the routine DiffCalculate of chapter 9, which finds the distance between an item and the specified point. For each item in the list, its distance from the point is calculated. If this is closer than the previous nearest, the item is remembered in Nearest.

```
PROCEDURE Locate (x, y : INTEGER;
                  VAR Where : GCommandLink) : BOOLEAN;
VAR Diff, NewDiff : REAL; Nearest : GCommandLink;
BEGIN
  Diff := MAX (REAL);
  Nearest := NIL;
  Where := CurrentShape^.first;
  WHILE Where<>NIL DO
    NewDiff := DiffCalculate (Where, X, Y);
    IF NewDiff<Diff THEN
      Diff := NewDiff;
      Nearest := Where
    END;
    Where := Where^.Next
  END;
  IF Nearest=NIL THEN
    RETURN FALSE
  ELSE
    Where := Nearest;
    RETURN TRUE
  END
END Locate;
```

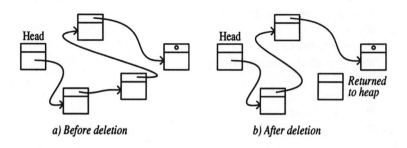

a) Before deletion   *b) After deletion*

Figure 12.2 Deletion from a linked list

166 Modula-2 Applied

Deletion from a list is also straightforward, again it requires the manipulation of pointers. Referring to figure 12.2, which shows an item being deleted, before and after the event, deletion is just:

```
IF item to be deleted (Item) is first in the list THEN
   head of the list should point to one after Item
ELSE
   previous item should point to one after Item
END;
Deallocate (Item)   (* that is, return it to the heap *)
```

The diagram package allows the user to specify one or many items to be deleted. Those items are marked: the boolean Marked in the GCommand is set true if the item is selected. The basic operation then is to examine each item in turn and if it is to be deleted then it is removed. This requires a pointer to scan through the list, and another one to remember the previous element so that when an item is deleted, the Next part of previous item should be changed. When an item is deleted it must be erased from the screen, by being drawn in the EraseColour and then the memory space deallocated. The operation is basically as follows:

```
P := CurrentShape^.first;
Prev := NIL;
WHILE P<>NIL DO
  IF P^.Marked THEN
    P^.Marked := FALSE;
    DrawItem (P, EraseColour);
    temp := P;   (* remember address of P to delete it *)
    IF Prev=NIL THEN
      CurrentShape^.first := P^.Next
    ELSE
      Prev^.Next := P^.Next
    END;
    P := P^.Next;
    GCommandDeAllocate (temp)
  ELSE
    Prev := P;
    P := P^.Next
  END
END
```

The procedure GCommandDeAllocate is used to dispose of an item. This requires more than just deallocating the memory: if the item being deallocated is a string then the memory for the string must be deallocated as well. Also, if the item is a head, then the whole of the list is also removed.

```
PROCEDURE GCommandDeAllocate (VAR L : GCommandLink);
BEGIN
   IF L<>NIL THEN
      CASE L^.Gtype OF
         string  : DEALLOCATE (L^.str, SIZE (L^.str^) ) |
         head    : DeAllocateList (L^.first);
                   DEALLOCATE (L^.name, SIZE (L^.name^) ) |
         program : ProgramDeAllocate (L^.programptr);
                   DeAllocateList (L^.first);
                   DEALLOCATE (L^.name, SIZE (L^.name^) )
      END;
      DEALLOCATE (L, SIZE (L^) );
      L := NIL
   END
END GCommandDeAllocate;
```

and DeAllocateList just deallocates each item in the list. As all of the list is being deallocated, not just some, this is straightforward. One point to note is that the pointer must progress through the list. However, after one element is deallocated its memory cannot be accessed, therefore the next item in the list must be determined before the current item is removed. Thus:

```
PROCEDURE DeAllocateList (VAR S : GCommandLink);
VAR Snext : GCommandLink;
BEGIN
   WHILE S<>NIL DO
      Snext := S^.Next;            (* remember next item *)
      GCommandDeAllocate (S);      (* deallocate this one *)
      S := Snext                   (* move on *)
   END
END DeAllocateList;
```

Block selection

The erase command is one of many which allows the user to select a group of commands for processing. The user specifies one item in the manner used by Modify; all items within a window; the last item entered (if this is chosen n times, the last n items entered are selected); the entire shape; or the group chosen previously. The boolean MarkedPrev is set if the item was selected the previous time, so this is used when the 'Previous' option is used. A pointer Last is used to indicate the item chosen when the 'last' option is selected: each time this option is chosen the item referenced by this pointer is marked and the pointer is moved one along the list. When the user has selected all items, he can accept the commands or quit. When an item is selected it is Marked. The procedure GetSelection returns TRUE if at least one item has been selected.

```
PROCEDURE GetSelection() : BOOLEAN;
BEGIN
  Last := CurrentShape^.first;
  AnyMarked := FALSE;

  LOOP
    CASE Select (Specify,Window,Last,Prev,Entire,Accept,Quit) OF
      'S' : GetPoint (x, y);  (* user specifies a position *)
            IF Locate (x, y, P) THEN Mark (P) := TRUE END |
      'W' : GetWindow (x1, y1, x2, y2);(* user defines a window *)
            P := CurrentShape^.first;
            WHILE P<>NIL DO
                IF InWindow(P, x1, y1, x2, y2) THEN Mark (P) END;
                P := P^.Next
            END |
      'L' : IF Last<>NIL THEN
               Mark (Last);
               Last := Last^.Next
            END |
      'P' : P := CurrentShape^.first;
            WHILE P<>NIL DO
                IF P^.MarkedPrev THEN Mark (P) END;
                P := P^.Next
            END |
      'E' : P := CurrentShape^.first;
            WHILE P<>NIL DO
               Mark (P);
               P := P^.Next
            END |
      'A' : P := CurrentShape^.first;
            WHILE P<>NIL DO
               P^.MarkedPrev := P^.Marked;
               P := P^.Marked
            END;
            RETURN AnyMarked |
```

```
    'Q' : P := CurrentShape^.first;
          WHILE P<>NIL DO
            IF P^.Marked THEN
              P^.Marked := FALSE;
              DrawItem (P, NormalColour)
            END;
            P := P^.Next
          END;
          RETURN FALSE
    END (* of CASE *)
  END (* of LOOP *)
END GetSelection;
```

The procedure Mark marks the item as being selected and draws it in a different colour to indicate to the user that it has been marked:

```
PROCEDURE Mark (I : GCommandLink);
BEGIN
  I^.Marked := TRUE;
  DrawItem (I, HighLightColour);
  AnyMarked := TRUE
END Mark;
```

Double lists in the diagram package

A diagram is a list of shapes, and each shape is a list of GCommands. The list of GCommands is achieved by a linked list, so is the list of shapes. Thus the data structure for the package consists of two lists embedded, as shown in figure 12.3. The Next field of a head or a program is the next shape. Thus as well as there being routines to insert into and delete from a shape, there are also routines for inserting and deleting shapes.

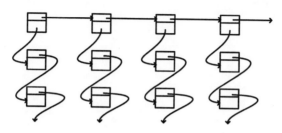

Figure 12.3 Diagram structure

Conclusion

In this chapter the concept of the heap has been introduced as a means of allocating space for data dynamically. Also one data structure for using the heap has been introduced, the one-way linked list. In subsequent chapters other dynamic data structures are introduced.

Exercises

The linked lists given above are used for connecting associated data whose order is irrelevant. Another use for such lists is for sorting data. In this, for example, the first item in the list has the lowest value, the next one has the next lowest value, etc. Thus when an item is to be inserted, the program should scan through the list until the correct position is found and insert the new element there. When searching the list, if the item searched for is less than the current item, there is no point in looking further on in the list, because the list is sorted so that all elements further down the list must be greater than the current one, so the search can stop then.

A collection of data is to be stored in a sorted list. The data should include the name of students and the mark each has been given. The list should be sorted according to marks.

Define suitable data types for a linked-list, and write procedures to:

1) list all students and their marks in the list.

2) search through the list to report any student who has a given mark.

3) add data about another student to the list.

References

1 Niklaus Wirth *Algorithms and Data Structures* Prentice-Hall 1986

2 Niklaus Wirth *Programming in Modula-2* Fourth Edition 1988 Springer-Verlag

13 Help Utility: Stacks and Linked Lists

The help facility provided with the diagram package is quite sophisticated. It is designed to provide an on-line manual, so that the user can find out what to do without having to search through an actual manual, nor should he be given lists and lists of data on the screen. Instead, at a press of a key the user is provided with some useful comments pertinent to his current action.

Therefore the program must keep track of what it is doing, and so be able to provide the appropriate help at any time. Thus at various stages of the program the pertinent help is loaded. When that stage is ended, this help is then removed and the previous state of help returned. This requires a data structure which allows new elements to be added, and subsequently removed: the last one added being the first removed. Thus the data structure needed is a stack.

The actual help data will not be provided in the package itself, but in a normal text file. This allows the file to be updated easily using a standard editor. In the file there are a number of sections of data, each one pertinent to a part of the package. These are tagged suitably so that the program can find the appropriate part when it is required and display it to the user. It is inefficient to scan through the file each time help is needed, so at the start of the program the file is read and the name and start position of each section is noted. Then when help is required, that position is found and the text read. For fast operation the various names are sorted in a linked list structure: it is faster to search through sorted data than unsorted data.

Thus in this chapter, stacks and sorted linked lists are described. Also described is the technique for reading a file from a particular position in the file, not just from the beginning, that is, random access.

13.1 Stacks

A stack is a data structure which allows the user to add items to it and remove items from it, with the one removed being the one at the top of the stack, that is, it is the last one added. This can be achieved with a very simple linked list.

Thus each element in a stack could be defined by the following:

```
StackPointer = POINTER TO Stack;
Stack = RECORD
          ActualData : SuitableType;
             (* what this is depends on the application *)
          NextTop : StackPointer
        END;
```

A stack requires an indication of the top of the stack. This is a pointer to the first element, and hence of type StackPointer. Then pushing an item on to the stack consists of getting the new item to point to the current top of stack, and making the stack pointer point to the new item.

```
PROCEDURE Push (Item : SuitableType);
VAR NewSP : StackPointer;
BEGIN
   ALLOCATE (NewSP, SIZE (NewSP^) );
                               (* get space for top of stack *)
   NewSP^.ActualData := Item;        (* load actual data *)
   NewSP^.NextTop := TopOfStack;     (* set stack pointer *)
   TopOfStack := NewSP
END Push;
```

Removing an item from the top of the stack consists of loading the TopOfStack with the next element of the stack and disposing of the top of the stack:

```
PROCEDURE Pop (VAR Item : SuitableType);
VAR WasSP : StackPointer;
BEGIN
   IF TopOfStack<>NIL THEN
      Item := TopOfStack^.ActualData;
      WasSP := TopOfStack;
      TopOfStack := WasSP^.NextTop;
      DEALLOCATE (WasSP, SIZE (WasSP^) )
   END
END Pop;
```

This is a simple form of linked list, made easy because items are added to and removed from the top of the list.

Note that, in the final implementation of the above, checks are needed to verify, for example, that sufficient space is available from the heap, and suitable action provided if such checks fail.

13.2 Sorted linked lists

A sorted linked list is simply one in which the data in the list are in order. Thus new data are not added at the front or end of the list, but in the correct position to maintain the order. In figure 13.1 a sorted list is shown before and after an insertion. Insertion into the list is relatively complicated and time consuming. However, searching through a sorted list is on average faster than searching a random list, and in the diagram package the list will be searched more than having items added to it.

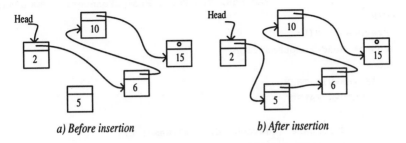

a) Before insertion   *b) After insertion*

Figure 13.1 Insertion into a sorted linked list

In the diagram package, the sorted list is used to store the names of the key words in the help file and the position of the associated data. Thus the data structures used are:

```
CONST PromptMax = 20;

TYPE  PromptName = ARRAY [0..PromptMax] OF CHAR;
      PromptPointer = POINTER TO PromptPosition;
      PromptPosition = RECORD
                          Name : PromptName;
                          FilePos : LONGCARD;
                          Next : PromptPointer
                       END;

VAR HeadPromptPosition : PromptPointer;   (* marks head of list *)
```

The routines to insert into and search the linked list use a common search routine, ListSearch. This searches through the list for the specified name. If the name is found, the procedure returns TRUE and a pointer to the found element is returned. Otherwise FALSE is returned, and two pointers return the address of the element when the search was stopped and the address of the previous element. The latter pointer can then be used to insert items into the list.

The algorithm is simple. The search begins at the start of the list and loops until a result is found. If the end of the list is reached, the search is unsuccessful. Otherwise, if the search name equals the name in the current element, the search is complete. If it is less than the name then the name is not in the list, because the list contains names in order. Otherwise the search continues with the next element. This is another example of multiple RETURNs from a loop/procedure, justifiable because it provides the most direct implementation of the algorithm.

174 Modula-2 Applied

```
    PROCEDURE ListSearch (SearchName : ARRAY OF CHAR;
                          VAR Pos, PrevPos : PromptPointer) : BOOLEAN;
    BEGIN
      PrevPos := NIL;
      Pos := HeadPromptPosition;
      LOOP
        IF Pos=NIL THEN
          RETURN FALSE
        ELSE
          CASE Compare (SearchName, Pos^.Name) OF
            -1 : RETURN FALSE |
             0 : RETURN TRUE |
             1 : PrevPos := Pos;
                 Pos := Pos^.Next
          END
        END
      END
    END ListSearch;
```

For searching, the above is called. If the routine returns TRUE, the data have been found, and are pointed to by Pos.

For inserting, the above routine is also used. If PrevPos is NIL, the new item is added to the start of the list, as for the stack. Otherwise the item is added after the element referenced by PrevPos and before the one pointed to by Pos. If the new data have been stored in memory pointed to by NextPrompt, this is achieved by:

```
    IF NOT ListSearch (NextPrompt^.PromptName, Pos, PrevPos) THEN
      IF PrevPos = NIL THEN
        NextPrompt^.Next := HeadPromptPosition;
        HeadPromptPosition := NextPrompt
      ELSE
        NextPrompt^.Next := Pos;
        PrevPos^.Next := NextPrompt
      END
    END;
```

13.3 The help facility

The initial stage of the help facility is to scan through the help file and remember the positions of each of the sections of help. The start of each section is marked by the character '~' followed by the name of the section. Thus the initial procedure scans through the file and each time a '~' is found, the following string is read and the current file position remembered. These are then added into the sorted linked list of such data. The algorithm is:

```
HeadPromptPosition := NIL;
Open Help File;
WHILE NOT EOF DO
  Get Next Char;
  IF char is '~' THEN
    Read In String;
    Remember Position in File;
    Insert the sting and position into list
  END
END;
Close Help File
```

Determining the position in the file is simple. If the file is described by the file variable HFile, then the TopSpeed routine GetPos (HFile), from the module FIO, returns a LONGCARD with the current file position. This action is encoded in the routine InitHelp.

Help facility in use

At each stage of the program when new help is required, the program calls:

```
PushHelp (Help Category name)
```

In response to this, the help utility searches for the name in the linked list, obtains memory for an item to be put at the top of the stack, initialises the memory and adds it to the stack.

Then, whenever the user requests help, the item from the top of the stack is read, and so the appropriate file position is found. Then the algorithm is:

```
Open help file;
Seek to specified position;
LOOP
  IF End Of File THEN
    EXIT
  ELSIF Next char from file = '~' THEN
    EXIT  (* as is start of next record *)
  ELSE
    display char
  END
END;
Close file
```

176 Modula-2 Applied

Starting to read from the specifed position is achieved by the TopSpeed routine:

```
Seek (HFile, FilePos);
```

When the program has finished its current action, and the current help is inappropriate, PopHelp is called and this removes the help level from the top of the stack.

Another procedure provided empties the help stack. This is called from the main loop to ensure that there have been as many PushHelps as PopHelps, which may have occurred if the user pressed the abort key (see chapter 5). The action of this procedure is simply:

```
WHILE HelpStackPointer<>NIL DO PopHelp END;
```

These routines are contained within a module, Help. Again, the relevant procedures and data types are hidden within the module, so the user does not need to know the mechanisms involved, but only calls the routines InitHelp, PushHelp, PopHelp and EmptyHelp.

Invoking help

The user is able to invoke help at any time by typing control-Q. This is achieved very easily by an addition to the keyboard buffer handling routines of chapter 5. Now procedure CheckKey (which checks if a key has been pressed, and reads it if so, and puts it in the buffer if it is not the abort character) is extended: if the key entered is the abort character, the appropriate longjump occurs, otherwise if it is the help character, the help procedure is called. The character is added to the buffer if it is neither of these. Again, to make this general, the user is able to specify the particular key and the action to be taken. The latter is achieved by telling the buffer routine the name of the procedure to be run if the key is detected. This requires another procedure in the buffer module of chapter 5 which initialises its three associated variables:

```
PROCEDURE HotKey (ch : CHAR; HKeyProc : PROC);
BEGIN
   HotKeySet := ch <> 0C;
   HotKeyChar := ch;
   HotKeyProc := HKeyProc
END HotKey;
```

Then in CheckKey, the following check is made when a key is pressed if the character read is not the abort character:

```
ELSIF HotKeySet AND (ch=HotKeyChar) THEN HotKeyProc
```

Thus if enabled and the appropriate character is entered, the procedure stored in variable HotKeyProc is run. In this case the procedure displays help on the screen.

Help in action

Whenever help is required a new window appears on the screen, and help is displayed in it. At the end, the window disappears and what was on the screen previously is returned. This requires the program to save the previous screen contents in memory before writing the help. The procedure SaveWindow is used. At the end, the RestoreWindow procedure is called.

The help module, like the string edit routine described in chapter 8, is a general utility which can be used with any program. This requires that the utility knows about the device into which the help is displayed. In the diagram package the help is displayed in a window, but this may not be so in other programs. Therefore, in addition to scanning the help file, the InitHelp procedure sets up certain procedure variables which are used by the utility to determine the characteristics of the output device.

The procedures set up include those to position the cursor and determine the cursor position, find the size of the output device and clear the screen. Also there are two procedures to initialise the help and to end it. In this case, the initialisation saves the screen and the end routine redisplays the contents.

The actual display of the help consists of more than just displaying the text. First it ensures that the help fits within the window. Thus each word is read from the file and only displayed on the current line if there is space for it, otherwise the word is shown on the next line. Also when the window is filled, the utility allows the user to read the screen and then hit a key to get the next part, or ESC to abort.

Exercises

1) Write routines to print and delete an item from a sorted linked list.

2) Write routines to push and pop integers on/off a stack.

3) Dijkstra's stacking method for converting normal expressions to reverse Polish takes each item of the original expression in turn, and the items are pushed onto one of two stacks, the result stack and the temporary operator stack. The algorithm is given below and is illustrated in figure 13.2. Implement the algorithm and test it on expressions like

$3 + (4 * 5 + 6) - 8 * 9$

178 Modula-2 Applied

Initial	Op Stack	Result	Comments
3+(4*5+6)-8*9			
+(4*5+6)-8*9		3	Push 3 direct
(4*5+6)-8*9	+	3	Put + on Op
4*5+6)-8*9	+(	3	Put (on Op
*5+6)-8*9	+(	34	
5+6)-8*9	+(*	34	
+6)-8*9	+(*	345	
6)-8*9	+(+	345*	+ displaces *
)-8*9	+(+	345*6	
-8*9	+	345*6+	) empties Op to (
8*9	-	345*6++	
*9	-	345*6++8	
9	-*	345*6++8	
	-*	345*6++89	
		345*6++89*-	Empty Op

Figure 13.2 Conversion to reverse Polish

```
FOR each item from expression DO
   CASE item type OF
     number : Push On to Result Stack |
     operator : WHILE top of Operator Stack <> '(' AND
                Precedence of item from expression <
              that of operator on top Of Operator Stack DO
                 Pop off Operator stack, Push onto Result
              END;
              Push Item On to Operator Stack |
       '(' : Push Item On to Operator Stack |
       ')' : WHILE Operator Stack not empty AND
                  Top Of Operator Stack <> '(' DO
               Pop off Operator Stack, Push onto Result
             END;
             IF Top of operator stack is '(' THEN
                Pop '(' off Operator Stack
             ELSE
                Error ('Mismatch of brackets')
             END
   END
END;
WHILE Operator Stack not empty DO
   IF Top Of Stack ='(' THEN Error ('Bracket mismatch') END;
   Pop off Operator Stack and Push onto result stack
END
```

14 Two-way Linked Lists

The linked lists described in the last two chapters are one-way lists, that is, each item in the list has a means of indicating the position of the next item in the list. This enables the program to move through the list, and there are many applications for such lists. However, it is sometimes required that the program should be able both to go on to the next item in the list, and be able to return to the previous item. This is accomplished using a two-way list.

The application in the diagram package where these are used is in a module which allows the user to select an item from a list. This is a more advanced implementation of the technique given in chapter 6: the user is able to select from a list by moving a cursor up and down through the list. The technique presented here is more general than that given earlier as it is used whenever a selection is made, not just for selecting a command from the main loop.

Once again, the module described here is a general purpose module, written to be used in the diagram package, but equally applicable in other programs. Therefore, as in the case of the string edit module, procedure variables have been used so that the screen is controlled through the appropriate procedures. The module is called SELECTOR.

14.1 Two-way linked lists

A two-way linked list is just like a one-way linked list except that it has an extra element, a link to the previous item in the list, as well as a link to the next item. Thus a record defining an item for a list could be defined as follows:

```
ListPointer = POINTER TO TwoWayList;
TwoWayList  = RECORD
                 Previous, Next : ListPointer;
                 < then any relevant data >
              END;
```

If P is a variable of type ListPointer, which points to an item in the list, moving on to the next one is achieved by:

```
P := P^.Next
```

and moving back to the previous item is:

```
P := P^.Previous
```

180 Modula-2 Applied

In a one-way list, the end of the list is marked by having an item whose Next field has the value NIL. This is also true in a two-way list. In addition, the Previous field of the first item also has a value NIL.

Again, as with one-way lists, another variable points to the first item in the list. In the above, this variable is of type ListPointer.

Insertion into a two-way list

When inserting into a one-way list, the Next pointers need to be adjusted. The process for inserting into a two-way list is similar, except that here both the Previous and Next pointers must be changed. To insert an item, pointed to by PNew, after the element pointed to by P, the code is essentially:

```
Next part of PNew^ := Next part of P^;
Next part of P^ := PNew;
Previous part of PNew^ := P;
Previous part of (Next part of PNew^)^ := PNew;
```

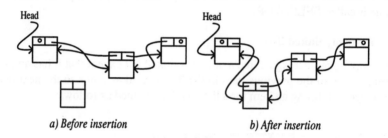

a) Before insertion *b) After insertion*

Figure 14.1 Insertion into a two-way linked list

This is shown in figure 14.1. However, checks are needed when adding at the start or end of a list. Thus the detailed coding is:

```
IF P=NIL THEN   (* adding at start of list *)
  PNew^.Previous := NIL;
  PNew^.Next := HeadOfList;
  HeadOfList := PNew
ELSE
  PNew^.Next := P^.Next;
  P^.Next := PNew;
  PNew^.Previous := P
END;
IF PNew^.Next<>NIL THEN PNew^.Next^.Previous := PNew END
```

Deletion from a two-way list

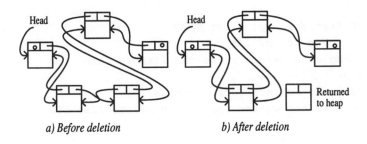

a) Before deletion   *b) After deletion*

Figure 14.2 Deletion from two-way linked list

Removing an item from a list also involves pointer manipulation. The basic algorithm to remove node P^, shown in figure 14.2, is as follows:

```
Next part of (Previous part of P^) := Next part of P^;
Previous part of (Next part of P^) := Previous part of P^
```

Again, checks are needed at the start and end of lists. So the actual code is of the form:

```
IF P^.Previous=NIL THEN
   HeadOfList := P^.Next
ELSE
   P^.Previous^.Next := P^.Next
END;
IF P^.Next<>NIL THEN P^.Next^.Previous := P^.Previous END
```

14.2 The selection application

The SELECTOR module contains routines which allow the user to select an item from a list of items. Routines are provided, therefore, for producing the list, as well as selecting from it. Sometimes the list contains commands which can be in any order, so commands are added to the start of the list. At other times, for example when selecting from a list of file names, it is better for the list to contain sorted data. Here adding into a sorted list is required.

The start of a list needs certain information, including whether it is a sorted list, thus a record is used to define the top of a list. Therefore a routine is provided which creates the top of a list. Then there is a routine for adding another item to the list.

Also there is a routine for deleting a complete list. Finally, of course, there are routines for selecting from a list. Thus the selection process involves:

```
IF list does not exist THEN
  Create top of list;
  Add each selection to the list in turn
END;
Get user to select from option;
IF list not wanted again THEN Delete list END
```

Thus these routines use the heap, to obtain memory for each item in the list, and to return the memory when the list is not required again.

In use, the list is displayed, the current choice is indicated and the user is able to move up and down the list. It is possible that the list will be too large to fit into the window, so the user needs to be able to scroll up and down through the list. Therefore the program needs to know the first item in the list which is actually displayed in the window.

In the diagram package the commands are listed in one column in the window on the right of the screen. However, in the general case it must be possible to have multiple columns from which the user can select an item.

The length of the commands in the list will vary depending on the application, so this is selectable. The variable length is again best achieved by not containing the string in the list, but having a pointer to the memory in which the string is stored.

Data types

The implementation of the technique requires some suitable data structures as well as algorithms for their manipulation. Data structures are needed for both the head of the list and members of the list. The head needs the following information:

The number of elements in the list

The number of the first element to be drawn (called ScreenOffset)

The maximum length of the messages

The current choice in the list

The first item in the list

Whether the list is sorted.

An item in the list needs the following:

A pointer to the string describing the item

The associated character by which the item can be selected (see chapter 6)

The number of the item

Pointers to the previous and next items in the list.

This is best achieved using a variant record:

```
TYPE Select = POINTER TO SelectRecord;
     MessageType = ARRAY [0..80] OF CHAR;
     SelectRecord = RECORD
                        CASE IsHead : BOOLEAN OF
                          FALSE : Message : POINTER TO MessageType;
                                  IdentChar : CHAR;
                                  Number : CARDINAL;
                                  Next,
                                  Prev : Select |
                          TRUE  : NumEntries,
                                  ScreenOffset,
                                  MessageLength : CARDINAL;
                                  CurrentChoice,
                                  FirstItem : Select;
                                  IsSorted : BOOLEAN
                        END
                    END;
```

The items in the record directly implement the requirements given above.

Creating a list

Forming a list consists of setting the head of the list, and then adding items to it. The creation procedure is effectively:

```
  PROCEDURE CreateSelect (VAR Top : Select;
                          sorted : BOOLEAN) : BOOLEAN;
  BEGIN
     IF Able to Get Memory for Top THEN
        Initialise Top^ suitably;
        RETURN TRUE
     ELSE
        RETURN FALSE
     END
  END CreateSelect;
```

Adding an item to the list is achieved by:

```
PROCEDURE AddSelect (Top : Select;
            mess : ARRAY OF CHAR; IdChar : CHAR) : BOOLEAN;
VAR New : Select;
BEGIN
  IF Able to get Memory for New and the Message THEN
    Copy mess into memory;
    initialise New^ suitably;
    adjust Top suitably (e.g. increment NumEntries);
    add New into the list starting at Top;
    RETURN TRUE
  ELSE
    RETURN FALSE
  END
END AddSelect;
```

Where adding New into the list is achieved by:

```
IF Top^.FirstItem=NIL THEN    (* adding first item *)
  Top^.FirstItem := New
ELSIF Top^.IsSorted THEN       (* add into sorted list *)
  add New into list at the appropriate spot
ELSE                           (* add as first item in list *)
  New^.Next := Top^.FirstItem;
  IF New^.Next<>NIL THEN New^.Next^.Prev := New END;
  Top^.FirstItem := New
END;
```

Adding into a sorted list is achieved by:

```
Ptr := Top^.FirstItem;
LOOP
  IF Ptr^.Message^ > new^.Message THEN
    insert New before Ptr;
    EXIT
  ELSIF Ptr^.Next=NIL THEN
    insert new after Ptr;
    EXIT
  ELSE
    Ptr := Ptr^.Next
  END
END
```

Deleting a list consists of deleting each item from the list, so this is easier than deleting a specific item from the list. The routine is:

```
Ptr := Top^.FirstItem;
Deallocate (Top);
WHILE Ptr<>NIL DO
   Deallocate (Ptr^.Message);
   NextPtr := Ptr^.Next;
   Deallocate (Ptr);
   Ptr := NextPtr
END
```

Selection

The selection of items is achieved using a general routine, DoSelect, which displays the items on the screen, and allows the user to move up and down through the list. The general algorithm is as follows:

```
IF list not on screen THEN DrawList END;
LOOP
   CASE ReadChar() OF
      UpArrow     : GoBack (NumberColumns) |
      LeftArrow   : GoBack (1) |
      Home        : GoBack (to top of screen) |
      PgUp        : GoBack (a 'window worths') |
      RightArrow  : GoForward (1) |
      DownArrow   : GoForward (NumberColumns) |
      End         : GoForward (to bottom of screen) |
      PgDn        : GoForward (a 'window worths') |
      Enter       : EXIT
   ELSE
      Search to see if character is an 'identify' char
   END;
   IF NOT KeyPressed() THEN Tidy Up END
END;
Tidy Up
```

'Tidy Up' looks to see if the choice has changed, and if so repositions the cursor on the screen. If any movement has caused the cursor to move on to an item not shown on the screen, then the list must be redrawn so that the cursor position is visible, that is, the ScreenOffset field of the top record should be changed.

186 Modula-2 Applied

Moving backwards or forwards through the list is accomplished by the procedures GoBack and GoForward which are passed the number of moves to make. GoBack is shown below, and GoForward is of the same form:

```
PROCEDURE GoBack (num : CARDINAL);
BEGIN
  WHILE (num>0) AND (CurrentChoice^.Prev<>NIL) DO
    CurrentChoice := CurrentChoice^.Prev;
    DEC (num)
  END
END GoBack;
```

14.3 Selection routines provided

The basic selection routine, DoSelect, is local to the select module and so it is called indirectly. The user program calls the following procedures:

```
PROCEDURE GetSelect (Top : Select) : CHAR;
  DoSelect (Top);
  RETURN Top^.CurrentChoice^.IdentChar;
```

This returns the character associated with the option selected. It is used for selecting a command from one of many.

```
PROCEDURE StringSelect (Top : Select;
                       VAR str : ARRAY OF CHAR);
  DoSelect (Top);
  Copy (str, Top^.CurrentChoice^.Message^)
```

This returns the string selected. It is used, for example, for selecting a file name from a list of names.

These routines require that the list of items from which the selection is made is already set up, by calling CreateSelect once and AddSelect often. However, for ease of use, two other routines are provided which form lists automatically. The first allows a selection from three choices:

```
PROCEDURE ThreeSelect (s1 : ARRAY OF CHAR; c1 : CHAR;
                       s2 : ARRAY OF CHAR; c2 : CHAR;
                       s3 : ARRAY OF CHAR; c3 : CHAR) : CHAR;
```

This forms a list with the three strings, makes the selection and then deletes the selection. If s1 is an empty string, it is not added to the list, so the selection is made from s2 and s3. This is used, for example, when the user chooses the quit option, a double check is made:

```
IF ThreeSelect ('',0C, 'Yes do quit','Y',
                'No do not quit','N') = 'Y' THEN
   EXIT     (* from the main loop of the program *)
END;
```

The other special case allows the selection of a number from a list.

```
PROCEDURE NumberSelect (s : ARRAY OF CHAR;
         min, max : CARDINAL; VAR ans : CARDINAL);
```

A list is formed with the string s followed by each number in turn from min to max, and the user selects from that. This is used for example, to select the current colour, which is in the range 1 to 8:

```
NumberSelect ('Colour ', 1, 8, colour);
```

So the list displayed is Colour 1, Colour 2, etc.

The type Select is another opaque type. It is defined in the definition file by:

```
TYPE Select;
```

and only declared to be a pointer type in the implementation module. The selection module also has a routine for specifying the procedure variables. The procedures required include those for reading and writing characters, positioning the cursor, selecting colours, etc. Thus the module is a self-contained library module which can be used in various programs.

Conclusion

This chapter has presented another useful data structure, the two-way linked list, and described a useful library module containing facilities for selecting commands in a user friendly manner. At this stage of the book, most of the diagram package has been described. The part remaining is that which allows the user to define a shape by a program, and that is the topic of the next five chapters.

Exercises

1) Using the directory routine from chapter 10, write a procedure which forms a two-way linked list full of file names in alphabetical order.

2) Another application of two-way linked lists is for an editor. An editor allows the user to change a file containing lines of code. Each line of code consists of a series of characters. At any time the cursor is positioned on one line. From there the user can insert new characters, delete characters or move the cursor around in the line or to another line. This can be achieved with double linked lists. Each item in the list must contain the actual string and pointers to the previous line and the next line.

Define suitable data types.

Write a routine to insert a new line into the structure and to delete a line.

Write routines to read a text file into such a structure.

Extend the program to allow the user to move up and down through the text.

Using the edit string routine as a basis, modify the above to allow the user to edit a line, and to insert automatically a new line when the current line is full, and delete a line when the user deletes the start of the current line.

15 Editor

This chapter is the first to describe that part of the diagram package which allows the user to specify a shape by a program, rather than using a series of items entered interactively. The processes needed are to enter the program, analyse it and then execute it. The first stage, entering the program, requires an editor, the topic of this chapter.

The editor is another part of the diagram package, and so is used with the windows system. The text being edited is displayed in the main window, where the diagrams are drawn normally. Again, although written for the diagram package, the editor can be used in other programs not requiring the graphics windows. Therefore the editor module is a self-contained library module which makes use of procedure variables. The module is called EDITOR.

15.1 Basic methods

The author has tried four different structures for editors, and believes that the latest is the best. The first method is described in the exercise at the end of the previous chapter. Essentially each line of the file is represented by an element in a two-way linked list. Space is provided for the entire contents of a line in each record.

The advantages of this method include the ease with which lines of text are moved around. A line can be moved from one position to another by just adjusting pointers. Also, movement between lines is easy. The main problem with the method is its inefficient use of memory. Each line requires, say, 80 bytes for the actual data. Often a line is much shorter than that, particularly when writing programs, so there is waste. However, sometimes a line is long, so a limit of only 80 bytes may be a problem. Increasing this number only aggravates the first problem. A better structure is one which automatically handles lines of different length.

The second method tried had two areas of memory, one containing the text before the current position, the other having the rest of the text. These two areas were just array buffers with pointers indexing into them, similar to the keyboard buffer described in chapter 5.

Moving along through the file consisted of transferring the top of the 'after' memory to the 'before' memory, moving backwards being the reverse. Loading into one area was achieved by storing the data at the position indicated by the index pointer and then moving the pointer. Adding an item to the memory was achieved by adding a new character to the 'before' memory. Deleting the current character consisted of removing the top of the 'after' memory.

This simple idea was easy to implement, and again should have been quick to operate, as large amounts of data do not have to be moved when a new character is inserted. However, in practice, a great deal of data shuffling is required. When a new character is added, the VDU screen needs to be updated. If the cursor is on the right of the screen, this may mean that the whole screen needs to be redrawn. This requires moving the cursor to the first character to be displayed, by transferring bytes from the top of the 'before' memory to the 'after' memory, then progressing forwards reading characters from the memory and displaying them on the screen, and then returning to the 'current' cursor position, again by transferring characters. This made the method unacceptably slow.

The third method tried stored the data being edited in a large area of memory, but stored the actual line being edited in a separate area. Thus, when the user moves to a new line, that line is copied from the memory into the buffer, the line is edited (where characters may be added or removed) and then the line is copied back into the memory when the user moves to another line. If the size of the line is increased, the rest of the memory has to be moved forwards to make space for the extra memory; but if it is decreased, the rest of the memory is moved backwards, and then the line is copied back into the memory. However, moving large amounts of data is needed only after a line has been edited, not after the insertion or deletion of each character, so the system ought to be quite quick.

One problem with this method is that redrawing the contents of the screen potentially requires displaying both the current line, which is in the buffer, and displaying other lines, which are in the main memory. Therefore two different display routines are needed, which is inelegant.

The final method chosen, and the one used in the diagram package, was the same as the third except that the current line was not removed from the memory. This means that when any character is inserted, the rest of the memory must be moved down to make space for the new character. However, moving a block can be done very efficiently, so this is not a problem. Usually the editor is used on small programs, so small amounts of data are moved. However, even if a 32000 byte file were being edited, and a character was added to the start of the memory, requiring 32000 bytes to be moved, this would take around 10 ms, which is not a problem.

One restriction for this structure is the maximum size of the buffer. This means that a very large file cannot be edited. For the diagram package this is not really a limitation. It is not envisaged that the user will want to specify a shape by a particularly large program. However, to be more general, the module could be modified to keep some of the buffer in memory and the rest in a file.

15.2 Editor data structure

The main data structure for the editor module is a record holding all the pertinent information for the data being edited. This requires the actual data buffer as well as, for example, the cursor position, whether the data have been displayed, etc. As the allowable size of the data buffer may depend upon the application program, once again the actual buffer is not part of the record, instead there is a pointer to the buffer in the record. The data structures declared are as follows:

The Editor

```
dummyArray = ARRAY [0..MAX(CARDINAL)] OF CHAR;
DataLink = POINTER TO dummyArray;
EditorRec = RECORD
             CsrRow, CsrCol,            (* cursor position *)
             WindowOffset,(* column displayed in first column *)
             FileRows,     (* first row actually displayed *)
             FileLines,    (* number of lines in a file *)
             DataPtr,      (* current position in file *)
             DataEnd : CARDINAL;   (* position of end of file *)
             InsertMode, (* are chars inserted or overwritten *)
             HaveChanged,  (* has a change to data been made *)
             IsOnScreen : BOOLEAN; (* has data been displayed *)
             Name : ARRAY [0..20] OF CHAR;    (* name of data *)
             DataArrayPtr : DataLink;(* points to actual data *)
             DataMax : CARDINAL;       (* size of data buffer *)
           END;
```

The first stage is to initialise a record for the file to be edited. This is achieved by the procedure InitEditorRec which is passed the record to be initialised and the size of the buffer, and which requests sufficient memory from the heap for the buffer, and initialises the rest of the record:

```
PROCEDURE InitEditorRec (VAR ERec : EditorRec;
                         size : CARDINAL) : BOOLEAN;
BEGIN
  IF Available (size) THEN
    ALLOCATE (ERec^.DataArrayPtr, size); (* get buffer memory *)
    < Initialise rest of ERec (e.g. CsrRow := 1, CsrCol := 1) >
    RETURN TRUE
  ELSE
    RETURN FALSE
  END
END InitEditorRec;
```

Then, if an existing file is to be edited, the file is opened and each character in turn is inserted into the array, then the file is closed. One point to note is that, on IBM PCs the end of a line is marked by two characters, return and linefeed. Two characters are not really needed, thus within the array a single character, return, is used to mark the end of a line.

The edit procedure is then called to edit the contents of the array: this is described below. Then the contents can be saved. This requires creating the file, writing each character in turn and closing it. When a return character is found, both it and the corresponding linefeed are written to the file.

192 Modula-2 Applied

Procedure variables

To make the editor also usable in programs other than the diagram package, procedure variables are again used (see chapter 8). The following procedures used by the editor, whose actions are described in chapter 4, are implemented using procedure variables:

```
ReadChar, WriteChar, KeyPressed, GotoXY,
WhereX, WhereY, InsertLine, DeleteLine, ClrScr, ClrEol,
TextColour, TextBackGround.
```

In addition there is a procedure DisplayMode, which sets the mode of where the characters are written. Normally, they are written into the edit window. However, the line above the window is also used (to record the cursor position, the state of 'insert' or 'overwrite' mode, etc). Another area is used for displaying help, and a fourth is used for prompts, like asking for the string to be found. Procedure DisplayMode is used to switch between these modes.

Other variables used specify the size of the window and the colours used for editing, printing messages, etc.

15.3 Edit procedure

The main editor procedure is effectively:

```
IF text not displayed THEN display text END;
Do suitable initialisation;
REPEAT
  Edit the current line;
     (* this edits the line and sets the variable LineMove
        which indicates by how many lines the cursor should
        be moved: if LineMove is 1, then the editor should
        be moved onto the next line; if it is -2, then the
        editor should move back two lines, etc. *)
  IF LineMove>0 THEN
     MoveOn (LineMove)
  ELSIF LineMove<0 THEN
     MoveBack (-LineMove)
  END
UNTIL User has hit ESC
```

The procedure which edits the current line is:

```
IF current line is not displayed THEN
   redraw screen suitably
END;
REPEAT
   Analyse Next Char
UNTIL (User has hit ESC) OR (LineMove<>0)
```

Redrawing the screen suitably is quite involved. If the current line (determined by CsrRow) is just off the top of the screen or off the bottom, it is quicker to use the InsertLine or DeleteLine procedure to scroll the screen and then redraw one line, than to redraw the whole screen. Also to be considered is that the user can have lines so long that they do not fit into the display. So when the position is off the right, the whole screen must be redrawn with the first character of a line that is actually displayed not being the first character of the line: any character at a position less than the value WindowOffset is not drawn. This value is adjusted suitably in the procedure OnScreen.

OnScreen checks that the current position is not to the left or the right of the screen. If the cursor is not on the screen, WindowOffset is adjusted suitably, the whole screen is redrawn and the procedure returns FALSE. If, however, the cursor is on the screen, OnScreen does not redraw the screen, and returns TRUE. The procedure is effectively:

```
IF CsrCol <= WindowOffset THEN    (* if to left of screen *)
   REPEAT
      DEC (WindowOffset, 16)
   UNTIL CsrCol > WindowOffset;
   DrawWholeScreen;
   RETURN FALSE (* screen changed : cursor was offscreen *)
ELSIF CsrCol > WindowOffset+WindowWidth THEN
   REPEAT
      INC (WindowOffset, 16)
   UNTIL CsrCol <= WindowOffset+WindowWidth;
   DrawWholeScreen;
   RETURN FALSE
ELSE
   RETURN TRUE
END
```

Given the WindowOffset, the procedure which draws a line is as shown below. The index DataPos specifies the position in the data array, and when the procedure ends, DataPos is left at the end of the line.

```
Column := 1;
WHILE Data[DataPos] <> Return DO
  IF (Column > WindowOffset)
      AND (Column < WindowOffset+WindowWidth) THEN
    WriteChar (Data[DataPos]);
  END;
  INC (Column);
  INC (DataPos)
END;
```

Thus the start of the edit line procedure is effectively:

```
IF CsrRow just above the screen THEN
  CsrRow := 1;
  IF OnScreen() THEN
    InsertLine (at row 1);
    Draw first line
  END
ELSIF above top of screen THEN
  REPEAT
    INC (CsrRow, WindowLength)
  UNTIL CsrRow on the screen;
  IF OnScreen() THEN DrawWholeScreen END
ELSIF CsrRow on bottom line THEN
  DEC (CsrRow);
  IF OnScreen() THEN
    Delete (row 1);
    Draw bottom line
  END
ELSIF CsrRow below bottom of screen THEN
  REPEAT
    DEC (CsrRow, WindowLength)
  UNTIL CsrRow on the screen;
  IF OnScreen() THEN DrawWholeScreen END
END;
```

The action of the 'Analyse each character' procedure is to read a character and test it. If it is a 'normal' character, then it is inserted into the text. If it is a control character, that is actioned. For example, LeftArrow moves the cursor to the left, which is achieved by decrementing CsrCol, UpArrow moves up to the previous line, so LineMove is set to -1; Delete will delete the character at the cursor position, etc.

Inserting a character is done by a procedure which inserts a string of characters. Normally this is a string of length one. However, when tab is input, this is converted to a series of spaces, so a longer string is inserted, and this is handled automatically by the same procedure. Also, when a string is replaced by a longer string, this requires inserting a string of characters. The Insert routine is effectively:

```
IF InsertMode THEN
   Insert Space into the data buffer for the string
ELSIF String exceeds current line THEN
   Insert Space for extra characters in line
END;
Copy String into memory;
Move Cursor to end of string;
IF OnScreen() THEN Redraw changed part of the line END
```

Inserting a 'return' is more complicated: again this involves adding a string, with the return character as the last element in the string.

```
Make space for string;
Copy string into memory;
INC (FileLines);    (* increment number of lines in file *)
CsrCol := 1;    (* move cursor to the start of the line *)
LineMove := 1;              (* set to move to next line *)
IF OnScreen() THEN Redraw rest of screen END
```

For deletion there are three procedures, delete backwards (for removing the previous character), delete forwards (for removing the character at the cursor position) and deleting a return. The procedure DeleteBackwards is:

```
IF not at start of line THEN
   go back one place;
   DeleteForwards
ELSIF not at start of file THEN
   go back to end of previous line;
   DeleteForwards
END
```

Procedure DeleteForwards is:

```
IF at end of line THEN
  Delete End Of Line
ELSE
  Remove character from memory;
  IF OnScreen() THEN redraw rest of line END
END
```

and the procedure to delete the end of the line is:

```
IF NOT at end of file THEN
  Remove return character from memory;
  DEC (FileLines);
  IF OnScreen() THEN redraw rest of the screen END
END
```

In fact the part of the DeleteBackwards procedure which says 'go back to end of previous line' and 'delete forwards' is achieved by setting LineMove to -1, so as to go back to the previous line, and a variable called AutoChar is given the DeleteForwards character: normally AutoChar has value 0C. Thus the program leaves the routine which handles the current line, and then returns to it working on the previous line. This checks that the cursor is on the screen, and then processes the next character. Normally AutoChar has value 0C, so the next character is read from the keyboard. However, in this case AutoChar has a different value, so its value is taken as the next character instead of reading the keyboard. AutoChar has the DeleteForwards character, so the routine to DeleteForwards is called.

AutoChar is also used in the Find and Replace routines. When the program has searched the file to find the next occurrence of the search string, it must ensure that the line in which the string is found is displayed suitably. So when the 'analyse next character' routine is called, it is suitably diverted at the start if AutoChar is set to 'Find'. The start of the 'analyse next character' routine is:

```
IF (AutoChar=Find) AND SearchGoesOn() THEN RETURN END;
  (* SearchGoesOn returns true if after processing the
     string found, the search should continue to the next
     position on a new line *)
IF AutoChar<>0C THEN
  EditChar := AutoChar;
  AutoChar := 0C
ELSE
  EditChar := ReadChar()
END;
(* Then EditChar is analysed *)
```

The SearchGoesOn procedure is:

```
IF found the search string THEN
   IF (find and replace) AND (should replace) THEN
      Replace string
   END;
   IF user presses ESC THEN (* to abort find and replace *)
     AutoChar := 0C;
     RETURN FALSE
   ELSE
     RETURN TRUE
   END
ELSIF Search successfully for next occurrence of string THEN
   Set LineMove suitably;
   RETURN TRUE
ELSE
   Print that cannot find string;
   AutoChar := 0C;
   RETURN FALSE
END;
```

The above description should provide enough information to allow the user to follow the actual procedures in the EDITOR module.

The editor routines allow the user to enter a program describing a shape. The next stage is to analyse the program, to verify that it is correct, and to then obey the program so as to draw the shape. These topics are described in the next few chapters.

16 Lexical Analysis

After the user has entered a program which describes a shape, that program must be analysed to check that it is syntactically correct, before being executed. The first stage in the analysis is to divide the program into separate items, like numbers, words, operators, etc. This process is called lexical analysis, and is the main topic of this chapter. See also Bornat[1].

When an item is identified, it must be classified as being a number, operator, reserved word, or a user defined word. Therefore a means is required by which the type of any string of characters is determined. This should be achieved by storing such words and their types in a suitable structure which the program can search. A structure which can be searched rapidly is required. One technique, hashing, is given here. Another, trees, is given in the next chapter.

16.1 Separation of items

The main part of a lexical analyser returns the next item from the program. This should skip spaces, ends of lines and comments, and then identify the next item. In the diagram package, the analyser is processing a program stored in an array of characters (the buffer in the EditorRec, described in the previous chapter), and so it indexes into the array. A global variable, LexPointer, is used as the index. This is initially set to point to the start of the array, and is then moved on through the array by the lexical analyser, when the next item is to be found. Another variable, LexRows, indicates which row in the program is currently being analysed.

The first stage of the algorithm to find the next item is to skip spaces, etc. This moves LexPointer so that it addresses the next element. The algorithm is:

```
InComment := FALSE;
LOOP
  IF LexPointer at end of program THEN RETURN FALSE END;
    (* return 'no next item' as at end of file *)
  ch := Data [LexPointer];
  IF ch=' ' THEN
    INC (LexPointer)      (* move past a space *)
  ELSIF ch=Return THEN
    INC (LexPointer);     (* move past a return *)
    INC (LexRows)         (* keep count of which row in file *)
  ELSIF ch=CommentChar THEN  (* comments enclosed in #s *)
    InComment := NOT InComment;
    INC (LexPointer)
  ELSIF InComment THEN
    INC (LexPointer)      (* inside comment, so skip char *)
```

```
    ELSE
        EXIT
    END
END;
```

The variable ch now contains the first character of the item. This is a letter if the item is a name, a digit if the item is a number, a quote if it is a string and any other character is probably an operator. So the next stage is:

```
IF IsLetter (ch) THEN
   AnalyseName
ELSIF IsDigit (ch) THEN
   AnalyseNumber
ELSIF (ch="'") OR (ch='"') THEN
   AnalyseString
ELSE
   AnalyseOperator
END;
```

When an item is found, pertinent information about that item must be stored, usually in a record. In many analysers, the item is stored in the record. However, this can impose limits as to the length of an item, and many compilers restrict the number of significant letters of identifiers. In the diagram package there are no such restrictions. As the program being analysed is stored in an array in memory, the record is given the start position of the item, its length and, of course, its classification. Therefore the routine to analyse a name must determine the start position and the length of the name, and similarly for numbers, strings, etc.

A name is a series of characters, starting with a letter and followed by a series of letters or digits. Examples include FRED, Item15, ReadChar, etc. Analysing a name consists of the following:

```
Store start position of name in the record;
REPEAT
   INC (LexPointer);
UNTIL Data[LexPointer] is not a letter or a digit;
Remember length of name;
Classify name   (* how this is done is described later *)
```

A number is slightly more complicated. The diagram package operates on floating point numbers, which can come in various forms. Examples are:

    1   13.89   0.56   1.67E-3   156E+7

Thus a number can have a series of digits, one dot, one E, and a + or a -, but only immediately after an E. This can be tested using a series of booleans indicating if the last character was an E, whether an E has been found and if a dot has been found. Note that -1.5 is treated as the unary operator '-' followed by a separate number 1.5. The routine to analyse a number is:

```
GotDot := FALSE;
LastWasE := FALSE;
GotE := FALSE;
Remember start position;
REPEAT
  INC (LexPointer)
UNTIL Data[LexPointer] is not a valid number character;
Classify as number
```

Checking that a character is a valid number is as follows:

```
CASE Data[LexPointer] OF
       '.' : IF GotDot OR GotE THEN
                 RETURN FALSE
             ELSE
                 LastWasE := FALSE;GotDot := TRUE;RETURN TRUE
             END |
       'E' : IF GotE THEN
                 RETURN FALSE
             ELSE
                 LastWasE := TRUE; GotE := TRUE; RETURN TRUE
             END |
    '+', '-' : IF LastWasE THEN
                 LastWasE := FALSE; RETURN TRUE
               ELSE
                 RETURN FALSE
               END |
     '0'..'9' : LastWasE := FALSE; RETURN TRUE
       ELSE    RETURN FALSE
END
```

A string is a series of characters enclosed by two " or two '. This is analysed by a routine which is passed the start string character. Its action is to scan the array until the corresponding end of string character is found. Strings cannot overflow from one line to another, so a suitable check is needed. The procedure is:

```
Remember start position;
LOOP
  INC (LexPointer)
  IF Data[LexPointer] = start string character THEN
     EXIT
  ELSIF Data[LexPointer]=end of line THEN
     Report Error ('String exceeds end of line');
     RETURN FALSE
  END
END;
Store end position of string;
Classify as string
```

Processing an operator is again quite simple. Operators are either single characters, like + or - or > or =, or double characters like >= or <>. The analyser must identify these and classify them. In the diagram package an operator type is:

```
OperatorType =
       (plus, minus, times, divide, and, or, equals,
        notequals, less, lessequals, more, morequals,
        assign, comma, colon, leftroundbrac,
        rightroundbrac, leftsquarebrac, rightsquarebrac,
        unaryminus, unaryplus, not);
```

These require little comment. 'assign' is the assignment operator :=. The last three are unary operators, that is, they act on one value, whereas a binary operator operates on two values. Thus the minus in -3 is unary, though the minus in 4-3 is a binary operator. Determining whether a + or - is a unary or binary operator is achieved by remembering the last item identified. Consider the following:

$$-3 - 4 \qquad 4 + -3 \qquad 2 * (-3 + 5) - 6$$

From these it can be seen that a + or - is a unary operator if it is the first item in the expression or the previous item was an operator, including an opening bracket, but not if it was a closing bracket.

The lexical analyser uses a boolean variable, CouldBeUnary, which is set true at the start of an expression, and set suitably after each item has been analysed, to determine if the next + or - is unary or binary.

An operator must be classified as to its type and given a precedence value. As explained in the section on reverse Polish notation in chapter 11, the precedence of an operator is the degree to which an operator binds with other items, and so determines the order in which the expression is evaluated. For example, the expression 3 + 4 * 5 is evaluated as the sum of 3 and the product of 4 and 5 because

202 Modula-2 Applied

* has a higher precedence value than +. Brackets have the highest precedence value, then unary operators, then the binary operators.

The processing of operators is achieved by one large CASE statement acting on the current character. It calls the procedure GetOperator which classifies the item as an operator, and is passed the operator type, its precedence value and the number of characters which form the operator. The operator identification is achieved by:

```
CASE Data [LexPointer] OF
   '+' : IF CouldBeUnary THEN
            GetOperator (unaryplus, 10, 1)
         ELSE
            GetOperator (plus, 7, 1)
         END |
   '-' : IF CouldBeUnary THEN
            GetOperator (unaryminus, 10, 1)
         ELSE
            GetOperator (minus, 7, 1)
         END |
   '*' : GetOperator (times, 8, 1) |
   '/' : GetOperator (divide, 8, 1) |
   '&' : GetOperator (and, 5, 1) |
   '!' : GetOperator (or, 4, 1) |
   '~' : GetOperator (not, 10, 1) |
   ':' : IF Data[LexPointer+1]='=' THEN
            GetOperator (assign, 1, 2)
         ELSE
            GetOperator (colon, 3, 1)
         END |
   ',' : GetOperator (comma, 2, 1)
   '=' : GetOperator (equals, 6, 1) |
   '<' : IF Data[LexPointer+1]='='THEN
            GetOperator (lessequals, 6, 2)
         ELSIF Data[LexPointer+1]='' THEN
            GetOperator (notequals, 6, 2)
         ELSE
            GetOperator (less, 6, 1)
         END |
   '>' : IF Data[LexPointer+1]='=' THEN
            GetOperator (moreequals, 6, 2)
         ELSE
            GetOperator (more, 6, 1)
         END |
```

```
'(' : GetOperator (leftroundbrac, 20, 1) |
')' : GetOperator (rightroundbrac, 20, 1) |
'[' : GetOperator (leftsquarebrac, 20, 1) |
']' : GetOperator (rightsquarebrac, 20, 1)
END
```

GetOperator sets the operator type and precedence, moves LexPointer on, and sets CouldBeUnary appropriately. Its action is effectively:

```
Remember Start Position;
INC (LexPointer, LengthOfOperator);
Store end position;
Classify as Operator;
Store OperatorType and Precedence;
CouldBeUnary := (OperatorType <> rightroundbrac) AND
                (OperatorType <> rightsquarebrac)
```

The routines which handle numbers and names also set CouldBeUnary suitably.

16.2 Identification of names

The above procedures separate items into numbers, operators and names. Names need further processing: is a name a user defined name, or is it a special name? For example, IF, LOOP, etc. are reserved control words in the programming language, and LINE or SIN are reserved procedures. Also user names might be the name of a procedure or a variable: their type must be stored also. Thus once a name has been found it must be classified. Reserved words could be processed by code like:

```
IF name='IF' THEN
    say name is the control word IF
ELSIF name='THEN' THEN
    etc.
```

However, this would be slow and inefficient, and it does not allow the processing of names introduced by the user.

Therefore a data structure is needed in which the reserved names are stored, with other data defining the type of name, and into which user defined names can be added as they are identified. Then the classification of a name consists of searching the structure for the appropriate name and hence finding its type. This can be achieved in various ways, but should be made efficient.

One method is to use linked lists. To speed up the search the list should contain sorted data, so that the whole list does not need to be examined in order to determine that a name is not in the list. Thus the routines described in earlier chapters for searching and adding to sorted lists can be used.

However, when a large number of items are added, the list will grow long, and so searching can be slow. Thus linked lists are rarely used. Two alternatives to linked lists will be discussed: trees and hashing. Trees are described in the next chapter, as they can be used in various applications and come in many forms. Hashing is given here: see also Wirth[2].

16.3 Hashing

The basic idea of hashing (or key transformation) is to perform a suitable operation on the data to yield a number which determines where the data are stored. Thus if a DataRec is a record containing all the pertinent information on a data item (in the diagram package this would be the name and whether it was a reserved word or user defined, etc.), hashing could be achieved by defining an array

```
HashArray = ARRAY [0..HashMax] OF DataRec;
```

And a new item of data would be stored in the array at position:

```
HashArray [ HashCalc (data) ];
```

where HashCalc processes the DataRec to return a value between 0 and HashMax.

If a DataRec contains a string, name, a simple HashCalc procedure is one which sums each character in the string and returns that number MOD HashMax+1.

```
PROCEDURE HashCalc (data : DataRec) : CARDINAL;
VAR ans, ct : CARDINAL;
BEGIN
  ans := 0;
  FOR ct := 0 TO Length (data.name)-1 DO
    ans := ans + ORD (data.name[ct])
  END;
  RETURN ans MOD (HashMax+1)
END HashCalc;
```

In many ways this idea is good. There is a slight problem that the data stored in the hashing array are unsorted. However, this is only a problem if a sorted list of names in the array is required. Many assemblers and compilers produce such lists. Another problem is that a large array is always required, which can be wasteful.

The main problem, though, is that of collisions. Two different strings processed by HashCalc may return the same number. Making HashMax a large prime number helps to reduce the problem, but is not foolproof.

Various methods are suggested for handling collisions. One method is to perform the hashing calculation as normal, but when a collision is detected (the element in the array has already been used), to search neighbouring elements in the array until an empty position is found. There are various problems with this, including the ultimate problem that the array may become full.

A better method is to have some means whereby many elements can be effectively found at the same point. This can be achieved by making each element in the hashing array the start of a linked list of data. Thus searching for an element consists of performing the hashing calculation, and then looking in the associated linked list for the data. If the array is quite large, and a good hashing calculation is used, these lists should be short and so the search will be rapid.

For this method, the hashing array is defined by

```
Link = POINTER TO DataRec;
HashArray = ARRAY [0..HashMax] OF Link
```

Initially each element in HashArray is set to NIL. Then searching for an element consists of searching in the linked list whose head is:

```
HashArray [ HashCalc (data) ]
```

And the routines for handling linked lists, given earlier, can be used.

Hashing is quite a good method of handling data. However, the author prefers tree structures because, for example, they can be analysed elegantly, so the diagram package uses trees not hashing.

Conclusion

This chapter has described the first stage in the analysis of a program, the lexical analysis whereby each item of the program is determined separately and classified. One method of rapid searching of names from a data structure is given, hashing. An alternative method, using trees, is given in the next chapter.

References

1 Richard Bornat *Understanding and Writing Compilers* Macmillan Education 1979

2 Niklaus Wirth *Algorithms and Data Structures* Prentice-Hall 1986

17 Trees

When the lexical analyser has found an identifier, it needs to decide what that identifier represents; is it a reserved word, an operator, a user defined symbol, etc? This can be done, as illustrated in the last chapter, using the hashing technique. An alternative method is to use a binary tree, and this is the topic of this chapter. Trees can be used for representing various data, and so are applicable in many programs. The structure is neat and elegant, as are the routines for manipulating trees.

17.1 Linked lists and trees

A linked list is a sequential list of data. To search for an item in the list, the list is scanned from the start until the item is found, or it is decided that the item is not in the list. This can take a long time if the list is long. An analogous problem is when the data are stored in an array. The sequential search of an array is as follows:

```
PROCEDURE Search (First,Last:CARDINAL;VAR Index:CARDINAL):BOOLEAN;
BEGIN
   Index := First;
   WHILE (Index<=Last) AND (Array[Index]<>SearchData) DO
     INC (Index)
   END;
   RETURN Index<=Last    (* true if found data *)
END Search;
```

However, if the data in the array are in order, the binary search method is better. Here the middle element is tested: if this is the required data the search stops; if this is greater than the required data, then the data cannot be further in the list, so the search continues in the first half; otherwise the second half is searched. Thus:

```
PROCEDURE Search (First,Last:CARDINAL;VAR Index:CARDINAL):BOOLEAN;
BEGIN
   IF First>Last THEN RETURN FALSE END;          (* data not there *)
   Index := (First + Last) DIV 2;                (* find middle position *)
   IF Array[Index]=SearchData THEN
     RETURN TRUE
   ELSIF Array[Index]>SearchData THEN
     RETURN Search (First, Index-1, Index) (* look in first half *)
   ELSE
     RETURN Search (Index+1, Last, Index) (* look in second half *)
   END
END Search;
```

This is illustrated in figure 17.1.

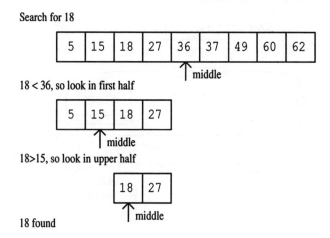

Figure 17.1 Binary search of an array

A binary tree structure is an attempt to arrange the data so that a binary-type search can be used, as opposed to the sequential structure provided by linked lists.

17.2 Tree structures

A one-way linked list can be represented by data structures of the form:

```
ListPointer = POINTER TO ListElement;
ListElement = RECORD
                <appropriate data>
                Next : ListPointer
              END;
```

For the last element, the Next field is NIL, and there is a pointer which references the first element in the list.

A binary tree structure is similar, except that there are two pointers, one referencing an item which contains data less than the current element, and one referencing an element whose data are greater. The data structures are in the form:

```
TreePointer = POINTER TO TreeElement;
TreeElement = RECORD
                <appropriate data>
                Less, More : TreePointer
              END;
```

208 Modula-2 Applied

Again, the ends of a tree are indicated by pointers whose value is NIL, and another pointer references the first element in the tree.

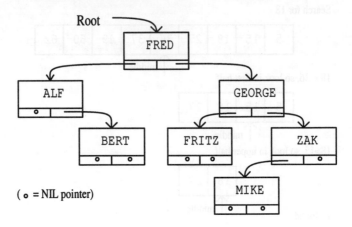

(o = NIL pointer)

Figure 17.2 A tree structure

For any element in the tree, all data found by following the path pointed to by Less will have data less than the element, whereas all data found in the 'more path' will be greater than the current element. An example of such a tree is shown in figure 17.2. Given this arrangement of data, a binary-type search can be adopted. So an algorithm to search the tree is one which examines the element in the tree referenced by a pointer P, and decides on a suitable action. The following routine returns a pointer to the element containing the data being searched for, or NIL if the data are not in the tree:

```
PROCEDURE Search (P : TreePointer;
                  SearchData : DataType) : TreePointer;
BEGIN
   IF P=NIL THEN
      RETURN NIL
   ELSIF SearchData = P^.Data THEN
      RETURN P
   ELSIF SearchData < P^.Data THEN
      RETURN Search (P^.Less, SearchData)
   ELSE
      RETURN Search (P^.More, SearchData)
   END
END Search;
```

If the top of the tree is referenced by a pointer TreeTop, the above is called by:

```
NodeFound := Search (TreeTop, Data);
```

To illustrate this procedure consider the search for FRITZ in figure 17.2. The first call to Search acts on the top of the tree, and compares FRED with FRITZ. As FRITZ is greater than FRED, if FRITZ is in the tree it will be in that part of the tree referenced by the More pointer of the FRED node. Thus the GEORGE node is searched next. As FRITZ is less than GEORGE, the item pointed to by the Less pointer is searched next. There FRITZ is found, so the search is complete.

A search for ABIGAIL would be unsuccessful: ABIGAIL is less than FRED, so the node referenced by the Less element of FRED, the one containing ALF, is examined next. ABIGAIL is less than ALF, the Less pointer is used again. This is NIL, so the search routine will return NIL.

Note that initially the tree may contain no data, so TreeTop will have a value NIL. This will create no problem in the above, as the first test made is to check if the pointer has the value NIL.

The definition of a tree is recursive (an element in the tree references other such elements), therefore it is not suprising that the search routine above is recursive, as are most routines which access trees.

A routine to list all elements in the tree in order is another example of a recursive tree routine (in fact it is an INORDER recursive routine, as opposed to PREORDER or POSTORDER (see next chapter)). As all elements found by searching the tree on the path pointed to by Less have values less than the current element, these should be printed first. All items referenced by More have values greater than the current element, so the current element should be printed next, and then all the rest (which have greater values). Hence the routine is:

```
PROCEDURE Print (P : TreePointer);
BEGIN
  IF P<>NIL THEN
    Print (P^.Less);    (* print all data less than current *)
    < Print the data associated with P^ >
    Print (P^.More)     (* print all data more than current *)
  END
END Print;
```

and is first called by

```
Print (TreeTop)
```

These routines illustrate the comment given at the start of the chapter that tree structures are neat and elegant, as are the routines which process trees. In the next sections some more elegant routines are given.

Insertion into trees

Insertion in a tree is an extension of the search routine, and is achieved by adding a new element to the bottom of the tree at the appropriate position. ABIGAIL is added to the tree of figure 17.2 by getting suitable memory from the heap and then the Less pointer of node ALF is changed from NIL to point to this memory. Similarly, to add NATALIE to the tree, the More pointer of the node with data MIKE should be changed from NIL to point to the memory containing NATALIE.

```
    PROCEDURE Insert (VAR P : TreePointer;
                      NewData : DataType) : TreePointer;
    BEGIN
      IF P = NIL THEN
        IF Available (SIZE (P^) THEN
          ALLOCATE (P, SIZE (P^));
    (* this changes P from NIL to point to the new memory *)
          <Initialise P^ suitably, incl. Less := NIL; More := NIL >
          RETURN P
        ELSE
          RETURN NIL
        END
      ELSIF NewData = P^.Data THEN
        RETURN P     (* data already in tree at P, so return P *)
      ELSIF NewData < P^.Data THEN
        RETURN Insert (P^.Less, NewData)
      ELSE
        RETURN Insert (P^.More, NewData)
      END
    END Insert;
```

The above inserts NewData into the tree, returning a pointer to the place where the data are put (if the data are already there, a new node is not added into the tree, instead the procedure returns a pointer to the found data). The routine is called by:

```
    NewPointer := Insert (TreeTop, Data);
```

The pointer P is passed as a variable pointer, which is important because P may be changed. If P is NIL, the algorithm has found the place where the new data should be added, so P is changed to point to the new memory. For an empty tree, TreeTop is NIL, so the first call to Insert will change TreeTop to point to memory where the data are stored. Similarly for the recursive call Insert (P^.Less, NewData), when P^.Less is NIL, the pointer P^.Less is changed from NIL to point to the new data.

Deletion from a tree

In general, deleting a node from a tree is more complicated, although for some cases it is easy. If the node to be removed is at the bottom of the tree, it is easy to delete. For example, with reference to figure 17.2, if the node with MIKE in it is removed, the Less pointer of the ZAK node should be changed from pointing to MIKE to having the value NIL; then the node MIKE should be deallocated. Similarly, removing a node for which either its Less or More pointers has the value NIL is easy as it is effectively deleting from a linked list. For example, to delete ZAK, the More pointer of GEORGE should be replaced with the Less pointer of ZAK, and then ZAK deallocated (see figure 17.3a). Note that, deleting a node from the bottom of the tree is a special case of deleting a node for which either Less or More is NIL; that is, it is like removing an entry from the end of a linked list.

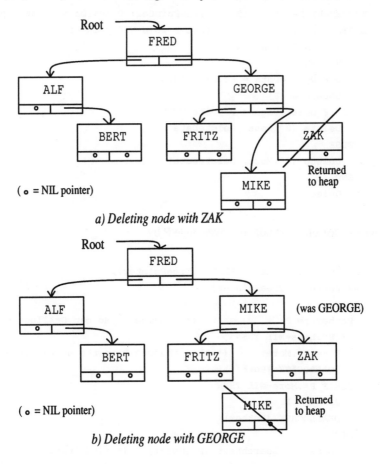

Figure 17.3 Deletion from a tree structure

However, to remove a node which has both its Less and More pointers referencing other nodes is more complicated. The basic technique is to replace the data contents of the node being deleted with data from a node whose Less or More pointer has the value NIL, and then delete this other node. This second node should be the one which comes immediately before or after the node to be deleted if the tree were printed in order. For example, if GEORGE were to be deleted, the node which comes after GEORGE is MIKE, so the name GEORGE should be replaced with MIKE, and the node with MIKE in it should be deleted. This is shown in figure 17.3b. Finding MIKE is achieved by searching the More tree of GEORGE, always following the Less path, until a node is found whose Less pointer is NIL.

A procedure to delete the specified data is as follows:

```
PROCEDURE Delete (VAR P : TreePointer; DeleteData : DataType);
BEGIN         (* again note that P is a VAR pointer *)
  IF P = NIL THEN
    RETURN
  ELSIF DeleteData = P^.Data THEN
    DoDelete (P)
  ELSIF DeleteData < P^.Data THEN
    Delete (P^.Less, DeleteData)
  ELSE
    Delete (P^.More, DeleteData)
  END
END Delete;
```

where DoDelete actually removes node P by:

```
PROCEDURE DoDelete (VAR P : TreePointer);
VAR Pother : TreePointer;
BEGIN
  Pother := P;              (* remember P so can DeAllocate *)
  IF P^.Less=NIL THEN
    P := P^.More;     (* this changes P in the actual tree *)
    DEALLOCATE (Pother)
  ELSIF P^.More=NIL THEN
    P := P^.Less;
    DEALLOCATE (Pother)
  ELSE
    Pother := SearchNext (P^.More);   (* find 'next' node *)
    P^.Data := Pother^.Data;          (* copy its data *)
    DoDelete (Pother)                 (* delete the 'next' node *)
  END
END DoDelete;
```

and SearchNext finds a node whose Less pointer is NIL by:

```
PROCEDURE SearchNext (P : TreePointer) : TreePointer;
BEGIN
  IF P^.Less=NIL THEN
    RETURN P
  ELSE
    RETURN SearchNext (P^.Less)
  END
END SearchNext;
```

In action, to delete ZAK from the tree in figure 17.2, Delete calls itself recursively until the node with ZAK is found, and then DoDelete is called having been passed the pointer to ZAK, that is the More pointer of GEORGE. The More pointer of ZAK is NIL, so DoDelete replaces the More pointer of GEORGE with the Less pointer of ZAK.

To delete GEORGE from figure 17.2, Delete calls itself recursively until the node with GEORGE in it is found. Then DoDelete is called being passed the More pointer of FRED. As both pointers of GEORGE are not NIL, SearchNext is called looking for a node whose Less pointer is NIL. First the node pointed to by ZAK is examined: its Less pointer is not NIL, so the search continues on the node MIKE, whose Less pointer is NIL, so this is the node returned to DoDelete. The data contents of GEORGE (not its pointers) are replaced by those of MIKE, and then the MIKE node is deleted by DoDelete (which is easy as its Less and More pointers are NIL).

17.3 Balanced trees

When trees were introduced in this chapter, the comparison was made between a linear search and a binary search of an array, and the linear search of a linked list and the binary search of a tree. This comparison is strictly valid only when the number of nodes in the 'less' part of a tree differs from that in the 'more' part by at most one, that is, the tree is balanced. If this is the case, then a comparison at one node will allow the program to decide that half of the data can be ignored, as is the case of a binary search of an array. This requirement is true for every node in the tree.

If the elements in figure 17.2 were added in the order ALF, BERT, FRED, FRITZ, GEORGE, MIKE and ZAK, the tree would be a linear list, as shown in figure 17.4. Thus the advantages of a tree over a list would be lost.

However, ensuring that a tree is perfectly balanced is a complicated process. Each time a new element is added, potentially every node in the tree must be examined and/or modified to ensure that the tree remains balanced. The program may then spend much of its time balancing a tree.

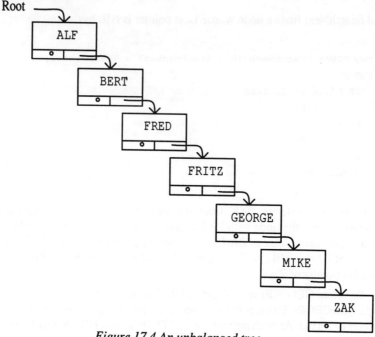

Figure 17.4 An unbalanced tree

An alternative is the redefinition of a balanced tree proposed by Adelson-Velskii and Landis[2] (see also Wirth [1]). They defined that an AVL tree is balanced if for every node in the tree, the height of its Less subtree differs from the height of its More subtree by at most one.

This seems a reasonable criterion, as the height of the tree determines the maximum number of comparisons needed in a search. So when each node is analysed, about half the maximum number of comparisons can be obviated.

The tree in figure 17.2 is not perfectly balanced as there are 2 nodes in the Less subtree of FRED and 4 in its More subtree. However it is AVL balanced; for example, the height of the Less tree of FRED is 2 and that of its More tree is 3. Similarly, all other nodes are also AVL balanced.

Maintaining an AVL balanced tree is also easy. Each time a new node is added, at maximum only one node on the tree may need rebalancing, and often no extra rebalancing is required. This is shown in Wirth[1] and is borne out by a few examples.

If ZEBERDEE were added to the tree of figure 17.2, it would be added to the More part of ZAK. In this case the tree is now more balanced, as the difference in height at node ZAK is changed from 1 to 0.

If however NATALIE were added, she would be added to the More side of MIKE, so the difference in height at node ZAK would be 2. This would require rebalancing. Rebalancing consists of shifting pointers, and the resultant tree is shown in figure 17.5. Note that only nodes ZAK, MIKE and NATALIE have been changed, so only one balancing action is required.

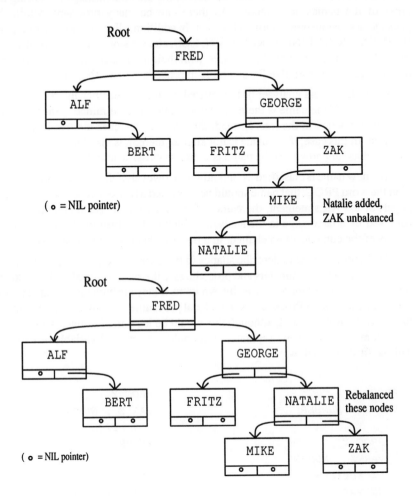

Figure 17.5 Keeping a tree AVL balanced

Maintaining a balanced tree is only worthwhile if speed is essential, and that data are added to the tree very much less often than the tree is searched. This is because maintaining balanced trees requires processing every time data are added to the tree, and so slows the insertion process. This time is only saved if the search through trees is made faster as a result of the balanced tree. Routines for maintaining balanced trees when data are inserted into and deleted from a tree are left to the reader as exercise: more information is given in Wirth[1].

17.4 Trees in the diagram package

Trees are used in the program analyser part of the diagram package for storing the types of the names encountered. As there can be many programs within the package, a separate tree is formed for each. In addition, all the reserved words, like IF, THEN, PROC, LINE, CIRCLE, SIN, COS, etc. are stored in a 'reserved word' tree. These names are stored in the tree with their associated data types (whether they are a control word like IF, or a built-in procedure like LINE or SIN).

When the lexical analyser has identified a name, it searches the reserved tree for the name. If the name is there, its classification is determined. Otherwise, the name is not added to the tree. Instead, the analyser searches the tree local to the program. In this case, if the name is not already there, it is inserted in this tree and classified as 'unknown'. If the name is there, its classification is determined.

Any new name is classified as 'unknown'. However, if the name occurs directly after the word PROC, that name should be classified as a procedure, and if the name is part of a VAR statement, the name refers to a variable. Such classification is achieved by a later stage in the analysis, which is described in chapter 19. More details of the contents of an element in a tree are also given in chapter 19.

The language used to describe shapes in the package defines that the scope of names of variables, parameters and procedures is the same as for Modula-2, except that the same name cannot be used by two items if they are both visisble at the same time. For example, if Procedure X has a local procedure Y, both procedures cannot have a variable of name Z, although this would be legal in Modula-2. However, if Procedures X and Y were separate, both could have a local variable of name Z. This is illustrated below:

```
PROC X                              PROC X
VAR Z : NUMBER                      VAR Z : NUMBER
                                      <action>
  PROC Y                            ENDPROC
  VAR Z : NUMBER
    <action>                        PROC Y
  ENDPROC                           VAR Z : NUMBER
                                      <action>
  <action>                          ENDPROC
ENDPROC
     illegal                                legal
```

This is achieved in the diagram package, by storing with each name a boolean to indicate if it is still 'visible'. When the tree is searched, using routines similar to those given above, if a name is marked invisible the search routine ignores the node and carries on searching.

```
PROCEDURE Search (VAR P:TreePointer; Data:DataRec) : TreePointer;
BEGIN
  IF P=NIL THEN
    InsertNewData (P);
    RETURN P
  ELSIF Data < P^.Data THEN
    RETURN Search (P^.Less, Data)
  ELSIF Data > P^.Data THEN
    RETURN Search (P^.More, Data)
  ELSIF NOT P^.Visible THEN
    RETURN Search (P^.More, Data);
  ELSE
    RETURN P
  END
END Search;
```

When a name is added, it is visible. However, when the end of a procedure is found, the tree is searched and names defined in the procedure are made invisible:

```
PROCEDURE Hide (P : TreePointer);
BEGIN
  IF P<>NIL THEN
    Hide (P^.Less);
    Hide (P^.More);
    IF P^ defined in Current Procedure THEN
      P^.Visible := FALSE
    END
  END
END Hide;
```

17.5 Multiway trees

The trees discussed in this chapter are binary trees, that is a node in the tree can reference two other nodes. However, multiway trees can be used, where one node can reference many other nodes. One application of these is Bayer's B-Trees. These can be used for storing tree structures in files where to minimise the number of disc accesses, as much data as possible is stored in each sector. This topic is beyond the scope of this book, but more information can be found in Wirth[1].

Conclusion

Tree structures provide an elegant method of storing data. They can be searched rapidly, using simple recursive routines. One application in the diagram package for their use is for storing names identified by the lexical analyser. They can also contain arithmetic expressions, and this is the topic of the next chapter.

Exercises

1) A data file contains data about electronic components: capacitors, resistors or inductors. Each component is described in the file by its type, (C, R or L), its value (in Farads, Ohms or Henrys) and its tolerance.

Write a program to read each item in turn from the file.

Write a routine to compare two components, where it is defined that

a capacitor < an inductor < a resistor, and for two components

of the same type, their values are compared.

Modify the program so that it finds the smallest component.

Modify the program so that each component is added to a tree structure, and at the end the components are listed in order.

2) Write a program to read a Modula-2 source file and report the number of times that each reserved word is used. Print this information in alphabetical order of reserved words.

3) The disk which is associated with this book comes with the source code for the diagram package. This code is compressed so that it fits on the disk. Usually each byte of the source code is copied into the 'compressed' file, but strings are often replaced by 1 or 3 bytes. The source consists of ASCII characters in the range 0..127; the characters 128..255 are used for compression purposes, as follows:

All Modula-2 reserved words are replaced by one byte (in the range 160..250).

Other strings are written in full the first time they are encountered, but the position of the string in the compressed file is remembered.

Subsequently, a string is replaced by three bytes: 255 and then the two bytes which form the position of the string in the compressed file.

This is achieved by first forming a tree containing all the reserved words and associating a value in the range 160..250 with each word.

Then, as each new 'user' word is encountered it is added to the tree, and the current file position remembered.

Write a program to compress a file and expand a file.

Add other compression methods to your program.

References

1. Niklaus Wirth,*Algorithms and Data Structures* Prentice-Hall 1986

2. G.M Adelson-Velskii and E.M Landis *Doklady Aladzemia Nauk* SSSR146 1962 263-266; English translation in Soviet Math 3 1259-63

18 Expression Trees

Binary trees were introduced in the last chapter as a means of storing data in a structure which can be searched rapidly. Another use of trees is for storing arithmetic expressions, and this is the topic of this chapter. Tree structures again provide elegant data representation and their processing is achieved by elegant and recursive procedures.

In chapter 11, reverse Polish notation was described as a method of representing arithmetic expressions in a form simple to evaluate. The disadvantage of the notation is that it is different from that in everyday use: humans are more used to infix. Another reason for not using reverse Polish is that the processing of infix notation into a tree structure is in fact not much more complicated than converting from infix to reverse Polish.

18.1 Expression trees

The basic idea of an expression tree is that nodes in the tree contain numbers (or names of variables, etc.) and operators. Operators process other data, so nodes with operators reference those nodes which have such data. Thus each node contains appropriate data and pointers which may point to other nodes. For more information, see Graham[1] or Rohl[2].

Examples of expression trees are shown in figure 18.1. Note, in particular, that 2-3-4 is represented in the manner shown in figure 18.1c, and not by that in 18.1d. Unary operators are represented by nodes which reference only one other node (as in figure 18.1f). The expression of figure 18.1g includes brackets, which are unnecessary as an expression tree is unambiguous: the expression could be represented as shown in figure 18.1h.

Trees which contain either numbers or operators could be represented by the following data types:

```
TYPE Operator = (plus, minus, times, divide,
                 leftbrac, rightbrac, unaryplus, unaryminus);
     ExpressionPointer = POINTER TO ExpressionRecord;
     ExpressionRecord = RECORD
                         Left, Right : ExpressionPointer;
                         CASE IsOperator : BOOLEAN OF
                           FALSE : Value : INTEGER |
                           TRUE  : OpType : Operator;
                                   OpPrecedence : CARDINAL |
                         END
                        END;
```

220 Modula-2 Applied

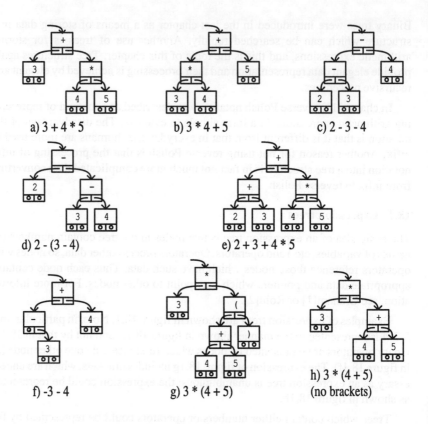

Figure 18.1 Various expression trees

Evaluation of expression trees

Evaluation of a tree is also straightforward, and recursive. Any node in a tree is evaluated simply. If the node is a number (or variable), then the value of that node is the value of the number. If the node contains a binary operator, the node value is the result of evaluating the nodes to the left and right of the current node and processing them by the operator. A unary operator processes the result of the evaluation of its one subtree.

For example, for the expression in figure 18.1a, the result is the sum (because of the + in the top node) of the evaluation of the node with 3 and that with a *. The former is evaluated as 3, the latter has a value of the product of 4 and 5. Similarly, the value of the tree in figure 18.1f is the sum of -3 and 4. The following procedure evaluates a tree.

```
PROCEDURE Evaluate (P : ExpressionPointer) : INTEGER;

  PROCEDURE EvaluateOperator() : INTEGER;
  VAR temp : INTEGER;
  BEGIN
    WITH P^ DO
      CASE OpType OF
        plus      : RETURN Evaluate (Left) + Evaluate (Right) |
        minus     : RETURN Evaluate (Left) - Evaluate (Right) |
        times     : RETURN Evaluate (Left) * Evaluate (Right) |
        divide    : temp := Evaluate (Right);
                    IF temp=0 THEN
                      ReportError ('Divide by zero');
                      RETURN 0
                    ELSE
                      RETURN Evaluate (Left) DIV temp
                    END |
        unaryplus : RETURN Evaluate (Right) |
        unaryminus: RETURN - Evaluate (Right) |
        leftbrac  : RETURN Evaluate (Left) |
        rightbrac : ReportError ('Bracket unexpectedly found');
                    RETURN 0
      END
    END
  END EvaluateOperator;

BEGIN
  IF P=NIL THEN
    ReportError ('Referencing a NIL pointer');
    RETURN 0
  ELSIF P^.IsOperator THEN
    RETURN EvaluateOperator()
  ELSE
    RETURN P^.Value
  END
END Evaluate;
```

Other processing of expression trees

Other procedures can be used to handle expression trees. For example, the following procedure prints a tree as a reverse Polish expression:

```
PROCEDURE PrintReversePolish (P : ExpressionPointer);
BEGIN
  IF P<>NIL THEN
    PrintReversePolish (P^.Left);
    PrintReversePolish (P^.Right);
    PrintItem (P)
  END
END PrintReversePolish;
```

where PrintItem prints the number or the operator (left to the reader as an exercise). Note that this is a POSTORDER recursive procedure (compare the INORDER procedure of chapter 18 for printing a tree). By POSTORDER is meant that the processing of the current item is done after that of the subitems. INORDER means that the current item is done between the subitems. To show this in action consider the tree of figure 18.1a.

The left side of the + will be printed (i.e. 3), then the right side, then the +. The right side of the + is the left of the * (the 4), the right of the * (the 5), then the *. Thus the result is:

$3\ 4\ 5*+$

which is the reverse Polish equivalent of $3 + 4 * 5$.

Reverse Polish notation consists of the two data, then the operator. Forward Polish is the operator, then the data. Therefore the (PREORDER) procedure to print an expression in forward Polish is simply:

```
PROCEDURE PrintForwardPolish (P : ExpressionPointer);
BEGIN
  IF P<>NIL THEN
    PrintItem (P);
    PrintForwardPolish (P^.Left);
    PrintForwardPolish (P^.Right)
  END
END PrintForwardPolish;
```

18.2 Forming an expression tree

The algorithm to convert an infix expression into an expression tree is simple and elegant, consisting mainly of only two mutually recursive procedures. However, because of its mutually recursive nature, an explanation of the algorithm is not easy. To ease the explanation, it will be assumed that numbers and only two operators are allowed, namely + and * (see also Rohl[2]).

Such an expression can be defined as follows:

Expression is a Term1
Term1 is a Term2, or Term2 + Term2, or Term2 + Term2 + Term2, etc.
*Term2 is a Factor, or Factor * Factor, or Factor * Factor * Factor, etc.*
Factor is a Number

Therefore a procedure to form an expression tree from a Term1 is:

```
PROCEDURE Term1 (VAR TreeTop : ExpressionPointer);
BEGIN
   Term2 (TreeTop);
      (* form a tree, pointed to by TreeTop,
        containing a Term2 *)
   WHILE NextItemFromExpression = '+' DO
     Make TreeTop a node with a + in it, whose
         Left pointer references the previous TreeTop;
     Term2 (TreeTop^.Right)
         (* i.e make TreeTop^.Right point to a Term2 *)
   END;
END Term1;
```

Where a Term2 is made by:

```
PROCEDURE Term2 (VAR TreeTop : ExpressionPointer);
BEGIN
   Factor (TreeTop);
      (* form a tree, pointed to by TreeTop and
        containing a Factor *)
   WHILE NextItemFromExpression = '*' DO
     Make TreeTop a node with a * in it, whose Left
         pointer references the previous TreeTop;
     Factor (TreeTop^.Right)
         (* i.e make TreeTop^.Right point to a Factor *)
   END;
END Term2;
```

Where Factor is:

```
PROCEDURE Factor (VAR TreeTop : ExpressionPointer);
BEGIN
  IF NextItemFromExpression = Number THEN
    Allocate memory pointed to by TreeTop;
    Put the Number in TreeTop^;
    Get next item from the expression
  ELSE
    ReportError ('Number expected')
  END
END Factor;
```

These procedures can be seen in action when converting 3 + 4 * 5 into a tree.

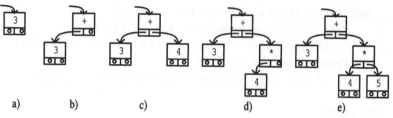

a)   b)   c)   d)   e)

Figure 18.2 Formation of an expression tree

Term1 is called first, which calls Term2, and this calls Factor. Here the first item in the expression is examined, it is a 3, so a tree is formed containing only 3: see figure 18.2a.

The program returns to Term2. The next item in the expression is not a *, but a +, so the while condition in Term2 fails, and the program returns to Term1. As the next item in the expression is a +, the while condition in Term1 is true. Thus a node is formed for the +, whose Left pointer refers to the current TreeTop (i.e. to the 3), and TreeTop is now set to point to the +. The tree is as shown in figure 18.2b.

Term2 is now called which forms a tree whose root is TreeTop^.Right. This it does by calling Factor, which forms a node for the 4, so the complete tree is as in figure 18.2c. Then, as the next item in the expression is *, the while condition in Term2 is true, so the tree will be as in figure 18.2d. Remember that the TreeTop used by Term2, is in fact the TreeTop^.Right from Term1. Then Term2 will call Factor, and attach the 5 to the Right node of TreeTop of Term2, as in figure 18.2e. The end of the expression has now been reached, so the while of Term2 will be false, so the program will return to Term1. The while condition there will also be false, so Term1 will end also, and the expression tree is formed.

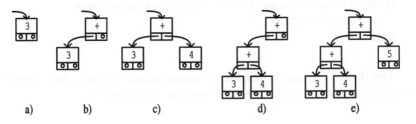

Figure 18.3 Formation of an expression tree

The expression 3 + 4 + 5 will grow in the stages shown in figure 18.3. Here Term1 calls Term2. Term2 calls Factor, each time, but the while condition of Term2 is always FALSE, so the program always returns to Term1.

In the above examples, two levels of term are allowed, one for + and one for *. In the general case, more levels are needed. So Term1 calls Term2, which calls Term3, etc., until at last Factor is called. The only difference between each Term procedures is the condition for the while loop: Term1 looks for +, Term2 looks for *, etc. Therefore, one recursive Term procedure can be used:

```
PROCEDURE Term (VAR TreeTop : ExpressionPointer;
                Level : CARDINAL);
BEGIN
   IF Level >= MaxLevel THEN
      Factor (TreeTop)
   ELSE
      Term (TreeTop, Level + 1)
   END;
   WHILE NextItemInExpression is an operator
         whose precedence level is Level DO
      Form New TreeTop with operator, whose Left is TreeTop;
      Term (TreeTop^.Right, Level + 1)
   END
END Term;
```

In fact Level is not the type of operator, + or *, etc., but the precedence value of the operator.

One slight change is needed to Term to allow for unary operators. In an expression tree, a unary operator is represented by a node whose Left pointer is NIL and whose Right pointer references the next node (see figure 18.1f). Therefore if procedure Term is processing a unary operator, it should not call Factor before starting the while loop. So in the above, the line Factor (TreeTop) should be replaced by:

```
   IF NextItemInExpression <> Unary operator THEN
      Factor (TreeTop)
END;
```

One further change is needed to accommodate brackets. An expression containing numbers, brackets, + and * only, can be defined as:

Expression is a Term1

Term1 is a Term2, or Term2 + Term2, or Term2 + Term2 + Term2, etc.

*Term2 is a Factor, or Factor * Factor, or Factor * Factor * Factor, etc.*

Factor is a Number, or (Expression)

So procedure Factor must be changed to handle Numbers or (, then expression, then). An expression is analysed at this stage by Factor calling Term at the lowest level. So Term calls Factor, and Factor can call Term. Thus Term is directly recursive and Factor and Term are mutually recursive.

If Factor finds a (, it puts the (in the tree, analyses an expression which it puts as the Left subtree of the node with the (, and then expects a) which it will put as the Right subtree of the (. A closing bracket is only legal after a recursive call to Term from Factor. Note that the brackets need not be inserted into the tree.

The final version of the expression analyser can now be written. If the lexical analyser stores details about the next item in the expression in a global variable of type ExpressionRecord, then the analyser consists of three procedures, Factor and Term (described above) and another, NewExpr.

NewExpr calls the heap manager to get memory for a new node. Into this new node the details of the current item are stored, and its two pointers are set according to two parameters which are passed to the procedure. These allow Term to make the top of the tree a node with an operator whose left subtree is the top of the current tree, by passing the current tree top as a parameter to NewExpr. The procedure is:

```
PROCEDURE NewExpr (VAR Top : ExpressionPointer;
                   NewLeft, NewRight : ExpressionPointer);
BEGIN
   IF Available (SIZE (Top^) THEN
      ALLOCATE (Top, SIZE (Top^));
      Top^ := NextExpr;
      Top^.Left := NewLeft;
      Top^.Right := NewRight;
      LexicalAnalyse (NextExpr) (* Get next item from expression *)
   END
END NewExpr;
```

Procedure Factor is as follows:

```
PROCEDURE Factor (VAR TreeTop : ExpressionPointer);
BEGIN
  WITH NextExpr DO
    IF IsOperator THEN
      CASE OpType OF
        leftbrac : NewExpr (TreeTop, NIL, NIL);
                                    (* put bracket in tree *)
                   Term (TreeTop^.Left, 0);
                                    (* form expression *)
                   IF NextExpr.IsOperator AND
                       (NextExpr.OpType = rightbrac) THEN
                     (* is there a ) after the expression ? *)
                     NewExpr (TreeTop^.Right, NIL, NIL)
                                    (* yes, so put in tree *)
                   ELSE
                     ReportError (') expected')
                   END |
        rightbrac : ReportError (') unexpected')
              ELSE  ReportError ('Operator not expected')
      END
    ELSE
      NewExpr (TreeTop, NIL, NIL)   (* put Number in tree *)
    END
  END
END Factor;
```

Procedure Term is:

```
PROCEDURE Term (VAR TreeTop : ExpressionPointer; Level : CARDINAL);

  PROCEDURE CorrectLevel() : BOOLEAN;
  BEGIN
    WITH NextExpr DO
      IF IsOperator THEN
        RETURN OpPrecedence = Level
      ELSE
        RETURN FALSE
      END
    END
  END CorrectLevel;
```

```
    BEGIN (* of Term *)
      IF Level >= Max THEN
        IF NOT (CorrectLevel() ) THEN Factor (TreeTop) END
      ELSE
        Term (TreeTop, Level + 1)
      END;
      WHILE CorrectLevel() DO
        NewExpr (TreeTop, TreeTop, NIL);
        Term (TreeTop^.Right, Level + 1)
      END
    END Term;
```

Initially the lexical analyser is called to get the first item from the expression. Then the expression is analysed by

```
Term (Top, 1);
```

It should be noted that the final implementation of the above needs checks to abort the algorithm when, for example, insufficient heap is available in NewExpr, or the lexical analyser finds an illegal item, etc. These checks are not given as they complicate the algorithm, but are left to the reader as an exercise!

18.3 Expression trees in the diagram package

In the diagram package, the code which analyses a program describing a shape makes use of the expression analyser, and this calls the lexical analyser. In addition to the numbers and simple operators described above, the lexical analyser is able to classify items as operators such as >, >=, :=, etc., names of user defined procedures and variables, control words like IF and THEN, and built-in procedures like LINE, SIN, COS, etc. The expression analyser must therefore be able to handle all of these as well.

Variables, procedure names and controlwords are handled very much like numbers: when a suitable place is found, a name, like a number, is added into expression trees in procedure Factor, by calling NewExpr.

One slight change to the above allows the processing of procedures and their parameters, and array indexing. When a procedure and its parameters are added to the tree, it is useful to form one tree containing the procedure name and its parameters. A tree for

LINE (100, 200, 4000, 500)

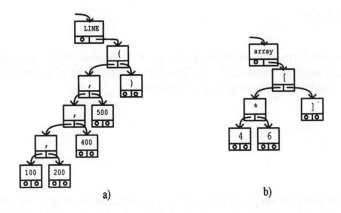

Figure 18.4 More complicated trees

is shown in figure 18.4a. This is achieved simply. In Factor, if the item following the name is a bracket, the name is added by calling NewExpr. Then the node with the bracket is added to the Right side of the node with the name.

```
NewExpr (top, NIL, NIL);
IF Next Item is a leftroundbrac THEN
   Factor (top^.right)
END;
```

Similarly, for arrays an element of the form

*array [4 * 6]*

should be formed into a tree like that shown in figure 18.4b. Again this is achieved by putting the array name into a tree, then forming a tree, containing the square brackets and their contents, pointed to by the Right pointer of the node with the array name. When an array variable is added in Factor, the following code is used:

```
NewExpr (top, NIL, NIL);
IF Next Item is a leftsquarebrac THEN
   Factor (top^.right)
END;
```

One point to note about the analyser is that, if the following is analysed:

230 Modula-2 Applied

```
    3 * 4 5 + 6
```

the analyser will form a tree containing only 3 * 4. If the analyser is called again, it will form a separate tree with 5 + 6. This fact is used in the diagram package analyser. Consider the following program fragment.

```
IF x > y THEN
    x := 6 * 7
ENDIF
```

The program analyser keeps on calling the expression analyser until an error is detected or the end of the program reached. Thus, for the above, the expression analyser will be called five times, so five separate trees will be returned containing:

IF

x > y

THEN

*x := 6 * 7*

ENDIF

This is ideal for analysing the program. How this information is used is considered in the next chapter.

Conclusion

Expression trees are presented in this chapter as a suitable structure for storing arithmetic expressions. These can then by processed by simple recursive routines. Procedures have also been presented for converting an infix arithmetic expression into an expression tree. These essentially consist of two mutually recursive procedures. The next stage is to verify that the tree contains valid information. How this is achieved, and the rest of the analyser, is the topic of the next chapter.

Exercises

1) Write a program which allows the user to enter a simple infix arithmetic expression, and which then converts the expression into a tree structure, evaluates the result, and prints the expression in reverse Polish form.

2) Write a procedure to convert a reverse Polish expression into a tree structure. This is quite straightforward, the algorithm being similar to that used to evaluate a reverse Polish expression:

```
FOR each item in the expression DO
  IF number THEN
    Push on to a stack
  ELSIF binary operator THEN
    Make Tree whose node is the operator and whose Left
    and Right subtrees are the two items popped from the
    top of the stack;
    Push top of this tree onto the stack
  ELSIF unary operator THEN
    Make Tree whose node is the operator and whose Right
    subtree is popped from the top of the stack;
    Push top of this tree on to the stack
  END
END
```

3) Extend the above so as to convert a reverse Polish expression into its equivalent forward Polish expression.

References

1 Neill Graham *Introduction to Computer Science* West 1982

2 J.S. Rohl *Recursion via Pascal* Cambridge University Press 1984

19 The Analyser

In this chapter the rest of the analyser is considered. This builds on the lexical analysis and the expression tree structures of the preceding chapters. A full description of such analysis, including considerations of syntax analysis, methods of specifying the syntax, etc., is beyond the scope of this book. Instead, the aim here is to illustrate the basic concepts used in the diagram package, which the user can examine in more detail by studying the program source on the accompanying disk. More details can be found in the various references, Bornat[1], Wirth[2], Gries[3].

The analyser has two functions to perform: to check that the program is syntactically correct, and then to obey the program. If any syntax errors are found, the analyser stops, reports the error, and invokes the editor with the cursor placed at about the position of the error. If the program is correct, however, it is obeyed. The output of the program is normally a series of lines, circles, rectangles, strings, etc., and these are both displayed on the screen, so that the user can check that the program has had the desired effect, and stored in a linked list of GCommands (as described in chapter 12). Therefore the program will generate a usershape, just like one entered interactively, which can be used by any other shape (or itself). The analysis, obviously, takes time. However, once analysed, the shape will be redrawn as quickly as any other user defined shape.

The analyser continuously calls the expression analyser, which forms an expression tree. Each tree is checked to see that it is of the correct form, and is then stored in a suitable structure. When the program has been analysed completely, it is obeyed, and this is achieved by traversing the structure. These stages are described here.

19.1 Data structures

The basic data structures used are the two tree structures used for storing names and arithmetic expressions. The former is used by the lexical analyser to look up the type of symbol, the latter is used to represent the next arithmetic expression found in the program.

The lexical analyser categorises an item by an ItemType:

```
ItemType = (progend, unknown, operator, controlword, procedure,
            type, constant, variable, parameter);
```

Some of these need further clarification types, that is, to specify the particular operator, controlword, type or procedure:

```
OperatorType = (plus, minus, times, divide, ...);
ControlType  = (var, proc, endproc, return, if, etc.);
TypeType     = (undefined, number, varnumber, array, charstring);
ProcType     = (mainProc, lineProc, circleProc, ...,
                sqrt, sin, ... userProc);
```

Full definitions of these are given in DIAGIDEF.DEF.

All names found by the lexical analyser, both reserved and user defined, are stored in the symbol tree. The former are controlwords like IF and THEN, the built-in procedures like LINE, CIRCLE, SIN, and ABS, and other reserved words like the types NUMBER and ARRAY. The latter include the names of procedures, variables and parameters declared in the user program.

A SymbolRecord defines any symbol (or name). This is an element in a tree, so it contains pointers to subtrees (of type SymbolPointer), indications of the position of the name in the data file, classification of the symbol (an ItemType) and associated data. The associated data include the sort of controlword or type (a ControlType or TypeType); the procedure (if inbuilt or user defined, and the associated parameters and instructions which form the procedure); and for variables and parameters, their value and such information as the procedure in which they were defined. A complete definition of the record is given in the definition module DIAGIDEF.DEF.

A program defining a usershape is stored in a record which includes an Editor-Rec (see chapter 15) for storing the program, and a SymbolRecord classified as a procedure. Procedural SymbolRecords contain the necessary data to define the instructions of the procedure. As the complete program can be considered a procedure, this is reasonable.

Components of arithmetic expressions are stored in ExpressionRecords, which contain pointers to sub-expression trees (ExpressionPointers) and the necessary data: whether it is a number, operator, controlword, procedure, variable, etc., and associated data, such as the type and precedence of an operator, or a pointer into the symbol tree to a SymbolRecord which defines the controlword, variable, etc. A complete definition is also in DIAGIDEF.DEF.

More details on these and associated data structures are given as the chapter proceeds. The complete analyser is encoded in the five modules DIAGIDEF, DIAGILEX, DIAGIEXP, DIAGISYN and DIAGINTR, which contain, respectively, the global definitions, the lexical analyser, the expression analyser, the syntax analyser and the interpreter which obeys the analysed program.

The basic analysis is achieved by using the results of the expression analyser. So the first stage is to consider the results of this analysis.

19.2 Results of the expression analyser

As stated in the previous chapter, the expression analyser processes the next part of the program and puts this into a tree structure. For example, the program fragment:

```
LOOP
  IF x>SIN(y) THEN
    EXIT
  ELSE
    x := x + 1
    LINE (x, y, x, SIN (y))
  ENDIF
ENDLOOP
```

would be analysed by ten calls of the expression analayser, which would return trees containing the following:

LOOP	IF	x>SIN(y)	THEN	EXIT
ELSE	x:=x+1	LINE(x,y,x,SIN(y))	ENDIF	ENDLOOP

Thus an expression tree can contain a controlword, like IF or LOOP; an arithmetic expression, like x>SIN(y) or x := x + 1; or a call to a procedure, either a built-in one like LINE, or a user defined procedure.

Two checks are needed on these: one verifies that the contents of the expression are correct and the other checks that such an expression is valid at that point in the program. For example, if s is a STRING and x a NUMBER, the statement

$$x := s + SIN(y)$$

is incorrect. Similarly, the call to procedure LINE requires that the four parameters passed are all of type NUMBER. Given that the only types allowed in the language are NUMBER, ARRAY (of NUMBER), VARNUMBER (which is a variable NUMBER passed to a procedure) and STRING, and that all procedures return values of type NUMBER, this checking is easier than that required in Modula-2 with its many types, both built-in and user defined. This check must process ARRAYs suitably, if A is of type ARRAY, A[x+7] is of type NUMBER.

The second check, that the current expression is appropriate at the current point in the program, will ensure, for example, that an IF is followed by an expression tree which returns a NUMBER, and this is followed by a tree containing a THEN, etc.

19.3 Checking compatible types

Ensuring that the expression tree is filled with items of compatible types is achieved by a straightforward recursive procedure which analyses the given tree, and returns a value of the enumeration type, TypeType. It is:

```
PROCEDURE GetType (e : ExpressionPointer) : TypeType;
BEGIN
   IF e=NIL THEN
      RETURN undefined
   ELSE
     CASE e^.ItemType OF
        operator  : RETURN GetOpType() |
        procedure : RETURN GetProcType() |
        constant  : RETURN < type of constant > |
        variable,
        parameter : IF e^.Right=NIL THEN
                       RETURN < type of variable / parameter >
                    ELSIF (e^ is an array) AND
                          (e^.right^ is a []) AND
                          (GetType (e^.Right^.Left)=number) THEN
                       RETURN number
                    ELSE
                       RETURN undefined
                    END
        ELSE      RETURN undefined
     END
   END
END GetType;
```

where GetProcType and GetOpType are local procedures. GetOpType is:

```
PROCEDURE GetOpType() : TypeType;
BEGIN
   CASE e^.operatortype OF
     plus..colon    :     (* binary operators *)
                    IF GetType (e^.Left) =
                         GetType (e^.Right) THEN
                       RETURN GetType (e^.Left)
                    ELSE
                       RETURN undefined
                    END |
```

```
                unaryminus..not : IF GetType (e^.Right)= number THEN
                                     RETURN number
                                  ELSE
                                     RETURN undefined
                                  END |
          leftroundbrac :         RETURN GetType (e^.left)
                ELSE              RETURN undefined
         END (* CASE *)
         END GetOpType;
```

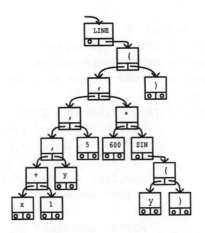

Figure 19.1 An expression tree

To appreciate GetProcType it is necessary to know the form of an expression tree containing a call to a procedure, and how the expected types of the parameters are stored. An expression tree for

```
LINE (x+1, y, 5, 600*SIN(y))
```

is shown in figure 19.1. As the precedence of the comma operator is low, the value of each parameter is separated from others by nodes containing a comma. Thus the basic operation of GetProcType (checking the procedure referenced by e) is:

```
IF there is a bracket at e^.Right THEN
           (* if any parameters *)
   ParameterCheck (e^.Right^.Left)
END;
```

where ParameterCheck is:

```
PROCEDURE ParameterCheck (p : ExpressionPointer);
BEGIN
  IF (p<>NIL) AND (p^ is a comma) THEN
    ParameterCheck (p^.Left);
    ParameterCheck (p^.Right);
  ELSIF NOT TypeCheck (GetType (p) ) THEN
    ReportError ('Type mismatch')
  END
END ParameterCheck;
```

This leaves the problem of checking that the type passed to TypeCheck is correct. For user defined procedures, a procedure is declared by a line of the form:

```
PROC Fred (x : NUMBER, y : ARRAY)
```

The name Fred is stored in the symbol tree and categorised as a procedure, and the values x and y are also stored in the tree, but categorised as parameters of the appropriate type. It is important that there should be an association of x and y with Fred. This is achieved by a linked list with Fred at the head, which points to x which in turn points to y. In fact, such a list contains all the parameters of the procedure, and any variable declared in the procedure.

At the start of GetProcType, a pointer (called NextParameter) is set to reference the first parameter in this linked list (in the above example it would point to x). Then all that is needed is for TypeCheck to verify that the type passed to it is that of the parameter referenced by NextParameter and then to move the pointer on. The part of TypeCheck which handles user defined procedures is given below:

```
PROCEDURE TypeCheck (ExpectedType : TypeType) : BOOLEAN;
VAR ok : BOOLEAN;
BEGIN
  IF procedure is user defined THEN
    IF (NextParameter=NIL) OR
       (NextParameter^<>parameter) THEN
      RETURN ExpectedType=undefined (* see below for why *)
    ELSE
      ok := ExpectedType = < type of NextParameter^ >;
      NextParameter := NextParameter^.Next;
      RETURN ok
    END
```

238 Modula-2 Applied

```
    ELSE
      (* see below for built-in procedures *)
    END
  END TypeCheck;
```

When every parameter in the expression tree has been checked, NextParameter should have moved off the end of the list of parameters, so it will be NIL or be referencing a local variable. This can be verified by calling TypeCheck when ParameterCheck has finished, for which the ExpectedType is 'undefined'. This is why, in the above, ExpectedType=undefined is returned if NextParameter=NIL or NextParameter^ is a local variable not a parameter.

This procedure needs slight modification for handling the built-in procedures like LINE, CIRCLE, SIN, TAN, etc. For these it is known, for example, that LINE expects 4 numbers, and that PLOTSTRING requires five numbers and then a string. So the procedure uses a number, ParameterNumber, to determine which parameter is being analysed. So, if the procedure is built in, the appropriate part of TypeCheck is:

```
INC (ParameterNumber);
CASE procedure type OF
  lineProc    : IF ParameterNumber<5 THEN
                  RETURN ExpectedType=number
                ELSE
                  RETURN ExpectedType=undefined
                END |
  stringProc : IF ParameterNumber=6 THEN
                  RETURN ExpectedType=string
                ELSIF ParameterNumber<6 THEN
                  RETURN ExpectedType=number
                ELSE
                  RETURN ExpectedType=undefined
                END |
  etc.
```

For the LINE procedure, ParameterNumber will equal 5 when all the parameters have been analysed (like NextParameter=NIL for user procedures). Hence the boolean value returned is ExpectedType=undefined.

Thus GetProcType checks the parameters of procedure e^ by:

```
PROCEDURE GetProcType() : TypeType;
BEGIN
  ParameterNumber := 0;
  NextParameter := FirstParameter of e^;
  IF e^ has any parameters THEN
    CheckParameter (e^.Right^.Left)
  END;
  TypeCheck (undefined);
  IF no error occurred THEN
    RETURN number
  ELSE
    RETURN undefined
  END
END GetProcType;
```

19.4 Checking next tree is appropriate

The next stage is a procedure which ensures that the next expression tree is appropriate, that is, an IF tree is followed by a numerical tree, which is then followed by a THEN, etc. As such checks are made, each tree is added into a structure which can be obeyed later. This stage is also achieved by a recursive procedure.

A program is a series of statements. These can be variable declarations, calls to procedures, assignments, control statements (like IF, LOOP, RETURN) or procedure declarations. These statements are terminated by the end of the program.

A procedure consists of its declaration, a series of statements (as above) then the control statement ENDPROC. Clearly, the statements after the procedure declaration and before the ENDPROC could be analysed by the same code which analyses the main statements in the program.

A LOOP statement consists of the word LOOP, a series of statements, then the ENDLOOP. This series could also be analysed by the same code. An IF statement has a series of statements after its THEN, which are terminated by an ELSIF, ELSE or ENDIF. Similarly, there are statements after any ELSE, terminated by ENDIF. Such statements can also be processed by the same procedure. A similar argument applies to FOR, REPEAT and WHILE loops.

This can be achieved by a procedure which keeps analysing statements until an 'end' is found, where an 'end' is the end of the program, or one of the statements ENDPROC, ENDLOOP, ELSE, ELSIF, ENDIF, ENDFOR, etc. The procedure AnalyseToEnd, uses a global ExpressionPointer, NextExpr, which contains the next tree formed by the expression analyser. Thus, when AnalyseToEnd terminates, NextExpr will contain the expression which caused the 'end'. Thus the code which called AnalyseToEnd can verify that NextExpr contains an appropriate 'end'.

AnalyseToEnd also needs to store each expression tree in a suitable structure so that the program can be obeyed. As a program is a series of statements, this could be a linear list of expression trees. However, a slightly better structure is one which separates the statements between the LOOP and the ENDLOOP, or between the THEN and the ELSE, etc., from the main statement list. This has the advantage that when the series of statements after the THEN have been obeyed, the program can just skip the ELSE tree, rather than having to skip all statements between the ELSE and the ENDIF.

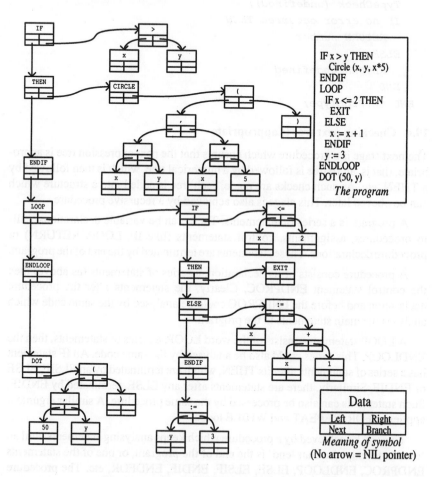

Figure 19.2 Structure of program fragment

This can be achieved by a linear list with branches. The main list contains the LOOP followed by the ENDLOOP, with the statements between them in the branch. The statements after a THEN or ELSE are also in branches. Similarly, a PROC and its ENDPROC are in the main list, with the procedure name and its parameters in the branch. The contents of the procedure are stored in a list referenced by the node in the symbol tree containing the name of that procedure. To illustrate this, consider figure 19.2 which shows the structure which would be formed in analysing the given part program.

This structure is achieved by extending the data structure used for representing expressions. Any node in an expression tree has pointers Left and Right, which reference other items in the tree, and the actual data (indicating if the node is a number, operator, controlword, etc.). Two more pointers allow a list of expression trees, with branches, so the structure of figure 19.2 can be realised:

```
ExpressionRecord = RECORD
                Next, Branch : ExpressionPointer;
                Left, Right  : ExpressionPointer;
                <etc>
              END;
```

Most correct trees are added to the current list. However, recursive calls to AnalyseToEnd cause instructions to be added to the branch.

AnalyseToEnd is passed a pointer, TopInstruction, (whose initial value is NIL) which will be given the first expression tree, i.e. the first instruction, and from which a list of instructions will be formed. Then each correct expression will be added to the end of the list. Adding to the end of the list is best achieved by remembering the end of the list: a variable, called Current, references the current last element in the list. The next expression, pointed to by NextExpr, is added to the end of the list by:

```
PROCEDURE AddNextExpr;
BEGIN
   IF TopInstruction=NIL THEN    ( if nothing in the list *)
     TopInstruction := NextExpr; (* add as first in list *)
     Current := TopInstruction
   ELSE
     Current^.Next := NextExpr;    (* add to end of list *)
     Current := Current^.Next
   END
END AddNextExpr;
```

Then AnalyseToEnd is:

```
PROCEDURE AnalyseToEnd (VAR TopInstruction :
                                  ExpressionPointer);
VAR Current : ExpressionPointer;
BEGIN
  LOOP
    IF any error detected THEN EXIT END;
    Expression (NextExpr);   (* get next expression *)
    CASE NextExpr^.type OF
      progend    : EXIT |
      operator   : IF GetType(NextExpr) <> undefined THEN
                     AddNextExpr
                   ELSE
                     ReportError ('Illegal operation')
                   END |
      procedure  : IF GetType (NextExpr) = number THEN
                     AddNextExpr
                   ELSE
                     ReportError ('invalid procedure')
                   END |
      controlword : CASE control word type OF
                      var     : CheckVar |
                      if      : CheckIf |
                      loop    : CheckLoop |
                      for     : CheckFor |
                      while   : CheckWhile |
                      repeat  : CheckRepeat |
                      return  : CheckReturn |
                      proc    : CheckProc |
                      exit    : AddNextExpr |
                      else, elsif, endif,
                       endproc, endloop : EXIT
                      ELSE    ReportError
                                   ('unexpected symbol')
                    END
    END
  END
END AnalyseEnd;
```

CheckVar, CheckIf, etc., are local procedures. CheckLoop is:

```
PROCEDURE CheckLoop;
BEGIN
   AddNextExpr;   (* put LOOP in structure *)
   AnalyseEnd (Current^.Branch); (* analyse loop contents *)
   IF NextExpr is tree with 'ENDLOOP' THEN
      AddNextExpr
   ELSE
      ReportError ('ENDLOOP expected')
   END
END CheckLoop;
```

and CheckIF is:

```
PROCEDURE CheckIf;
BEGIN
   LOOP  (* loop, as the same code after IF as ELSIF *)
      AddNextExpr;   (* add IF/ELSIF to tree *)
      Expression (NextExpr);
      IF GetType (NextExpr) <> number THEN
         ReportError ('Arithmetic expression expected'); EXIT
      END;
      AddNextExpr;
      Expression (NextExpr);
      IF NextExpr is tree with 'THEN' THEN
         AddNextExpr;
         AnalyseEnd (Current^.Branch);
          IF NOT (NextExpr is tree with 'ELSIF') THEN EXIT END
      ELSE
          EXIT
      END
   END;
   IF NextExpr is tree with 'ELSE' THEN
      AddNextExpr;
      AnalyseEnd (Current^.Branch)
   END;
   IF NextExpr is tree with 'ENDIF' THEN
      AddNextExpr
   ELSE
      ReportError ('Unexpected symbol')
   END
END CheckIf;
```

Procedures CheckWhile, CheckFor and CheckRepeat are similar to the above.

Procedure CheckProc calls AnalyseToEnd to check the statements after the procedure declaration and before the ENDPROC. These statements are then stored in a list referenced by the SymbolRecord containing the procedure name. Thus the instructions which form the procedure are directly referenced by the procedure. CheckProc must also process the procedure declaration. This consists of the procedure name and any parameters. These parameters are a series of statements of the form:

```
ParameterName : Type
```

separated by commas and enclosed by brackets. These are checked by a recursive procedure CheckVar. The analyser uses a variable CurrentProcedure to reference the current procedure. This enables the system to know in which procedure the variables and parameters are defined. As explained in chapter 17, at the end of the procedure all names defined in the procedure are made invisible. CheckProc is:

```
PROCEDURE CheckProc;
VAR WasCurrentProcedure : SymbolPointer;
BEGIN
  WasCurrentProcedure := CurrentProcedure;
  AddNextExpr;    (* add PROC *)
  Expression (NextExpr);
  Classify NextExpr as a procedure and set
     CurrentProcedure to name at top of NextExpr;
  IF NextExpr^ has parameters THEN
    CheckVar (NextExpr^.Right^.Left, FALSE)(* see below *)
  END;
  Current^.Branch := NextExpr; (* put paras as a branch *)
  AnalyseToEnd (CurrentProcedure^.FirstInstruction);
  IF NextExpr^ is 'ENDPROC' THEN
    AddNextExpr
  ELSE
    ReportError ('ENDPROC expected')
  END;
  Hide all names defined in CurrentProcedure;
  CurrentProcedure := WasCurrentProcedure
END CheckProc;
```

Procedure CheckVar analyses each parameter in turn to ensure that it is in the form Name : Type, and associates the type with the given name. It also forms the linked list of all parameters which is used by the procedure GetProcType. As the statements after a VAR are of the same form as the part of the parameter declaration between the brackets, CheckVar is used to check both. The boolean passed to CheckVar is true if local variables are being analysed, and false for parameters. CheckVar is:

```
PROCEDURE CheckVar (e:ExpressionPointer; IsVar:BOOLEAN);
BEGIN
   IF e^ is comma THEN
      CheckVar (e^.Left, IsVar);
      CheckVar (e^.Right, IsVar)
   ELSIF (e^ is colon) AND
         (e^.Left^ is unknown) AND
         (e^.Right^ is a type) THEN
      Set type of e^.Left^ to that in e^.Right^;
      IF IsVar THEN
         e^.Left^ := variable
      ELSE
         e^.Left^ := parameter
      END;
      Add e^.Left to list of items
         declared in CurrentProcedure
   ELSE
      ReportError ('Invalid declaration')
   END
END CheckVar;
```

The analysis of the complete program is thus achieved by first assigning to CurrentProcedure the address of the SymbolRecord of the record associated with the complete program, then calling AnalyseToEnd, and then checking that the end of the program has been reached:

```
CurrentProcedure := ADR (ProgramRecord^.Symbols);
AnalyseToEnd (CurrentProcedure^.FirstInstruction);
IF NextExpr^ <> ProgramEnd THEN
   ReportError ('Unexpected end of program')
END;
```

If no errors were detected, ProgramRecord^.Symbols will contain a reference to the linked list containing the instructions of the program. The next stage is to obey the program, by progressing through the list, obeying each instruction.

19.5 Obeying the program

When a program is obeyed, the associated expression trees are processed suitably. The output of this is usually a series of lines, circles, etc., which are added into a linked list of GCommands and drawn. A GCommand (chapter 9) which defines a program shape requires the following elements:

```
first : GCommandLink;
name  : GStringLink;
programptr : ProgramLink;
```

first contains the first GCommand that makes up the shape, name refers to the name of the shape, and programptr is a pointer to the record which defines the program (including the EditorRec and the SymbolRecord). The program is thus obeyed by following the instructions in the list starting in the SymbolRecord part of the programptr^ and adding GCommands to the list beginning with the GCommandLink, first.

Analysing the complete program is achieved by the code which analyses a procedure. Similarly obeying a program is achieved by a procedure which obeys any procedure. Thus the main action uses a procedure RunProc.

Inside a procedure is a series of statements, and these are stored as a list of expression trees. Also, the series of statements between LOOP and ENDLOOP, or after a THEN or an ELSE, or in FOR, REPEAT or WHILE loops, are stored as a list of expression trees. Therefore the major part of RunProc is achieved by a procedure, RunSeries, which obeys a list of expression trees. This is called at the start of RunProc, and called recursively when a LOOP, IF, FOR, REPEAT or WHILE statement is obeyed.

RunSeries obeys a series of statements, and it normally stops when the end of the series is found. However, any run-time error, like a divide by zero, or the user pressing ESC, stops the action. Also, a RETURN statement causes the program to abort the current procedure, and EXIT aborts the current LOOP. Therefore a variable is used to note such action:

```
foundType = (foundNowt, foundExit, foundReturn, foundAbort);
```

Initially this is set to foundNowt. However, if a run-time error is detected, foundType is given the value foundAbort, and this is used to terminate the action. When EXIT or RETURN is found, foundType is set accordingly and the current loop or procedure ended suitably. When a loop or procedure ends, foundType is reset from foundExit or foundReturn to foundNowt.

Thus the main action of the analyser is:

```
foundType := foundNowt;
dummy := RunProc (NIL, ADR (g^.Symbols));
```

RunProc is passed the parameter list of the procedure and a pointer to the SymbolRecord defining the procedure, and returns the numerical result of the procedure. For the main program, the parameter list is NIL and this result is ignored. The main action of RunProc is:

```
Allocate space for parameters and local variables;
Procedure^.Result := 0.0;
RunSeries (Procedure^.FirstInstruction);
IF foundType<>foundAbort THEN foundType := foundNowt END;
   (* this clears any foundReturn *)
Answer := Procedure^.Result;
DeAllocate space for all parameters and variables;
RETURN Answer
```

RunSeries moves along the list pointed to by ExprPointer. It uses procedure MoveOn to move to the next instruction. The action of RunSeries is:

```
LOOP
   CheckKey;  (* allow user to interrupt action *)
   IF any error THEN
      foundType := foundAbort
   END;
   IF (foundType=foundAbort) OR (ExprPointer=NIL) THEN
      EXIT
   END;
   CASE type of ExprPointer^ OF
      programend : EXIT |
      operator,
      procedure  : IF foundType=foundNowt THEN
                      dummy := Evaluate (ExprPointer)
                   END |
      controlword : CASE type of controlword OF
                  var    : doVar |
                  proc   : MoveOn; MoveOn |
                           (* passed PROC, ENDPROC *)
                  if     : doIf |
                  loop   : doLoop |
                  for    : doFor |
                  while  : doWhile |
```

```
                            repeat : doRepeat |
                            exit   : IF foundType=foundNowt THEN
                                        foundType := foundExit;
                                        EXIT
                                     ELSE
                                        MoveOn
                                     END |
                            return : IF foundType=foundNowt THEN
                                        Procedure^.Result :=
                                            Evaluate (ExprPointer^.
                                                Branch);
                                        foundType := foundReturn;
                                        EXIT
                                     ELSE
                                        MoveOn
                                     END
                      ELSE       EXIT
                      END (* CASE  of controlword*)
        END (* CASE of ExprPointer^ *)
    END (* LOOP *)
```

Procedures doIf, doLoop, doVar are local to RunSeries. The main part of doIf is:

```
LOOP
   IF (ExprPointer=NIL) OR (foundType<>foundNowt) THEN
      EXIT
   ELSIF Evaluate (ExprPointer^.Branch) <> 0.0 THEN
      (* if the IF boolean is true, obey the THEN clause *)
      MoveOn;  (* to the THEN *)
      RunSeries (ExprPointer^.Branch); (* do THEN clause *)
      EXIT
   ELSE
      MoveOn; MoveOn;  (* passed THEN to ELSIF/ELSE/ENDIF *)
      IF ExprPointer^ is ELSE THEN
         RunSeries (ExprPointer^.Branch);
         EXIT
      ELSIF ExprPointer^ is ENDIF THEN
         EXIT
      END
   END
END;
(* now keep moving on until find ENDIF: *)
```

```
WHILE (ExprPointer <> NIL) AND (ExprPointer^ <> ENDIF) DO
   MoveOn
END;
MoveOn;      (* past ENDIF *)
```

and the main part of doLoop is:

```
IF foundType=foundNowt THEN
   LOOP
      IF ExprPointer<>NIL THEN
         RunSeries (ExprPointer^.Branch);
         CASE foundType OF
             foundNowt : |
             foundExit : foundType := foundNowt;
                         EXIT
         ELSE            EXIT
         END
      ELSE
         EXIT
      END
   END
END;
MoveOn;      (* passed LOOP and ENDLOOP *)
MoveOn;
```

Procedures doFor, doRepeat and doWhile are similar to the above.

These require a routine to evaluate an expression, which is used for deciding if the expression following the IF is true, or for running any procedure. This is achieved by a routine similar to Evaluate given in the previous chapter, with only a few extensions to allow indexing into arrays and running procedures, so it is not given here.

Finally, considerations are required for handling variables. As shown in the definition of a SymbolRecord, a parameter or variable has an associated Value, defined as a ValueRecord (given in DIAGIDEF.DEF). This allows the value associated with the variable to be stored. It must be remembered that each time a recursive procedure is called, it needs its own copy of its local variables. This is normally achieved by a stack. However, the analyser does not have a stack, so a different approach is used.

At the start of a procedure, an ARRAY of ValueRecord is obtained from the heap. This is large enough to store details of the current parameters and local variables of the procedure. Then the current values of these parameters and local variables are copied from the appropriate SymbolRecords in the symbol tree into the array. At the end of the procedure, the reverse occurs: the values are copied from the array into the associated SymbolRecords, and the array is returned to the heap.

Conclusion

In this chapter, the basic philosophy of the analyser is given. The reader can obtain full details by consulting the listing of the modules DIAGISYN and DIAGINTR.

The analyser is an advanced feature of the diagram package, which allows interesting shapes to be drawn by the system. Some examples of these are given in the next chapter.

References

1 Richard Bornat *Understanding and Writing Compilers* Macmillan Education 1979

2 Niklaus Wirth *Algorithms + Data Structures = Programs* Prentice-Hall 1976

3 David Gries *Compiler Construction for Digital Computers* Wiley 1971

20 Miscellaneous Examples

In this final chapter a few techniques are described which can be used for producing some elegant drawings. These include Sierpinski curves, fractals and simple 3D images, which can be drawn using the diagram package by writing a suitable program to be interpreted by the analyser program. Thus this chapter provides some more examples of the language used in the diagram package.

20.1 Sierpinski curves

Figure 20.1 Sierpinski curves

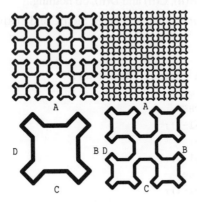

Figure 20.2 Individual Sierpinski curves

Sierpinski curves are from a class of 'space filling curves', which also include Hilbert and Wirth's W curves (see Wirth[1]). They can be drawn by a number of mutually recursive procedures. The same procedures draw both the simple shapes,

251

and the more complicated ones. Figure 20.1 shows four levels of Sierpinski curves superimposed. At first sight, drawing them looks complicated. However, there is a pattern to them. Consider figure 20.2, which shows the four levels drawn separately. Each level of curve consists of four shapes on the top, left, bottom and right, linked by the diagonal lines at the four corners. The four shapes can be labelled A, B, C and D (as in figure 20.2). The recursive curves draw these four shapes, so there are separate procedures for A, B, C and D.

Consider the level one A shape at the bottom left figure 20.2, which will be defined by A(1). This consists of a diagonal line, a horizontal line and another diagonal line. Shapes B, C and D have similar constituents, and will be defined by B(1), C(1) and D(1), respectively.

The level two A shape at the bottom right of figure 20.2b, A(2), consists of A(1), a diagonal line, B(1), a horizontal line, D(1), a diagonal line and then A(1). The three lines (between the calls to shapes at level 1), are those three lines required to draw A(1). For the complete level 2 curve, these lines are half the length of those in level 1. B(2), C(2) and D(2) are similar.

Similarly, A(3) consists of A(2), a diagonal line, B(2), a horizontal line, D(2), a diagonal line, A(2), and likewise for B(3), C(3) and D(3). Again the lines between the calls to shapes at level 2, are of the form which draw the level 1 shape, and the length of each line is half that of those used in a complete level 2 curve.

In general for any n>0, A(n) consists of A(n-1), a diagonal line, B(n-1), a horizontal line, D(n-1), a diagonal line, A(n-1), and similarly for B(n), C(n) and D(n). For n=0, A(n), B(n), C(n) and D(n), do nothing.

Thus four procedures, SierpA, SierpB, SierpC and SierpD, can be used, whose form is as follows:

```
PROCEDURE SierpA (Level : CARDINAL);
BEGIN
   IF Level > 0 THEN
      SierpA (Level-1);
      DiagonalLine;
      SierpB (Level-1);
      HorizontalLine;
      SierpD (Level-1);
      DiagonalLine;
      SierpA (Level-1)
   END
END SierpA;
```

with similar routines for SierpB, SierpC and SierpD. If the offset from one end of a diagonal line to the other has a value h in both the x and y directions, the horizontal and vertical lines have length 2*h. When many curves are drawn superimposed, as in figure 20.1, the value h is halved for each successive curve.

To draw a complete curve, two global variables are used, x and y, which specify the current position. As each line of the curve is drawn, so x and y are moved on. This is achieved by a procedure DrawTo which is passed the end of the next line (xn,yn), and which draws a line from the current position (x,y) to (xn,yn) and then stores (xn,yn) as the current position (x,y). Thus the first diagonal line above is drawn by

```
DrawTo (x+h, y-h)
```

the horizontal line is drawn by:

```
DrawTo (x+2*h, y)
```

and the second diagonal line is drawn by:

```
DrawTo (x+h, y+h)
```

A complete curve is achieved by setting x,y to the start of curve A, then curve A is drawn (which moves x,y to the end of curve A), then the diagonal line between curves A and B is drawn, then curve B, a diagonal line, curve C, a diagonal line, curve D and then the last diagonal line is drawn.

Thus the procedure is:

```
PROCEDURE DrawCompleteCurve;
BEGIN
    Initialise (x, y);   (* Position x, y at start of curve A; *)
    SierpA (level);
        (* this draws A, and moves x,y to end of curve *)
    DrawTo (x+h, y-h);
        (* draws diagonal line, and moves x, y to start of B *)
    SierpB (level);
    DrawTo (x-h, y-h);
    SierpC (level);
    DrawTo (x-h, y+h);
    SierpD (level);
    DrawTo (x+h, y+h)
END DrawCompleteCurve;
```

254 Modula-2 Applied

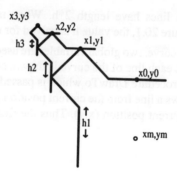

Figure 20.3 Start points of Sierpinski curve

All that is required is to determine the start point. Figure 20.3 shows part of a three level Sierpinski curve, with the start points of curve A for levels 1, 2 and 3, labelled x1,y1, x2,y2 and x3,y3. Another point x0,y0 and the middle of the curve xm,ym, and the line displacements h1, h2 and h3 are also shown. (Remember that h1 = 2 * h2 and h2 = 2 * h3.)

From these it can be seen that

```
x3 = x2 - 2 * h3              y3 = y2 - h3
x2 = x1 - 2 * h2              y2 = y1 - h2
x1 = x0 - 2 * h1              y1 = y0 - h1
```

Thus, if x,y is the start point of the previous curve, drawn using a given value h, the next level curve is drawn with the following start point x,y and h:

```
x := x - h;
h := h DIV 2;
y := y - h;
```

Initial values for h, x and y, assuming the size of the screen is some value ScreenSize, are:

```
h := ScreenSize DIV 4;
x := 2 * h;
y := 3 * h;
```

Where the initial value for x,y is x0,y0, as shown in figure 20.3.

The complete 'diagram package' program which draws Sierpinski curves of different levels superimposed is shown below. Note the use of forward definitions of the four mutually recursive procedures. These are needed because a procedure must be defined before it is used.

```
#Program to draw Sierpinski curves#
VAR Screen : NUMBER   Screen := 2048
  FORWARDPROC SierpA (Level : NUMBER)    #note Forward references#
  FORWARDPROC SierpB (Level : NUMBER)
  FORWARDPROC SierpC (Level : NUMBER)
  FORWARDPROC SierpD (Level : NUMBER)

PROC Draw (NumLevels : NUMBER)
VAR x : NUMBER, y : NUMBER, h : NUMBER, ct : NUMBER

  PROC DrawTo (xn : NUMBER, yn : NUMBER)
    LINE (x, y, xn, yn)
    x := xn    y := yn
  ENDPROC

  PROC SierpA (level : NUMBER)
    IF level > 0 THEN
      SierpA (level - 1)
      DrawTo (x + h, y - h)
      SierpB (level - 1)
      DrawTo (x + 2 * h, y)
      SierpD (level - 1)
      DrawTo (x + h, y + h)
      SierpA (level - 1)
    ENDIF
  ENDPROC

  PROC SierpB (level : NUMBER)
    IF level > 0 THEN
      SierpB (level - 1)
      DrawTo (x - h, y - h)
      SierpC (level - 1)
      DrawTo (x, y - 2 * h)
      SierpA (level - 1)
      DrawTo (x + h, y - h)
      SierpB (level - 1)
    ENDIF
  ENDPROC
```

```
  PROC SierpC (level : NUMBER)
    IF level > 0 THEN
      SierpC (level - 1)
      DrawTo (x - h, y + h)
      SierpD (level - 1)
      DrawTo (x - 2 * h, y)
      SierpB (level - 1)
      DrawTo (x - h, y - h)
      SierpC (level - 1)
    ENDIF
  ENDPROC

  PROC SierpD (level : NUMBER)
    IF level > 0 THEN
      SierpD (level - 1)
      DrawTo (x + h, y + h)
      SierpA (level - 1)
      DrawTo (x, y + 2 * h)
      SierpC (level - 1)
      DrawTo (x - h, y + h)
      SierpD (level - 1)
    ENDIF
  ENDPROC

  h := Screen / 4
  x := h * 2
  y := h * 3
  FOR ct := 1 TO NumLevels DO
    x := x - h
    h := h / 2
    y := y + h
    SierpA (ct)
    DrawTo (x + h, y - h)
    SierpB (ct)
    DrawTo (x - h, y - h)
    SierpC (ct)
    DrawTo (x - h, y + h)
    SierpD (ct)
    DrawTo (x + h, y + h)
  ENDFOR
ENDPROC

Draw (3)
```

Other space filling curves are given in Wirth[1] and the exercises at the end of the chapter.

20.2 Fractals

Another interesting set of shapes are fractals (see Mandelbrot[2]), and these can be drawn using the diagram package. The basic idea is straightforward. Associated with any fractal is an initiator and generator, both of which are a series of lines. The fractal operation is to replace each line of the initiator with a suitably scaled version of the generator. As the generator consists of a series of lines, this operation produces even more lines. Hence, the next stage is to replace all of these lines by a scaled version of the generator, etc. This process could continue indefinitely, so an arbitrary limit is used to stop the process.

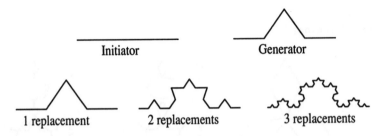

Figure 20.4 Fractal operation

An example is given in figure 20.4. The initiator is just one straight line, the generator consists of 4 lines, as shown at the top of the figure. The shapes generated, for increasing amounts of replacement, are shown at the bottom of the figure.

Assuming that the initiator and generator consist of arrays of x,y coordinates, the algorithm in Modula-2 is:

```
PROCEDURE Fractal;
VAR ct : CARDINAL;
BEGIN
   FOR ct := 2 TO NumberOfCoordinatesInInitiator DO
      MakeLine (Initiator[ct-1], Initiator[ct], 1)
   END
END Fractal;
```

where MakeLine is:

258 *Modula-2 Applied*

```
PROCEDURE MakeLine (C1, C2 : XYCoord; Level : CARDINAL);
VAR ct : CARDINAL;
    CPrev, CNext : XYCoord;
BEGIN
  IF Level >= MaxLevel THEN
    LINE (C1.X, C1.Y, C2.X, C2.Y)
  ELSE
    CalcXYCoord (Generator[1], CPrev);
    FOR ct := 2 TO NumberOfCoordinatesInGenerator DO
      CalcXYCoord (Generator[ct], CNext);
      MakeLine (CPrev, CNext, Level+1);
      CPrev := CNext
    END
  END
END MakeLine;
```

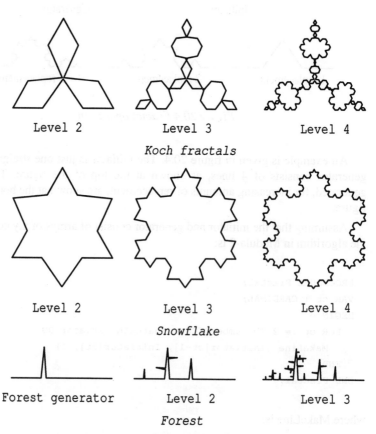

Figure 20.5 Some fractals

where CalcXYCoord returns the XY coordinate based on the generator position, suitably scaled to fit in the range C1..C2. Clearly, for the generator to replace the complete line C1..C2, the first coordinate of the generator has coordinate 0,0 and the last point has coordinate 1,0.

Some more fractals are shown in figure 20.5. The top three curves are Koch fractals: the initiator is a triangle, the generator is that shown in figure 20.4. Below these are 'snowflakes', whose initiator is the triangle used for Koch curves, and the generator is the same shape as for Koch, but with the peak pointing downwards. The three shapes at the bottom resemble a petrified forest. The initiator is a straight line, and the generator a line with a small peak, as shown in the figure.

The procedure given below allows the diagram package to draw a fractal, defined by arrays I and G, which contain the x,y coordinates of the initiator and generator respectively, and R the levels of replacement. These arrays are just arrays of numbers, with each coordinate stored by the x value in one location and the y value in the next. The diagram package procedure is:

```
PROC DrawFractal (I : ARRAY, G : ARRAY, R : NUMBER)

  PROC MakeLine (x1 : NUMBER, y1 : NUMBER,
                 x2 : NUMBER, y2 : NUMBER, level : NUMBER)
    VAR xp : NUMBER, yp : NUMBER,
        xn : NUMBER, yn : NUMBER, ct : NUMBER
    IF level = R THEN
      LINE (x1, y1, x2, y2)
    ELSE
      xp := x1
      yp := y1
      FOR ct := 4 TO HIGH (G) BY 2 DO
        xn := x1 + (x2 - x1) * G[ct-1] + (y2 - y1) * G[ct]
        yn := y1 + (y2 - y1) * G[ct-1] - (x2 - x1) * G[ct]
        MakeLine (xp, yp, xn, yn, level+1)
        xp := xn
        yp := yn
      ENDFOR
    ENDIF
  ENDPROC

  VAR ct : NUMBER
  FOR ct := 4 TO HIGH (I) BY 2 DO
    MakeLine (I[ct-3], I[ct-2], I[ct-1], I[ct], 1)
  ENDFOR
ENDPROC
```

260 Modula-2 Applied

The Koch, snowflake and forest fractals can be generated using the above procedure by code of the form:

```
VAR Initiator : ARRAY [1,8], Generator : ARRAY [1,10]

Initiator := [0.5, 0.08, 0.2, 0.6, 0.8, 0.6, 0.5, 0.08]
Generator := [0.0, 0.0, 0.3, 0.0, 0.5, 0.28, 0.7, 0.0, 1.0, 0.0]
DrawFractal (Initiator, Generator, 3)     # draw Koch #

Generator := [0.0, 0.0, 0.3, 0.0, 0.5, -0.28, 0.7, 0.0, 1.0, 0.0]
DrawFractal (Initiator, Generator, 4)     # draw inverse Koch #

VAR TreeI : ARRAY [1,4], TreeG : ARRAY[1,10]
TreeI := [0.2, 0.4, 0.8, 0.4]
TreeG := [0.0, 0.0, 0.3, 0.0, 0.33, 0.3, 0.35, 0.0, 1.0, 0.0]

DrawFractal (TreeI, TreeG, 4)     # draw forest #
```

20.3 Three-dimensional shapes

Another useful technique allows the user to draw 'real' three-dimensional objects on a two-dimensional screen. Clearly there will be an inherent loss of information unless some means is provided for giving the illusion of depth. This can be achieved by perspective projections. How a 3D object appears depends upon the position from which that object is viewed. Handling this requires the use of matrix transformations. In this section the very basic techniques for drawing 3D objects are given: these allow the generation of simple 'wire frame' images. More detail, including hidden line removal, shading, etc., can be found in various books; see for example Foley and Van Dam[3], Watt[4], Harrington[5] and Angell[6].

Coordinate systems and transformations

The techniques will be discussed by considering how to draw a wireframe cube. A cube can be defined by a set of lines between its corners. These are best defined as being at coordinates relative to, say, the centre of the cube. Thus these corners could be at points:

1,1,1   -1,1,1   -1,-1,1   1,-1,1   1,1,-1   -1,1,-1   -1,-1,-1 and 1,-1,1

How a cube should be drawn depends on the position from which it is viewed, that is the position of the eye. Some examples are given in figure 20.6. Therefore the first stage in trying to draw a cube is to redefine its coordinates in terms of their position relative to the eye. That is, each X,Y,Z coordinate must be transformed

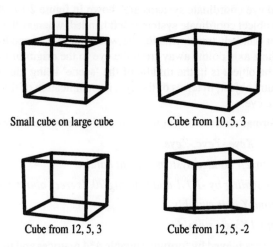

Small cube on large cube   Cube from 10, 5, 3

Cube from 12, 5, 3   Cube from 12, 5, -2

Figure 20.6 Some wire frame scenes

from being relative to the origin of the object to being relative to the eye. This can be achieved by a series of transformations, implemented using matrix techniques. In chapter 7, 3*3 transformation matrices were introduced for processing 2D coordinates. For 3D coordinates, 4*4 transformation matrices are needed. These are given below for translation by Tx,Ty,Tz, scaling by factors Sx,Sy,Sz, and rotation by A degrees about the x, y and z axes, for which c is COS(A) and s is SIN(A). These are just an extension of those given in chapter 7.

```
1  0  0  0    Sx 0  0  0    1  0  0  0    c  0  s  0    c  s  0  0
0  1  0  0    0  Sy 0  0    0  c  s  0    0  1  0  0   -s  c  0  0
0  0  1  0    0  0  Sz 0    0 -s  c  0   -s  0  c  0    0  0  1  0
Tx Ty Tz 1    0  0  0  1    0  0  0  1    0  0  0  1    0  0  0  1
 Translation    Scale         About x       About y       About z
```

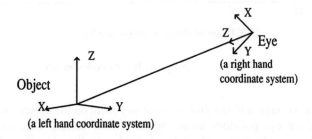

Figure 20.7 Object and eye coordinate systems

262 Modula-2 Applied

The object and eye coordinate systems are shown in figure 20.7. As explained in Angell[6], the object coordinate system is left handed, whereas the eye coordinate system is right handed: transformation between the two is needed. For the eye coordinates, the z axis points away from the eye to the origin of the object. Thus the centre of the object is in the middle of the 'scene' being viewed. Also, the z coordinate of any object, in terms of the eye, is an indication of the distance of the object from the eye.

The transformation from object to eye is achieved by the following:

Translate by -Xeye,-Yeye,-Zeye

Convert from left handed system to right handed

   (* done by scaling by -1,1,1 and rotating 90 degrees about X axis *)

Rotate around Y axis suitably

Rotate around X axis suitably

These actions are achieved by forming suitable 4*4 matrices and multiplying them together. This need be done only once for any given eye position, and the resultant matrix can then be used to transform any coordinate on the object into its equivalent eye coordinate.

Projection

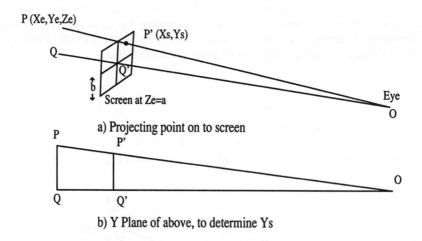

Figure 20.8 Eye to screen coordinates

The next stage is to determine where any point on the object (now defined in terms of the eye position) should appear on the screen. This process should, hopefully, include some indication of depth into the picture, and this can be accomplished by a perspective projection. The idea is to imagine that the screen on which the object is drawn is positioned between the eye and the object. Thus the position where a point on the image (P(Xe,Ye,Ze)) should appear on the screen (point P'(Xs,Ys)) is where the line from the eye to that image point intersects with the screen: this is shown in figure 20.8a. Calculating that point is achieved using similar triangles. Consider figure 20.8b, which shows the y plane of 20.8a: by similar triangles:

$P'Q' / PQ = OQ' / OQ$

i.e $Ys / Ye = a / Ze$ or $Ys = Ye * a / Ze$

and by a similar argument,

$Xs = Xe * a / Ze$

In the above a is the distance of the eye from the screen. If b is half the height of the screen, the above equations can be normalised so $-1<=Xs<=1$ and $-1<=Ys<=1$:

$Xs = (a / b) * Xe / Ze$ and $Ys = (a / b) * (Ye / Ze)$

Note that in the above, the screen coordinate of the point is achieved by dividing by the distance of the point from the eye, thereby including depth into the transformation. Thus, for objects along way off, their screen coordinate will tend to the middle of the screen, which is analagous to distant objects appearing on the horizon.

The ratio a/b is small if the screen is close to the eye, which has an effect like a wide angle lens on a camera, whereas a/b being large is like using a telephoto lens. A ratio a/b should be chosen so that the position of the eye is where the screen is normally viewed: a value of 6 is reasonable.

This ratio is fixed for any scene being viewed. Therefore it can be included in the transformation matrix by a final scaling matrix, which scales the object by (a/b, a/b, 1).

Any point (X,Y,Z) on the object can be transformed by the viewing transformation matrix, so as to yield a point (X',Y',Z'). This point can be transformed into normalised screen coordinates by the above equations. If the screen size is defined by Width and Depth, the actual screen position is:

$(X' / Z') * Width / 2 + Width / 2$, $(Y' / Z') * Depth / 2 + Depth / 2$

Using the techniques given above, any point on the object can be processed so as to generate its equivalent position on the screen. If the object is made up of lines, any of these lines can be drawn by calculating the screen position of the endpoints of each line and then drawing a line between them.

If the eye is sufficiently close to the object, it is possible that some of these lines will be outside the screen. Thus the lines must be clipped. This can be achieved by using the 2D line clipping algorithm, as given in chapter 7. Alternatively, it is possible to clip lines before the final transformation to the 2D screen coordinates, thus possibly saving some processing. How this is achieved is explained in the references.

The following program draws a simple wireframe cube, given a specified eye position. The first stage is to calculate the viewing transformation matrix (VTM).

264 Modula-2 Applied

Then, the endpoints of each line on the object are transformed, using VTM, to screen coordinates, and the line between them is drawn.

The two-dimensional transformation matrix is stored as a 16-element one-dimensional array. For this, an element at position row,col in the notional 2D matrix, has position (row-1)*4 + col. Such matrices are multiplied together by a procedure MatMult. Once the matrix has been calculated, each line of the cube is transformed and drawn by Line3D. The program is:

```
#Draw a cube given eye position#
VAR Xeye : NUMBER, Yeye : NUMBER, Zeye : NUMBER, VTM : ARRAY [1,16]

PROC MatMult (M1 : ARRAY, M2 : ARRAY, Mres : ARRAY)
#Multiplies M1 by M2, returning the result in Mres.
 All are 4*4 matrices#
VAR row : NUMBER, col : NUMBER, loop : NUMBER, ndx : NUMBER

  PROC Index (row : NUMBER, col : NUMBER)
    RETURN (row-1) * 4 + col
  ENDPROC # this calculates actual index given row and col #

  ndx := 1
  FOR row := 1 TO 4 DO
    FOR col := 1 TO 4 DO
      Mres[ndx] := 0
      FOR loop := 1 TO 4 DO
        Mres[ndx] := Mres[ndx] +
                   M1[Index(row, loop)] * M2[Index(loop, col)]
      ENDFOR
      ndx := ndx + 1
    ENDFOR
  ENDFOR
ENDPROC

PROC MakeVTM
#This procedure makes the viewing transformation matrix, VTM,
 given the current position of the eye, Xeye,Yeye,Zeye#
VAR T1 : ARRAY [1,16], T2 : ARRAY [1,16],
    r : NUMBER, r2 : NUMBER, cos : NUMBER, sin : NUMBER
  T1 := [1,0,0,0, 0,1,0,0, 0,0,1,0, -Xeye,-Yeye,-Zeye,1]
           #Translate by -Xeye,-Yeye,-Zeye#
  T2 := [-1,0,0,0, 0,0,-1,0, 0,1,0,0, 0,0,0,1]
           #Convert from left hand to right hand coordinates#
  MatMult (T1, T2, VTM)  #VTM is now both the above tranforms#
```

```
    r := SQRT (Xeye * Xeye + Yeye * Yeye)
    IF ABS (r) >= 1E-6 THEN
      cos := Yeye / r      sin := Xeye / r
    ELSE
      cos := 1             sin := 0
    ENDIF
    T1 := [cos,0,sin,0, 0,1,0,0, -sin,0,cos,0, 0,0,0,1]
    MatMult (VTM, T1, T2)                #rotate about Y axis#
    r2 := SQRT (r * r + Zeye * Zeye)
    IF ABS (r2) >= 1E-6 THEN
      cos := r / r2        sin := Zeye / r2
    ELSE
      cos := 1             sin := 0
    ENDIF
    VTM := [1,0,0,0, 0,cos,-sin,0, 0,sin,cos,0, 0,0,0,1]
    MatMult (T2, VTM, T1)                #rotate about X axis#
    T2 := [6,0,0,0, 0,6,0,0, 0,0,1,0, 0,0,0,1]
    MatMult (T1, T2, VTM)        #scale according to ratio a/b#
ENDPROC


PROC Transform (x : VARNUMBER, y : VARNUMBER, z : VARNUMBER)
#Transforms object position x,yz to eye position x,y,z using VTM#
VAR xt : NUMBER, yt : NUMBER
  xt := x       yt := y
  x := VTM[1] * xt + VTM[5] * yt + VTM[ 9] * z + VTM [13]
  y := VTM[2] * xt + VTM[6] * yt + VTM[10] * z + VTM [14]
  z := VTM[3] * xt + VTM[7] * yt + VTM[11] * z + VTM [15]
ENDPROC


PROC TwoDTransform (x : NUMBER, y : NUMBER, z : NUMBER,
                    xs : VARNUMBER, ys : VARNUMBER)
#Transforms x,y,z to screen coordinate xs,ys#
#Note screen depth and width is 4096, so half is 2048#
  Transform (x, y, z)
  IF ABS (z) >= 1E-6 THEN
    xs := (1 + x / z) * 2048     ys := (1 + y / z) * 2048
  ELSE
    xs := 2048                   ys := 2048
  ENDIF
ENDPROC
```

```
PROC LINE3D (x1 : NUMBER, y1 : NUMBER, z1 : NUMBER,
             x2 : NUMBER, y2 : NUMBER, z2 : NUMBER)
#Draw line between x1,y1,z1 and x2,y2,z2#
VAR xs1 : NUMBER, ys1 : NUMBER, xs2 : NUMBER, ys2 : NUMBER
  TwoDTransform (x1, y1, z1, xs1, ys1)
  TwoDTransform (x2, y2, z2, xs2, ys2)
  LINE (xs1, ys1, xs2, ys2)
ENDPROC

PROC DrawCube
    LINE3D ( 1.0,  1.0,  1.0,  -1.0,  1.0,  1.0)
    LINE3D (-1.0,  1.0,  1.0,  -1.0, -1.0,  1.0)
    LINE3D (-1.0, -1.0,  1.0,   1.0, -1.0,  1.0)
    LINE3D ( 1.0, -1.0,  1.0,   1.0,  1.0,  1.0)
    LINE3D ( 1.0,  1.0,  1.0,   1.0,  1.0, -1.0)
    LINE3D (-1.0,  1.0,  1.0,  -1.0,  1.0, -1.0)
    LINE3D (-1.0, -1.0,  1.0,  -1.0, -1.0, -1.0)
    LINE3D ( 1.0, -1.0,  1.0,   1.0, -1.0, -1.0)
    LINE3D ( 1.0,  1.0, -1.0,  -1.0,  1.0, -1.0)
    LINE3D (-1.0,  1.0, -1.0,  -1.0, -1.0, -1.0)
    LINE3D (-1.0, -1.0, -1.0,   1.0, -1.0, -1.0)
    LINE3D ( 1.0, -1.0, -1.0,   1.0,  1.0, -1.0)
ENDPROC

Xeye := 12  Yeye := 5  Zeye := 3
MakeVTM
DrawCube
```

The above program draws a wireframe cube. A scene made up of many such cubes, or other shapes, can be drawn using the method. More sophisticated scenes are those for which the only lines drawn are those which can be seen. For example, the surface at the back of a non-transparent cube is obscured from the eye, so its edges should not be drawn. Techniques for hidden line and hidden surface removal can be used to produce such effects. These, and techniques for shading, shadows and for handling smooth surfaces, and for producing ray-traced images, are beyond the scope of this book, and the reader is referred to the various references: Foley and Van Dam[3], Watt[4], Harrington[5], Angell[6], etc.

Exercises

1) Figure 20.2 shows four levels of Sierpinski curve drawn separated, as opposed to being superimposed. Modify the Sierpinski drawing program to draw the curves in this manner.

Miscellaneous Examples 267

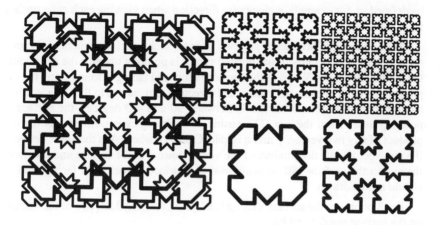

Figure 20.9 'RIC' curves

2) Figure 20.9 shows another space-filling curve produced by the author. In the figure are shown three layers superimposed and four levels separated. Write a program to draw these curves.

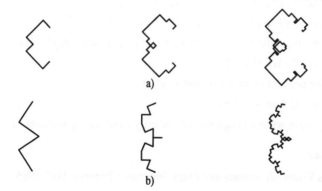

Figure 20.10 More fractals

3) Figure 20.10 shows some fractals. Determine their initiators and generators, and hence write a program to draw them.

4) The cubes shown in figure 20.6 are defined by a series of lines. A different method can be used so that only those surfaces facing the eye are drawn: so back faces are eliminated. For this method the cube is defined as a number of planes, where the coordinates of each corner of the plane are stored. These corners should

be defined in, for example, a clockwise direction when viewing each cube surface from the outside.

The vector cross product of any two lines on such a surface generates a vector normal to a surface. Only if that normal vector is pointing towards the eye should the surface be drawn. Whether the surface is forward facing is found using the dot product between this normal vector, and a vector from the eye to the surface. If the angle between these two vectors is between 90 and -90 degrees, the surface is pointing away from the eye. The cosine of such angles is positive. As the dot product of any two vectors p and q is |p||q| COS(A), where A is the angle between the two vectors, the dot product of the vector normal to the surface and one from the eye to the surface will be positive if the surface is backward facing, and so should not be drawn.

For 3 points on the surface x1,y1,z1, x2,y2,z2 and x3,y3,z3, two of the vectors on the surface are defined by:

(x1 - x2, y1 - y2, z1 - z2)

and

(x2 - x3, y2 - y3, z2 - z3)

for which the vector normal to the surface (xn, yn, zn) is given by:

xn = (y2 - y1) * (z3 - z2) - (z2 - z1) * (y3 - y2)

yn = (z2 - z1) * (x3 - x2) - (x2 - x1) * (z3 - z2)

zn = (x2 - x1) * (y3 - y2) - (y2 - y1) * (x3 - x2)

A vector from the eye, point xe,ye,ze, to the surface (xf, yf, zf) is

(x1 - xe, y1 - ye, z1 - ze)

The dot product of xn,yn,zn and xf,yf,zf is:

xf * xn + yf * yn + zf * zn.

Using these write a program to draw only front facing surfaces of a cube.

References

1 Niklaus Wirth *Algorithms and Data Structures* Prentice-Hall 1986

2 B. Mandelbrot *The fractal geometry of nature* W.H.Freeman & Co 1982

3 J.D.Foley and A.Van Dam *Fundamentals of Interactive Computer Graphics* Addison-Wesley 1981

4 Alan Watt *Fundamentals of Three-Dimensional Computer Graphics* Addison-Wesley 1989

5 Steven Harrington *Computer Graphics- A programming approach* McGraw-Hill 1983

6 Ian O Angell *High-resolution Computer Graphics Using C* Macmillan Education 1990

Index

8086 memory	62	Edit string	114
		Editor	188-197
Aborting	82	EGA graphics	59
Accessing ports	144	Eight Queens problem	13, 39
Arc drawing	69	Ellipse drawing	71
AVL tree	(see Tree)	Exclusive-Or	64, 67, 124
		Exporting	5
Backtracking	13		
Balanced tree	(see Tree)	File buffer	139
Bezier curves	48, 103	File names	130
Binary files	130, 137	File errors	131
Binary search	206	Files	130-142
Binary tree	(see Tree)	Fractals	257
BITSET	61, 100		
Bubblesort	37, 53	GOTO statement	82
		Graphics on PCs	59
CGA graphics	59		
Circle drawing	68	Hashing	198, 204
Clipping	76, 92, 99	Heap	158, 182, 226
COMEFROM	82	Help facility	171, 174-178
Constant arrays	24-26, 34	Hilbert curves	251
Cryptarithms	39	HPGL	47, 143, 155
Data base	139	Implementation modules	5
Definition modules	5	Importing	5
Diagram package	42	Infix notation	148, 222
Commands	44-47	Initialising structured	
Editor keys	47-48	variables	21
File structure	48	Inorder	209, 222
Modules	55-58	Interpreter	232
Programming language	50-52	Interrupts	81
Dijkstra's method	150, 177-178		
Directories	136	Keyboard buffer	80
Dynamic storage	158	Key codes on PCs	88

Knights tour 13, 39

Laser printer 96
Layout of programs 6
Lexical analysis 198-205
Libraries 5
Line drawing algorithm 32
Linked list 162-174, 204-206
   sorted linked list 170, 172-179
   two-way list 179-188
Local modules 3-5, 143, 147
Local variables 9, 14
Location of an item 127
Look up tables 74

Matrices 92-99, 260-261
   addition 106
   determinant 106
   multiply 265
Mid point subdivision 101
Modules 3
Multiple exits/returns 10, 109
Mutual recursion 222, 226, 251

Object orientated
   programming 3
Opaque types 75, 187
Open array parameters 108

Parallel port 144
Paths 135
PC memory map 60
Perspective projection 260, 262
Plotting text 72
Plotting 143
Pointers 62, 123, 159
Polish notation 148
Polling 81

Polyominoes 40
Postfix 143, 148, 156, 219, 221
Postorder 222
PostScript 47, 143, 150
Precedence of operators
   149, 202, 225
Preorder 222
Procedure variables 116, 143, 179, 187, 189, 192
Programming style 6

Quicksort 9-11, 141

Random access of files
   130, 138, 171
Random numbers 4
Reading pixels 63
Records 17, 119
Recursion 7, 209, 219, 226
Reverse Polish (see Postfix)

Scope rules 50, 216
Sequential file access 130
Serial communication 145-147
Serial port 144-145
Sets 61, 137
Sierpinski curves 251, 266
Software interrupts 59-60
Space filling curve 251, 266
Stack 149, 156, 171-172, 177-178
Strings 107-118
   conversion to numbers 113
Syntax analysis 232

Text files 130
Text on PCs 65
Three-dimensional images 260

Top-down programming 2
TopSpeed modules:
  Graph 15,
  IO 15, 58, 117, 132
  FIO 130-135, 139, 145, 175
  Lib 58, 67, 69, 83
  Storage 58, 160
  Str 58
  SYSTEM 69, 145
  WINDOW 116-117
Towers of Hanoi 7-9
Transformations 93, 260
Trees 206-250
  AVL 213
  balanced 213
  binary trees 206-218
  expression trees 219-250
  multiway tree 213
Triangle filling 35

Unary operators 200, 201

Variant records 119, 120
Vector characters 73
Vectors 268
VGA graphics 59

Windows 43, 59, 75
Wire frame images 260
Wirth's W curves 251
Writing pixels 63-64

Zooming in/out 92, 97

A $5\frac{1}{4}$-inch floppy diskette (IBM compatible) is available [ISBN 0–333–55454–X] containing the program which may be implemented using TopSpeed Modula-2. EGA/VGA graphics are required.

For details of availability and prices contact:
The Publisher for Computing
Macmillan Education
Houndmills
Basingstoke
Hampshire
RG21 2XS
UK